CHRIST'S ALTERNATIVE...
TO COMMUNISM AND ALL "ISMS" TODAY

THE 21ST CENTURY IN OUR TIMES SERIES

Series Editor: Anne Mathews-Younes, Ed.D., D.Min.
Associate Editor: Shivraj K. Mahendra (Ph.D. Candidate)

CHRIST'S ALTERNATIVE...

TO COMMUNISM
AND ALL "ISMS" TODAY

E. STANLEY JONES

DEDICATED TO

The memory of Stephen A. Graham
whose life parallels that of
E. Stanley Jones in its total
absorption and commitment to
Jesus Christ.

- Editor

CONTENTS

FOREWORD

BY MARCIA GRAHAM

One night while E. Stanley Jones was reading on board an ocean liner, the Inner Voice called him to "tackle" head-on Russia's great experiment with Marxist Communism. Many "isms" – jingoism, nationalism, militarism, materialism, racism, radicalism, fanaticism and sexism, to name a few, swirled about menacingly in the mid-1930s. They persist today in nations, institutions, terrorist movements, politics and politicians. No question, these relentless evils need to be exposed and confronted. Jones certainly did not neglect to unmask these prevalent scourges in his writings. However, near the end of World War I communism of the Russian ilk (Marxist-Leninist) struck the world stage with a "terrific thud."[1] This new order sprang up so forcefully in the midst of the world that in Jones' view not to meet the tough issues of Russian communism head-on would expose the Christian alternative as weak, hesitant and hopelessly inadequate.[2]

Initially, Jones deflected this divine "mandate" to present and interpret the Kingdom of God as Christ's alternative to materialistic,

1 E. Stanley Jones, *Christ's Alternative to Communism,* 1935, p. 34.
2 Ibid., p. 9.

godless communism. For many weeks he reasoned that he was not sufficiently qualified in social and economic "specializations" to address the problem of communism in Russia. Moreover, for all the books ably written at the time putting forth the Christian alternative, Jones sensed an "incompleteness." On the one hand, he felt the "pressure of Russia," and on the other hand he knew the bigger pressure of "something vast and overwhelming and challenging and adequate – the Kingdom of God." That the Kingdom of God was the "sweeping answer" to communism was inescapable. So, gradually it dawned on Jones that he would not overreach his "simple task" of presenting Christ in the face of the communist challenge because the interpretation of the Kingdom of God *was* his "field," his *raison d'etre*.[3]

Not unlike Soren Kierkegaard who felt impelled to reintroduce Christianity into Christendom, Jones, armed with the certainty that we must either offer something better than this new order of Marxist communism or "succumb to it," launched his life's work of unpacking the meaning of the unshakable Kingdom for world restoration.

Being persuaded that his calling was indeed to interpret the Christian message of the Kingdom of God along the lines Jesus revealed throughout his ministry, Jones determined to go to Russia. In 1934 he glimpsed up close and personal Russia's brand of communism. When he returned to India he went immediately to the Himalayas. For two months he and fellow Sat Tal Ashramites engaged in corporate study focusing on the Gospels' teachings of the Kingdom of God. What emerged was Jones' 1935 book *Christ's Alternative to Communism*.

Jones acknowledged that while the answer of the Kingdom of God as alternative was adequate, the interpretation of that answer would be

3 Ibid.
4 Ibid., p. 10.

"partial and incomplete."[4] Five years later *Is the Kingdom of God Realism?* appeared as the quintessential exposition of the Kingdom of God as Jones rediscovered it within the pages of the New Testament. His treatment of the Kingdom of God in this 1940 book is unsurpassed in its profundity. If the Church even now could but see, believe, receive, enter into and proclaim the Kingdom of God on earth as Jones, writing by the inspiration of the Holy Spirit, understood it, Christianity and Christians would be completely revolutionized and revived for authentic ministry, mission and witness. When Jones grasped the centrality of the Kingdom of God, its comprehensiveness, and its implication for every area of life, not only for the individual but also for the social as the only way to live life here and now, he rescued it, as it were, from beyond this life where it had been relegated to the future.

After traversing Russia and painstakingly investigating materialistic communism, Jones was convinced that the "whole basis of society" must shift from competition to cooperation.[5] To Jones the world's choice was narrowed to two: "atheistic communism and the Kingdom of God on earth."[6] Jones revealed his irrepressibly sanguine assessment thusly, "… the Russian experiment is going to help … Christianity to rediscover the meaning of the Kingdom of God upon earth. If it does it will mean such a mighty revival of the Christian spirit that will transform the earth."[7] Repeating his contention more forcefully, he wrote,

> they (Russian communists) were going to make us rediscover the meaning of the Kingdom of God on earth. And if we did and should apply it in its full meaning, it would prove to be the

5 Ibid., p. 16.
6 Ibid.
7 Ibid., p. 32.

greatest spiritual awakening since Pentecost and would dwarf even that in its world sweep. It may be that God is using the Communists to awaken Christendom to something neglected in its own gospel.[8]

In hindsight we do not see that this prediction happened (or has not yet happened). However, this should not prevent those who read and appreciate Jones' works from recognizing the truth and significance of his interpretation and analysis of the meaning of the Kingdom of God and the implications of the same for the Church today as being spot on.

What, then, is Jones' take on the Kingdom of God? To reiterate, Jones put forth the Kingdom of God concept, derived from scripture, in his attempt to delineate clearly Jesus' Master program and its content to be Christianity's answer to Russian communism. Jesus, Jones held, was "revolutionary" but he was a "constructive Revolutionary." Whereas Jesus' program was audacious and radical because based on love; communism, based on hate, was ruthless, iconoclastic, and despising of all that was past.

Jones directs his readers to Mary's Song in Luke's gospel. Mary saw that the new Kingdom would "precipitate revolution in the sum total of human living."

> He hath scattered the proud in the imagination of their heart.
> He hath put down princes from their thrones,
> And hath exalted them of low degree.
> The hungry he hath filled with good things;
> And the rich he hath sent empty away.[9]

---

8 Ibid., p. 33.
9 Ibid., p. 51.

Jones discerned four revolutions in Mary's Song: First, a general revolution tolerating no special privileges; second, a political revolution as clear warning to the rule of any in power who were out of sync with the new Kingdom; third, a social revolution, exalting those of low degree and eliminating all "privilege based on birth and property and social standing." Fourth, there would be economic revolution providing necessities for all as God intended and disallowing luxuries for the few.[10]

Jones concludes, "No wonder Bernard Shaw said that 'this song of Mary is the most revolutionary song that has ever been written in the history of Europe.' It is."[11]

Next Jones turns our attention to what he labeled the Nazareth Manifesto, enunciated by Jesus in his hometown synagogue close on the heels of his wilderness struggle:

> The Spirit of the Lord is upon me,
> Because he anointed me to preach good tidings to
> the poor [the economically disinherited];
> He hath sent me to proclaim release to the captives,
>   [the socially and politically disinherited]
> And recovering of sight to the blind, [the physically
>   disinherited]
> To set at liberty them that are bruised, [the morally
>   and spiritually disinherited]
> To proclaim the acceptable year of the Lord.
>   [the Lord's Year of Jubilee – a new beginning
>   on a world scale]
> The Spirit of the Lord is upon me – the dynamic behind
>   it all.[12]

---

10 Ibid., pp. 51-53.
11 Ibid., p. 54.
12 Ibid., pp. 41-42.

Jones believed that through this Manifesto, Jesus intended to "project into the soul of humanity" the true meaning of the Kingdom of God on earth. He also, in expounding on the key assertions contained in the Manifesto, aimed to expose the deceptions and inadequacies of the communist program to be on dangerously shaky ground.

Jones was accused of becoming obsessed with the Kingdom of God. This did not curtail his enthusiasm for the Kingdom of God as the "vast, indefinable and defining, radical, redemptive, refining, transforming, enlivening and powerful key to everything else there is. It is the answer to the whole of life because Jesus Christ made it so."[13] Jones never considered himself a professional writer. He wrote out of an "inner urge" to meet a perceived need.[14] He wrote almost thirty books, each aimed at a particular end. In 1934 *Christ's Alternative to Communism* appeared because the subject of communism was the pressing need facing Christianity and the world. In Jones' view the Kingdom of God more than met this pressing need.

In his later books, notably, *The Choice Before Us*, (1937), *Is the Kingdom of God Realism?* (1940), *The Unshakable Kingdom and the Unchanging Person* (1972), Jones enlarged, corrected and refined the Kingdom of God concept. Of course, the Kingdom of God was more than mere concept; it was *fact* writ large. It was from before the foundation of the world. He distinguished the Kingdom from the church. For the most part the Kingdom of God was confused as being the same as the church. Time and again Jones clarified the difference:[15]

---

13 Graham and Graham, *First the Kingdom*, 1994, p. 67.
14 Ibid., p. 69.
15 Ibid., p. 89.

1. The Church is a relativism.	1. The Supreme Kingdom, the Kingdom of God is Absolute.
2. Christ never made himself synonymous with the Church.	2. The Kingdom and Christ are Synonymous.
3. The Church may be and is the agent of redemption, of the "coming of that redemption."	3. The Kingdom is itself redemption – "not the subject of redemption – it offers it."
4. We are to build the Church, for it is "a relativism built more or less after the pattern of the absolute, the Kingdom of God."	4. We are not to build the Kingdom for it is already built. "For this 'Kingdom is built from the foundation of the world."

In essence the Church was to be the servant to the Kingdom. Jones pointedly reminded us that our highest loyalty is to the Kingdom making us bound to be "loyal to the Church to the degree that it is loyal to the Kingdom."[16]

Jones outlined our ontological relationship to the Kingdom of God. His reasoning was cogent and persuasive. God made us for the Kingdom. It is our native home. Until and unless we realized that we were made for the Kingdom, frustration would rule the day. Using everyday metaphors, Jones said that we were made for the Kingdom as a glove is made for the hand or air for the lungs.

Ethical implications were not overlooked. Jones maintained that we did not have to love our neighbor, but we wouldn't get along without him. Moreover, Jones apprehended that the Kingdom was Christocentric. Christ was the Perfect Person embodying and giving

---

16 Ibid.

15

expression to God's Perfect Plan or Program for humankind. To underscore the primacy of the Kingdom, Jones interpreted Jesus words in Matthew 6:33 thusly, "Seek first, last and in between the Kingdom of God…"

How did the Kingdom of God come? Jones discerned that based on Jesus' teachings it came both gradually and apocalyptically. Amazingly Jesus declared that the "location" of the Kingdom, to the shock of the religious elite of his day, was "within" them, in their midst. The Kingdom of God was not to be thought of exclusively as a distant goal, but rather as a fact now.

To conclude, here is a quote worth pondering:

The Christian faith has often been trying to fly with one wing – the living Christ as expression of the living order, the Kingdom as a task and hope. We are now seeing more clearly that to fly with one wing is to go around in circles, be that one wing the Person or the Order. It must be both – the Person and the Order. Each is unique but coming together they make an uniqueness unparalleled.[17]

As indicated earlier, Jesus taught "those who have ears to hear" that we are to "see it (Kingdom of God), believe it, receive it, enter into it and proclaim it." To repeat, that encapsulates our relationship to Christ and his Kingdom. Jones held that whether we recognized and embraced Kingdom principles or not they would work for us if we "stumbled" upon them.

I am convinced from having read practically all of E. Stanley Jones' books, some more than once, that he himself was possessed as much *by* the Kingdom as he possessed it. The book of Acts tells us that Jesus, before his ascension, talked with his disciples about the Kingdom of

---

17 Ibid., p. 130.

God. Was this a reiteration or reinforcement (perhaps both) of his earlier teaching on the Galilean and Judean hillsides. Or was this new content? Luke does not say. I am further convinced that the Holy Spirit imparted to Jones, through above and beyond revelation, all of what Jesus taught before temporarily leaving earth to return to heaven. If this is indeed the case, we can do no better than to delve into Jones' seminal exposition of the Kingdom of God. *Christ's Alternative to Communism* is not a bad place to start in our lifetime journey of rediscovering for our own edification, faith development, and spiritual enrichment of God's Kingdom on earth.

MARCIA GRAHAM

June 2019

PREFACE

TO THE 1951 EDITION

In this book, written sixteen years ago, I said that this generation, or at the most the next will have to decide between materialistic, atheistic Communism and the Kingdom of God on earth. I thought it would take a generation for this issue to come to a head. In half a generation the issue has become acute.

The book was written in 1935 before Russia had attacked Finland, had absorbed the Baltic States, and had turned imperialistic in general. The Russian experiment was apparently going to be demonstrated initially within Russia.

That meant that at that time we were more interested in the Russian experiment than afraid of her imperialism. Along with many others, my attitude toward the experiment was more sympathetic than it would be today. I see Russia now as a world danger.

Nevertheless, I find that the main issues I pointed out then have become intensified and the main prophecies fulfilled. I felt that force used in the means would persist in the ends, and it has been so. What Communists gain by force they must hold by force.

I felt that with no objective moral universe—the only morality being that which gets you to your goal of Communism—there would be a sense of expediency running through the whole. That has happened. We do not trust the word of Communists, on the whole, for they are ready to use truth or untruth if it, in their view, forwards the cause of Communism.

I was sure that the dictatorship of the proletariat would become a dictatorship over the proletariat, and it has been so. The state has not faded out, as orthodox Marxism prophesied, but has become more ubiquitous and dictatorial. It has become a police state.

But this book was primarily written not to emphasize the weaknesses or the strengths of Communism, but to present the Christian alternative to Communism. In rereading what I wrote I find myself holding to the main thesis of the book. That remains intact. There is a Christian alternative, and our emphasis should be to apply that alternative so that a soil might be created in which Communism could not grow.

But our attitude of fear and hysteria has thrown the emphasis so strongly upon hunting out supposed or real Communists that we have forgotten almost entirely that our main defense is an economy so sound that Communism becomes irrelevant.

Since this book was written, capitalism has shown signs of change. Profit sharing is modifying the system from being fiercely competitive to being fruitfully co-operative. That points in the right direction. The profit motive is legitimate and good provided the profits are shared widely.

Communism as a system is not the answer. It will break down ultimately through inherent weaknesses. We must be ready with a demonstration of the Christian answer. The Christian answer is the

Kingdom of God on earth. This book attempts to expound that answer and points to its application. I am gratified to know that the main plea is still relevant, and to my mind more relevant now than ever.

E. STANLEY JONES

January 3, 1951

PREFACE

TO THE 1935 EDITION

I had been reading a good deal on the great experiment in Russia for two reasons. One was the pressure I could feel in the whole of the East, and in the West, an indefinable sense of being pressed upon by an unseen and almost unknown something: that "something" was the fact of a new order in our world midst, with new principles and a different goal. This 'sense' rather haunted me. For I felt that its issues had not been fairly and squarely met. It gave one that sense of uneasiness that one has when he has a big, difficult, and unpleasant job on his hands, which he knows he has to tackle, but which he postpones by doing in the meantime various unimportant things, all the time knowing that, sooner or later, he must come to grips with the bigger thing. His absorption with the unimportant cannot quite make him forget the untackled task. It hangs over him. The sensitive minds in Christendom know that sooner or later they must come to grips with the issues raised by the Marxist experiment in Russia. But to do so would not mean a theological debate (had that been all there was involved, we should have been in the fray long ago), but the question of a new world-order. That is disturbing. Hence the hesitation. We read propaganda for and against the experiment, hoping that will settle it.

But it does not. For through the rifts of the clouds of controversy we see the fact of a new order emerging, different and challenging to the whole basis of present-day civilization.

In spite of the clouds, we can see that the Russians are making amazing progress; for instance, their literacy has gone up from 35 per cent in 1913 to 85 per cent today; instead of 3,500,000 pupils in 1912, there are now over 25,000,000 pupils and students; the circulation of daily papers is twelve times what it was in the Czarist days. They have risen from the eighth nation in total industrial production in 1927 to second today. Only the United States now surpasses them in total industrial production. And they have accomplished this in five years. The total output of Soviet products, excluding the agricultural, is 334 times what it was in 1914. They are in the process of creating in Moscow what will be the tallest and perhaps the most imposing building in the world, the parliamentary building and memorial to Lenin—symbol of the fact that they expect to surpass all the material and cultural achievements of the rest of the world. And in doing this there is a repudiation of all religion. These two facts of accomplishment and irreligion put together make the problem of Communism in Russia the untouched task of Christendom. The Christian world is uneasy, because it knows that with all its absorption in many unimportant things, it must sooner or later face this question with an adequate answer. And it is dawning upon it that the adequate answer will not be the production of an argument, but the production of a better order. That pressure is the pressure of a veritable thorn in the side of Christendom.

The second reason I had for reading all I could on Russia was that I was going to glimpse it for myself on my way back to India. I hoped to get the feel and the drift of the great experiment at first hand.

But all the books I read left me with a sense of incompleteness. Something had not been said. Many of the books were written from the Christian standpoint, and were able and incisive and moving. They were tremendous in letting us see what was happening in Russia, and moving in their appeal to the Christian world to do something about it. But when it came to putting up the Christian alternative the emphasis seemed weak or hesitating. They seemed to take it for granted that we know what the Christian alternative is. And that is not quite plain.

Just as I had felt the pressure of Russia on the one side, I had felt a bigger pressure on the other— something vast and overwhelming and challenging and adequate—the Kingdom of God. Our Christian writers have come in sight of it and its interpretation, but haven't interpreted it and presented it as a head-on and sweeping answer to Marxist Communism. As I sat one night reading on an ocean liner, the Inner Voice raised the question with me whether I should not attempt that interpretation. It was stronger than my words indicate—it was a call, almost a mandate.

I shrank from the task for many weeks. Questions which Marxism raises involve social and economic specializations which are not in my field. I am a simple interpreter of Christ to the East, and I must stick to my task. But then the increasing realization came that I should be sticking to my task if I were to attempt to interpret the Christian message in the light of the Communistic challenge. For to interpret the Christian message is my field.

Fortunately, when I returned from Russia I went straight to the Ashram at Sat Tal in the Himalayas where, with a group of about a hundred persons, we studied together for two months the Christian alternative to Communism. This gave me the immense advantage of getting the reactions and the corrections of the group to the message contained in this book. We emerged from those two months of corporate study with our hearts on fire. There was an open door before us. The Kingdom of God on earth was that open door. We had an answer, and we felt that it was an adequate one.

But while we felt that we had an adequate answer in the Kingdom of God, we knew that our interpretation of that answer would be partial and incomplete. Our hope is that this interpretation may at least throw open doors for possible advance. If this rough-hewn attempt stimulates more skilled and painstaking workers to correct and to polish the program presented in these pages, the author will be grateful. We shall need an army of thinkers and workers who will pool their thought and plans before an adequate Christian alternative will clearly emerge. It is now in the process of emerging. But our time is short. The world mind is being made up and we must be ready with an adequate program.

I take the announcement at Nazareth as the starting point of that program, but only as the starting point. If I seem to be putting more weight on it than it was intended to bear, which I do not believe to be the case, my inward justification is that I do not rest the program upon this announcement alone, but upon the sum total of the attitudes and teachings of the New Testament.

The writing of this preface is being done at about the geographical center of India. It is Sunday morning and my missionary colleague calls to me that Moscow is broadcasting in English and that I must come. The intelligent and able speaker ends up his address by announcing that a prize of a book will be given to the best answer, sent in by the radio listeners, to the following questions: "Why is there no unemployment in the U.S.S.R.?" and "Is there individual liberty in the Soviet system?"

Sunday morning, quiet and peaceful, in this ancient land of India— and those two questions intrude! No unemployment? In a world suffering the horrors of unemployment? There must be a catch somewhere. But whether there is or isn't, the whole question of the Russian Experiment is intruding into the Sabbath-like but ominous calm of the East, and into the struggling strenuousness of the West. The Christian answer must be unmistakable and clear—that is, if there is any Christian answer.

E. STANLEY JONES

December 2, 1934
Leonard Theological College
Jubbulpore, C. P., India

INTRODUCTION

THE COMING CRISIS: THE CHRISTIAN ALTERNATIVE

I am persuaded that Christianity is headed toward a supreme crisis—perhaps a decisive crisis. Events are leading up to a world decision. This generation, or at the most the next, will have to decide between materialistic, atheistic Communism and the Kingdom of God on earth. And this in both East and West.

For the foundations of society are crumbling before our very eyes. Many of the old securities are gone, or going. As I go about the world I find men with the feeling that the Germans must have had when the Hindenburg line began to crumble. Up to that moment they felt secure, after that—? That is where we are today. The old lines are giving way. Question marks about the future haunt us. Some of the reasons for this decay are obvious. Modern knowledge is breaking down the sense of compartmentalism in life and is giving us the conception of a unified world. But the organization of human life is too small to fit that conception. One able thinker diagnoses our difficulty thus: "The main disability under which the twentieth century is suffering arises from the fact that millions of human beings, who are the products of distinct cultural regions, have been thrust too suddenly into a planetary world entailing complex relationships on a world scale. Most of the mental equipment where with they are trying to make these adjustments—

assumptions, principles, attitudes, institutions—are out-of-date heritages of this earlier stage of things. For example, the present forms of political organization which grew up to meet local conditions and which today are struggling to solve international problems by means of colonial administrations, balances of power, and pretentious claims of national sovereignty are no more adapted to the demands of a planetary world than the venerable charters and the seaboard psychology of the thirteen colonies were fitted to incorporate into a commonwealth that vaster territory which lay to the west of the Alleghany Mountains."[1]

> **Christianity is headed toward a supreme crisis—perhaps a decisive crisis.... This generation, ... will have to decide between materialistic, atheistic Communism and the Kingdom of God ... in both East and West.**

While we accept this diagnosis as true as far as it goes, we would insist that our fundamental "disability" is deeper than the example given. Our main difficulties are not rooted in the political, they are rooted in the economic and the social, particularly in the economic. Most of our political difficulties are symptoms of a disease which is deep rooted in the economic. For our chief world-sickness is this: we are trying to respond to world unity while our economic life is based on competition. It is that fact which bedevils the whole world situation. Selfish and ruthless competition is at the basis of our daily struggle for livelihood. Of course it is softened here and there with

---

1 Archibald G. Baker, *Christian Missions and a New World Culture* (Chicago: Willett, Clark & Co., 1934), p. 10.

many a kindliness. It is the most insistent and ever-present incentive and urge. This spirit of selfish competition works its way from the individual clear up to the political and the international. It is at the basis of our world difficulty. For example, I sat on the same platform and heard Sir John Simon tell of the earnest, but pathetic and fruitless, efforts they were making to disarm the nations through the Disarmament Conference at Geneva. One could see at a glance wherein lay the difficulty: How can you ask nations to disarm in a world life based on competition? Can they throw away their very weapons of survival? These weapons are natural weapons if life is selfishly competitive.

But we have now arrived at the place in human development where we are beginning to see that, of all the outmoded conceptions, selfish competition is the most outmoded. It simply will not fit this new world which is striving to emerge. If we cannot base the future on cooperation, we perish, for all the great demands laid on us for the making of a new world have co-operation at their center. It is beginning to be realized that it is written in the very constitution of things that if we save our lives in selfishness, we lose them; but if we lose them in the collective good, we find them again. We may take that or leave it, but that is the fundamental law on which the future will be made or broken. I grant that the voice of lower nature is not clear at this point, for the law of competition seems to prevail there, but in the higher order into which we are striving to emerge co-operation is the very law of its life. Here "mutual aid" takes the place of "self against the rest."

Can our modern capitalistic society fit into a co-operative future? If it could, I for one would be most happy, for I do not like change, with all the upset that will be involved, nor am I committed to any alternative economic scheme. But I am afraid that the chances of its

29

doing so are heavily loaded against it. John Maynard Keynes is a capitalistic economist, but this is what he says: "Modern capitalism is absolutely irreligious, without internal union, without much public spirit, often though not always a mere congeries of possessors and pursuers." It is being weighed and is being found wanting. It is fundamentally incapable of responding to the world demand being laid on it, namely, that of producing and distributing enough for all and at the same time creating a world of brothers and sisters. It can produce—even Marx and Engels admitted the amazing productive capacity of capitalism—for that fits in with its own spirit of acquisitiveness; but it cannot distribute, for that cuts across its very nature. To distribute adequately and justly demands a motive which it simply doesn't have. When Wood says, "If that is all the trouble [unequal distribution of national income], capitalists should be intelligent enough to avert disaster," he seems very naive. "If that is all the trouble"! But that "trouble" is basic. It is the millstone around our necks as we strive to pull ourselves out of the morass. No amount of individual good will can atone for that basic "trouble."

The whole basis of society must be shifted from competition to cooperation. C. H. Dawson is right when he says that "the choice is not between an individualistic humanism and some form of collectivism, but between a collectivism that is purely mechanistic and one that is spiritual." In other words, the choice is between a materialistic, atheistic Communism and the Kingdom of God on earth.

I narrow the choice to those two, for I do not think that Fascism presents a permanent issue. It has the seeds of its own decay within itself. It is an attempt to hold the old order by force. It is true that here and there it modifies that order, but it leaves its essential nature unchanged. It succeeds —for a time. For it tightens up the old competitive spirit, makes it more selfish and ruthless and seemingly strong. But it is national fever instead of national strength. And fevers have a way of leaving devastating after-effects. Fascism is the flare-up of an impossible order—a flare-up just before the end.

But Russia with its materialistic Communism does present an issue—a real one. Object to it as we may, and as I do, on the basis of its lack of liberty, of its compulsions, of its ruthlessness, and its materialistic atheism, nevertheless it has founded society on a higher principle, namely, that of cooperation. That cooperation may be limited to those who share the same views and who fit into the regime, nevertheless, within that restriction the co-operation is a living thing and is open to all on equal terms. When Stalin said in an address to the Russian people, "In the Soviet Union, citizens, we have deposited the word 'Riches' in the archives of the nation," he said something that judges us to the very center. He did not mean collective riches, for they are feverishly striving to increase them and are succeeding in an amazing way, but he did mean the end of selfishly striving to be rich

> **The whole basis of society must be shifted from competition to co-operation.... the choice is between a materialistic, atheistic Communism and the Kingdom of God on earth.**

when to be rich means that other people become poor. We may squirm under that, we may hate it and cast it from us, but in the end it will judge us, for it is a higher ideal.

That higher ideal will dawn upon most of us only when it begins to produce a higher standard of material well-being in Russia than competition is able to produce in other countries. Up to now the level

31

of material life in Russia is lower than in most Western countries. So Russia can be dismissed by a wave of the hand as a land of famine and poverty. But when Russia makes up the leeway and begins to surpass the rest of the world—as she will probably do within the next ten years, if the present rate of advance is continued—then there will be the great awakening to the realities of the case. In the first Five-Year Plan they have laid the foundation of their industrial life by concentrating on the heavy industries. That has been accomplished. In five years they have gone from the eighth place to the second in total industrial production. In the second Five-Year Plan they will concentrate on the lighter industries, in other words, on things for themselves. They expect to double the standard of living by 1937; and if they succeed as well as they did in the first Five-Year Plan, they will accomplish it. In that case they will pull ahead of the West in material well-being. I predict that that will be the moment of the great crisis in the Western world. For the disinherited millions will understand that argument.

Russia worships the machine. The tractor seen on many posters is the new economic Messiah. On the veranda of a large cathedral in Leningrad I saw an agricultural machine parked—symbol of the fact that Russia had turned her back on religion and had put her faith in the machine. When I saw the ardency with which they worshiped the machine, I inwardly smiled and said to myself: "We too once worshiped the machine. They will come to our disillusionment." Then my smile wore away, for I saw there was a difference: we are afraid of the machine because we have it harnessed to private profit; it therefore constantly makes for overproduction and consequent unemployment and depression. It runs us periodically into a dead end. With them it is different. They are using the machine in the purposes of collective well-being and not of private profit; therefore there will be little or no danger of overproduction, for the products are distributed to raise the general standard of all. That standard will rise constantly as production increases. Therefore they have an open door. We haven't. We haven't— *unless we change our basis from competition to co-operation.*

That demand to change is laid on us by stern necessity. Our very survival depends on it. The question, then, comes: Will that change of basis come under the direction of materialistic, atheistic Communism or under the direction of the Kingdom of God on earth? You may forget your mother, you may forget your own name, but you dare not forget this issue as the supreme issue of the future —and of the present.

For everywhere this issue is arising in one form or another. The impress for change which is pressing upon the soul of the world is largely coming from Russia. A young Indian Christian professor said to me the other day: "I am shaken to my depths. I see the Russian Communists producing something in an unchristian way which we ought to, but cannot produce in a Christian way. My very spiritual life and my Christian faith depend upon the solution of this dilemma." A Hindu youth put it to me in this way: "We students stand with two sets of books in one hand and two sets in the other. In one hand we have Gandhi and Tolstoy, and in the other hand Lenin and Marx. We do not know whether to go the violent, irreligious way of Lenin and Marx or the nonviolent, religious way of Gandhi and Tolstoy." He represents the dilemma of many an Indian youth. "I am interested in what you say, for practically all the students of the university are Communists at heart or at least they are potential Communists," said an Indian graduate student to me. Potential Communists or potential followers of the New Kingdom—that is the dilemma of youth! Nor is youth alone affected by this impact. Even in places where one would not dream of it arising we find it pressing upon the souls of men. A Hindu, seemingly orthodox, for he had the marks of Vishnu upon his brow, arose at question time and said, "I don't believe in God any longer."

Surprised, I remarked: "My brother, I don't know which to believe—the words of your lips or the marks on your forehead. They speak contradictory things."

"Oh," he replied with a wave of his hand, "you can't tell what a man is thinking these days by the marks on his forehead. We are just waiting for Gandhi to play out, then what I represent begins."

I asked, "What do you represent?"

"I represent Communism," he replied.

Here was a man with all the signs of ancient orthodoxy intact and yet behind those symbols this fact of the Marxist challenge had possession. At question time in another place I was asked about my objections to Russian Communism. After I had said all I could in favor of it I was giving my objections. All the time I was giving the objections a Hindu lady with the orthodox caste marks upon her forehead was shaking her head in disagreement. The shaking of that woman's head is the shaking of a whole social system.

India, with her poorest and most exploited peasantry of the world, is tinder for this teaching. In the midst of many an Indian field there is the bleached skull of a bullock stuck up on a stick, a fitting symbol—a death-head the most prominent thing in these poverty-stricken villages. When the implications of the teaching of Communism dawn upon the mind of these peasants, a great upsurge will come. There are three great issues before India embodied in three persons: Mahatma Gandhi represents the demand for religious equality as he presses the rights of the Untouchables to temple entry; Doctor Ambedkar, the leader of the Untouchables, says he is not interested in this temple-entry, his demand

is for the doing away with caste —in other words, social equality;
Jawaharlal Nehru, the idol of youth, represents the demand for
economic equality. The first two men are free, the third is in jail, for the
demand for economic equality is the most far-reaching and dangerous
to the present order. One holds his breath when he sees the changes
which will come when the full impact of this teaching comes upon the
soul of India, with its ancient culture.

In China Communism is a more urgent and immediate issue than
in India. There is a race on in China between Communism and
Christianity, and Communism is leading. The old religions are out of it;
the race has narrowed down to these two. There is a Communist "cell"
in almost every school and college. This "cell" is supposed to multiply
like a living cell—and it does. A Communist student is planted among,
say twenty-five students, and he is supposed to win them to
Communism. He is more than a match for the twenty-five, for he is
certain of where he wants to go while the others are confused and
uncertain. If a soldier of the Nationalist armies is captured by the Red
Army, he is given the option of joining the Red Army or of being sent
home with three dollars in his pocket and Communist literature. That
last item is important. A missionary captured by the Communists in
China was held for some weeks and then released, but only after he had
been given a course in Communism. When I asked him whether he
thought it would spread, he replied, "I have watched it, for they are
passionately teaching." That counts.

At a Conference at which I was speaking in China a Communist
Manifesto was slipped into the pages of the hymn books between
meetings. This is symbolic of the fact that this movement, for good or
ill, is invading our very sanctuaries. And the point is this: if that
Manifesto represents a higher ideal and a greater passion for the
uplifting of man than does the hymn book, then they win. General

Chiang Kai Shek sends an appeal to the American people through a Christian bishop, saying that "all educated China is weighing the relative merits of Christianity and Communism and is deciding upon which to build the future of China." He asks the Christian people of America to help China to decide that question. Never in the history of modern missions has a more important appeal come to the West than that appeal. Of course there is the danger that, since the appeal comes from a military man and one known to be attached to the old order, Christianity may seem to be bound up with militarism and the old order. This must not be, for Christianity can only reply adequately to that appeal as it produces something better than either the old order or Communism has been able to produce.

In a Round Table Conference at Nanking a leading Chinese citizen said: "I am not a Christian, but let me say that all our eyes are on Christianity. If it can do anything to save our country, now is the time for it to exert its power. We will all follow it if it does." I repeat that the eyes of educated China are upon this issue: Will the future be determined by Russian Communism or by Christianity? The destiny of hundreds of millions hangs upon the answer to that question.

Is Communism an issue in Japan? It is, when Marx's *Das Kapital* is a best seller and when fourteen thousand students have gone to jail because of their Communist allegiances.

In regard to Turkey, an editor in that land says, "The youth of Turkey is spending vague and uncertain moments of torture and hesitation between the regimes of Capitalism and Communism."

Is there any significance in the fact that Wood tells us that Communism and "The Group Movement" are competing for the loyalty of the youth of Oxford University, and that two hundred and fifty undergraduates are said to have joined the October Club, a

Communist organization? Middleton Murry may be exaggerating when he says that "Communism is the one living religion in the Western world today," but it is significant that Murry, the author of *Jesus, Man of Genius*, should say so.[2] It is perhaps more significant still when a diplomat of high standing, himself not a Communist, should say to me in Russia, "I believe there is more spiritual power in these Russian people than is to be found in the churches of America." This too may be an exaggeration, but if it is, let us remember that it is made by a churchman and that it lets us see the issue. Maurice Hindus, who knows his Russia well, says that the Russian is "the most unified and hence the happiest man in Europe today."[3] I felt the force of this when a very intelligent young Russian woman said to me, "Tell the students of India that we are happy and that we send our greetings."

Those who try to make out a case that the Russian people are dumb driven cattle before their dictatorial taskmasters are deeply mistaken. There are discontented elements, especially among those who cannot fit into the new regime, but the great bulk of the Russian people are behind communism body and soul with an enthusiasm that is amazing. If you doubt it, watch the twenty-five thousand students who on holidays come and work voluntarily, picking and shoveling earth to help in the speeding up of the work of building the subway in Moscow. This is not a spasm, it happens on a lesser scale every school day after school hours, and this by both girls and boys. They are joined by workmen in other trades after their own working day is over. Listen to the chant of youth as they sing on their festival days, "We are making a new world."

---

2 John Middleton Murry was an English writer. As a prolific author, he produced more than 60 books and thousands of essays and reviews on literature, social issues, politics, and religion during his lifetime.

3 Maurice Gerschon Hindus, was a Russian-American writer, foreign correspondent, lecturer and authority on Soviet and Central European affairs.

With all their hearts they believe they are. I asked an intelligent young woman if the Russian people were drinking as much vodka as before the Revolution, and her answer was interesting: "How can they, when five out of six are studying after their working hours to improve themselves? They haven't time to think of vodka." There is no doubt that the apathy of the people has been broken up and that there is a passion to improve themselves. They have hope, and what they believe is an open door.

Come with me and look into the faces of the school children in the city of Baku. I asked the able, poised principal of this school if I might question one of her classes. It was a class picked at random, composed of children from twelve to fifteen years of age, there was no stage play and many ethnic backgrounds were represented. I asked them to tell me what they found in favor of the new regime. Up went their hands in eagerness. "Before my father was depressed in cultural life, now he is improving in his family life." "There were no such schools for working children, they were only for the rich." "Before we lived in a cellar, had no electricity, now we have a decent home." "Before the teachers beat the children, now they treat us kindly and there is no racial difference." "The cultural life of the workers has been improved, now we can have newspapers and magazines." "It was forbidden to Turkish girls to go to school, now we all go." "The food is better at home and in the school." "This school is on the site of a church; this is good, for the church did little for the education of the people; it gave no technical and political education, only religious education."

I stopped them and asked them to tell what they had against the present regime. "The government gives good orders, but there are people within the system who twist those orders and cause confusion. The bourgeoisie, still left in factories and offices, must be cleared out." They went on in a similar vein, but again I stopped them with the remark, "But all your criticisms are within the system; you have not criticized the system itself." There was a silence which I could see breathed astonishment, when one boy of about twelve broke it by blurting out in excitement: "But we have no criticism of the system itself. The system is all right." They believe that it is, and they believe further that it is only a question of time until the rest of the world will have to come to it. They say that just as America was the pioneer in political democracy in her day, so Russia today is the pioneer in economic democracy.

While questioning a group of young teachers I asked them to give what they had for and against the regime, and I found that they too were criticizing within the system, but were not criticizing the system itself. I interrupted and asked for the criticism of the system itself. They looked at me in astonishment. When I suggested that they were not free to criticize the system, and that they were therefore afraid to do so, they laughed at me in derision. It is quite true that they are not free to criticize the system, but they apparently believe with all their hearts that the system is all right, and that they have found the fundamental basis for human living.

The difference lies here: There is a doubt creeping across Western civilization about the whole system upon which life is founded. We are concluding that the competitive principle will not work except for the few. Adam Smith and his Manchester school of economics promised that the *laissez faire* doctrine would work out for the good of the greatest number. It has not. It cannot. It has left us with a world half overfed and the other half underfed. If Abraham Lincoln were here today, he would change his dictum of, "This nation cannot exist half slave and half free," and would say with infinite sadness, "This world of ours cannot exist half-stuffed and half-starved." And Lincoln would be right. God has given enough for all, but we his children have not yet learned to distribute it. And I am afraid that we cannot do it under the present system. I wish we could, but I am afraid we cannot, for production and distribution are in the hands of private profit. It must be changed over and used in the purposes of the collective good.

I am not a Communist, nor do I call myself a Socialist, but I am a Christian seeking for a solution of this problem. I am sure— desperately sure —that Christianity must give a lead at this place or abdicate. It is not enough to tell me that Christianity can and does change the lives of individual men. I know it, and am grateful beyond words for that fact. But it is not enough. Shall we rescue individual slaves and leave intact the slave system? Shall we reclaim individual drunkards and not touch the liquor traffic? Shall we pick up the wounded in war and leave intact the war system? Shall we pick up the derelicts of a competitive system and give them doles and leave the system to go on producing its poverty, its hates, and its exploiting imperialisms?

> **There is a doubt creeping across Western civilization about the whole system upon which life is founded. We are concluding that the competitive principle will not work except for the few.**

There were Christian slave owners who treated their slaves kindly, but this did not touch the basic injustice of their relationships. There are splendid Christians amid this present economic system who do much to soften it, but that very fact often hides the basic injustices. For instance, I was told in answer to this demand for a changed society that a man in charge of the work force of a factory was a slave driver and tried to browbeat his men into speeding up their work efforts. He produced only sullenness. But he was "changed," and called the men in and told them of the "change" and that hereafter he would treat them differently. The men responded and production was speeded up. At the directors' meeting the chairman told of this incident and ended by saying: "The manager says that it was religion that made this change. Whatever it was, we are glad that it has produced a better showing on this balance sheet." Here religion was used to produce more dividends—and incidentally to confuse the basic issues. The system was used toward the ends of private profit instead of the collective good, and religion merely softened somewhat its hard edges.

If merely to change individuals, however necessary that may be, is not enough, what shall we say of some of the less vital "activities" of the church in an hour like this? If competition as a world program is outmoded, so is much of the church life outmoded when we think of its world task. The Communists of Russia saw that the Protestant churches of Russia were about to sweep the country just after the Revolution, for their ideas fitted into many of the things under the new regime. They organized co-operatives, they gave themselves to the total uplift of the life of the people until, in the early days of the Revolution, these people were held up as models for Communistic youth to emulate. Then the Communists became frightened—this was dangerous. They forbade the church having any part whatever in social reconstruction. They could worship—that was all. They knew that they would thereby render the church innocuous. But we must not be too hard on the Communists at that point, for capitalistic society has practically demanded the same thing of the church. Let politics and economics alone! Business is business! They would reduce the church into the innocuous by reducing it merely to a worshiping institution. Much of the activity of the church today is dangerously near to trifling.

We are told that there was a Congress of the Russian Orthodox

Church in 1917, and that for two days they debated the question of whether a white or a yellow surplice should be used in a certain place in the church ceremony, while within six blocks of this Congress, at that very time, men were being shot down in the counterrevolution. Debating the question of white or yellow surplices while Russia was going through the travail of the birth of a new order! Let that picture haunt many of our conferences and committees where we deal with trivialities or pompous religious niceties while a world is being shaken to its depths. During the recent earthquake in India many of the pundits were surprised that the holy city of Benares was shaken too, for they had been taught that this sacred city was not connected with the rest of this sinful world. There is nothing exempt from this world-shaking movement for social reform, not even our sanctuaries.

Many in East and West are oblivious of this issue. They sense no coming storm. I was interviewed by a representative of a great metropolitan daily newspaper in America, in the midst of which I said, "In China the issue is clear-cut: Either Karl Marx or Jesus Christ will determine the future destiny of that land." He turned to me and asked, "Who is Karl Marx?" His mentality was that of a newspaper that was hunting for spicy local happenings, utterly oblivious of the great undercurrents that were remaking the world for good or ill. This mentality of the journalist was matched by that of the pastor in India who while interpreting for me stopped me when I used the word "Communism" and said, "I don't know that word." He had lived in a city which had just been rocked to its center by a strike of all the mill-workers—and Communists were largely leading it. The very day he said that he did not know the meaning of that word the Government of India had issued a proclamation proscribing Communistic organizations as unlawful in India. The British Government saw clearly that Communism was pushing against the very foundations of society as they now exist and was shaking them. The Christian pastor was living in another world.

No mere tinkering will do now. We must meet radicalism with a wiser and better radicalism. For we all see that change is needed. As I sit writing in this Himalayan retreat I am reminded of the time when these mountains were all ablaze around us with raging forest fires as they raced through the dry underbrush and the pine-needles. A newcomer to these mountains, living in one of the cottages near where the fire was coming, was seen with a watering can sprinkling the pine-needles around his house with water. Dampening pine-needles in the face of an approaching roaring furnace instead of clearing them away! Much of our religious effort seems dangerously near to dampening corporate injustice instead of clearing it away. No, that will not do now. It might have stayed things for a while once, but not now. We must go deeper.

But do not misunderstand me, for while I cry out against religious trifling at a time like this I do so because I am deeply convinced that Christianity has within it the program and the vitality for the remaking of the world, if we would discover it and apply it. A brilliant Hindu professor of science sat with us as we discussed *"Christ's Alternative to Communism"* at the Ashram this summer. After listening for some days he remarked: "Two things interest me. One is that I now see that there is really an alternative to Marxist Communism. I had thought there was none. And, second, I am amazed at the vitality of Christianity in facing such questions as these." I think that most of us who call ourselves Christians will be "amazed" as we go back again to discover within our Gospel an astounding program for the remaking of the world, and an amazing vitality to put that program into effect.

I am persuaded that the Russian experiment is going to help—and I was about to say to force Christianity to rediscover the meaning of the Kingdom of God upon earth. If it does, it will mean such a mighty revival of the Christian spirit as will transform the earth. God often uses instruments he cannot approve to make his children realize forgotten or neglected truths. It happened in Old Testament history, and it can happen again. For Christianity will fit better into a cooperative order than into a competitive order. It is not at home in an order where the weakest go to the wall and the devil takes the hindmost. In such a society Christianity is gasping for breath. It is not its native air. But its genius would flower in a co-operative order, for there love and good will and sharing, which are of the very essence of Christianity, should be at home.

> I am deeply convinced that Christianity has within it the program and the vitality for the remaking of the world, if we would discover it and apply it.

The night our train left Estonia for Leningrad I said to the bishop, my traveling companion: "Tomorrow morning, when we wake up, we shall be in Russia, and tomorrow morning will be Easter morning. So the first thing I shall say to you will be, 'The Lord is Risen,' and you are to answer, 'He is risen indeed.' We shall say this in affirmation of our own faith and as a witness against Christ-denying Russia." And thus it happened. It was the strangest Easter I ever lived through. For we spent the afternoon in the Anti-Religious Museum, which had once been the glorious Saint Isaac's Cathedral. The rest of the evening we spent hunting for open churches, but could find none, save a German church. Religion seemed to have collapsed like a house of cards. Christ was crucified again— dead and buried, with a "No-Resurrection" sign upon his grave. This was my first impression. But some time later, when I emerged at Baku at the other end of Russia, something else had formed in my heart. I had the feeling, ill-defined and fugitive, and yet with a certain definiteness about it, that something strange and paradoxical was happening, and it was this: Christ is rising again! His spirit is coming back to life in the passion for the underprivileged, in the belief in the common man, in the throwing open of the once select privileges of life to all who contribute. I had the feeling that a great deal of this was nearer to the spirit of Christ than much of the splendor and glory of the closed cathedrals. I saw a huge stone barring the door of one of these closed churches. The thought kept persisting, Was this stone that now barred the church door taken from against the door of the tomb of Christ, and would it now be easier for him to rise from that tomb and come back in his original spirit? At any rate, I had the feeling that they were going to make us rediscover the meaning of the Kingdom of God on earth. And if we did, and should apply it in its full meaning, it would prove to be the greatest spiritual awakening since Pentecost, and would dwarf even that in its world sweep.

It may be that God is using the Communists to awaken Christendom to something neglected in its own gospel. You remember that Jesus said: "A certain man had two sons, and he said to one son, 'Go and work in my vineyard,' and the son said, 'I will not,' but he went; and he said to the other son, 'Go and work in my vineyard,' and the son said, 'I will,' but he went not." And Jesus asked, "Which of these two did the will of his father?" The Communists are in many ways like the son who said he would not go and went—for they are doing many Christian things while denying the authority of Christ; but Christendom is dangerously near to the son who said he would go and went not, for we have said that we would enter into and establish the Kingdom of God, but have established something else in its place.

That "something else" which we have built up around Christ in the Western world is now being shaken to its depths. It must be, for it is shakable.

Russia hits one inwardly with a terrific thud. It knocks the breath out of one. One needs assurance. Will God not give a special word at an hour like that? I got it. In my daily morning readings while in Russia two passages were given to me with a kind of illumination about them. They were these: "For we have a kingdom which cannot be shaken," and, "Jesus Christ, the same yesterday, today, and forever." Amid the shock of things I emerged from Russia with two things: an unshakable Kingdom and an unchanging Person—a Program and a Person! I am persuaded that amid the clash of forces throughout the world these two things do remain. Many things in the Christian system are shakable and are crumbling. They should crumble, for they cannot stand the strain of the new demands laid on them. The hour of the Terrible Sifting has come. Christendom will have to pull up its roots from the present pagan order in which they are deeply embedded and plant them deep into the Kingdom of God and take its sustenance and life from it or it will perish. For the present order is shaken. Its weaknesses are breaking it down. But amid the crash of conditions two things remain: A Kingdom which I believe is the ultimate Order, and a Person who, I believe, is the ultimate Person. The one gives the Program for the remaking of the world and the other gives the power for the realization of that Program.

Forgive me if I repeat the issue as I close this Introduction. We must provide something better than Marxist Communism or succumb to it. The issue will not be settled by argument but by the actual production of a better order. The only way to beat them is to beat them to it.

But this means struggle and courage and faith and co-operation. For the forces of selfishness and exploitation are deeply intrenched. The church must learn anew the meaning of the cross—learn it by actually experiencing it. This coming travail will not be without blood. The Communists will not hesitate to shed the blood of others: we must not hesitate to shed our own. They will inflict suffering to bring in a new order: we must invite suffering to bring in God's new order. It would be easier to let all this alone and to retreat within the soul and there commune with God. It would be easier to do as the Russian Church did—retreat within its stately churches and go through ornate ritual while others grapple with these problems. Easier—and more deadly! As I was about to begin the writing of this book a request came signed by a hundred or more prominent church leaders asking me to write a book on "The Inner Life." I was deeply grateful for that request, and some day it must be answered. But it brought to a focus the conflict within me, and perhaps within the church: Shall we give ourselves to "The Inner Life" and let the question of a new world order alone? If we do, then our history will be the history of the Russian Church, and *"Ichabod"* will be written upon our drooping banners. On the other hand, amid the general breakdown and uncertainty we have a chance to guide the world into a new day. In the midst of the great confusion after the collapse of Czarism in Russia the only ones who had a definite program and real daring were the Communists. Kerensky had oratory but no program. The Communists seized power from his hesitating hand. In the midst of world confusion we must have more than oratory. Christianity has been preached to death. We must get hold of a program for world reconstruction and boldly apply it, lest again the Communists seize world power from the hesitating hand of Christendom.

We are now in the midst of a breathing space before the final issue is joined. We have time now to set our house in order, to define our attitudes and launch our Program. In all this the tempo matters mightily.

It is said that Dhrupa, an Indian sage, was asked by God what he wanted. He expressed his desire and it was given. Again he was asked and again his request granted. Asked the third time, Dhrupa replied, "I want nothing but to love God for the sake of God." For such an answer as this Dhrupa was made into the Pole Star and there he is today. That system will be the Pole Star of the future which leads men to ask not for their selfish and private ends, but for the good of the whole. In other words, that system will hold the future which loves most justly and deeply and widely and does most for man.

Which will be the Pole Star from which humanity will take its reckoning for its future course— Marxist Communism or the Kingdom of God on earth? Upon the answer to that question hangs the destiny of our society.

CHAPTER 1

GOOD NEWS TO THE
ECONOMICALLY DISINHERITED

W e must now address ourselves to the task of discovering, if possible, "Christ's Alternative to Communism." I am persuaded that the Christian forces of the world will not throw themselves behind this movement for the remaking of the total order unless they are sure that it is an integral part of their gospel. It must be something not imposed on the gospel as a changing social fashion, but the soul of its very soul. No movement ever took place that did not grow out of deep convictions. "The convictions of the heart are never stilled." The Russian Revolution was not a spasm, but grew out of convictions laid in the minds of many people for many years. The movement is now being fed by a very definite philosophy of life.

The Christian Revolution must be founded in convictions as deep as—and deeper than—Marxist Communism. It must rest upon principles that are the very foundations of the universe. It must go as deep as personal, individual need and spread as wide as human relationships extend. It must not only gather up into itself all the good in all other endeavors to remake the world, including Communism, and

CHRIST'S ALTERNATIVE TO COMMUNISM...

not destroy but complete and fulfill those endeavors, but it must go beyond them. Can we find such a conception as this in the Christian Gospels?

If it is there, it must be honestly there, and not constituting something smuggled into the account by "a species of exegetical legerdemain." We must not read meanings into the account and then triumphantly read them out again, for the universe will not back lies—not even religious lies.

> **The Christian Revolution must be founded in convictions as deep as—and deeper than— Marxist Communism. It must rest upon principles that are the very foundations of the universe.**

When we turn to the Christian gospel for a detailed program for world reconstruction, we shall find ourselves disappointed. No detailed program is there. "Then," says the critic, "the New Testament fails us—it does not give us the guidance we need at a time like this." I am not so sure that the absence of a detailed program is a fatal defect in the gospel. It may be its strength, for we soon outgrow rules of life. In a religion founded on rules one of two things happens: either the people in growing break the rules, or the rules are so strong that they break the people. But we never outgrow principles, for they are the same yesterday, today, and forever. Jesus therefore refused to give rules of life, but he did give principles, and those principles are as valid today as when they were first uttered. Had he given rules for the reconstruction of that simple age, would we not have outgrown them in this more complex age? And what about the complexities of the more complex tomorrows? But while all this is true we must not lose sight of the fact that the fundamentals of human nature change little from age to age. The sins which confronted Jesus in that age are fundamentally the ones which confront us in this age. The manifestations are different, but the sins are the same.

Jesus was right when he refused to give rules. But if we do not find rules, we do find principles— intimations and suggestions so definite and clear that we can mark out the road for the future. We can see quite clearly what his program is. That program is the Kingdom of God on earth. In this conception he announced a higher order, founded on love, good will, and brotherhood, breaking into and transforming and ultimately displacing the lower world order founded on greed, selfishness, exploitation, and unbrotherliness. That Kingdom is the ultimate order or goal of humanity. But while this Kingdom was his program in general, he put very definite content into it and marked out the lines of its advance when he made the great announcement in the little synagogue at Nazareth. After the years of silent brooding, after the clarification through the wilderness struggle, we should expect him to announce his program in the very beginning of his ministry. He did. Straight from that wilderness struggle he came to the synagogue and made known this program:

> The Spirit of the Lord is upon me, because he anointed me to preach good tidings to the poor; He hath sent me to proclaim release to the captives, and recovering of sight to the blind, to set at liberty them that are bruised, to proclaim the acceptable year of the Lord. And he closed the book. . . . And he began to say unto them, today hath this scripture been fulfilled in your ears.

In other words, "Today this program begins." When we analyze the program, we find:

1. Good news to the poor—the economically disinherited.

2. Release to the captives—the socially and politically disinherited.

3. The opening of the eyes of the blind—the physically disinherited.

4. The setting at liberty the bruised—the morally and spiritually disinherited.

5. The Lord's Year of Jubilee—a new beginning on a world scale.

6. The Spirit of the Lord upon me—the dynamic behind it all.

> **Jesus was right when he refused to give rules. But if we do not find rules, we do find principles—intimations and suggestions so definite and clear that we can mark out the road for the future.**

I believe that here we have the outline of the program which Jesus intended to project into the soul of humanity. Here he put the first content and meaning into the Kingdom of God on earth. The first meanings are important meanings, for they are foundational—the rest is superstructure.

But to get the importance of that announcement in the synagogue we must step back from it and see what preceded it. Jesus had identified himself with the people as they took the baptism of repentance at the hands of the Baptist. He who wore a stainless conscience took that baptism of repentance along with dishonest men and loose-living women as one of them. He identified himself with man's lowest point—at the point of his moral and spiritual degradation. It is not easy to give up one's good name, but

Jesus did just that. The reaction came. Into the wilderness he went to fight out the question of whether this was the way to proceed. Would the Kingdom come by pressures from without—by spectacular display, by dazzling miracle, by force, by compulsion? Or would it come by pressures from within—by his identifying himself with man, so that everything that falls on man would fall on him; so that all the time by these silent pressures he would project the Kingdom and its meanings further and further into the souls of men, until finally the vision would be seen and the new day dawn? Would he force from without, or would he lift from within?

At a glance it will be seen that one will be more expensive and a longer process than the other. One would mean an ideal with a club and the other would be an ideal with a cross. Out into the wilderness he went to fight it through. When he came to the end of the forty days in which the struggle was so intense that he forgot to eat, he was hungry and thought to leave the wilderness to get something to eat. "You need not," said the Tempter: "Live apart from all this—feed yourself on miracles. You are the Son of God; that is enough. You need not be the Son of man. Live apart on miracles." This is the temptation of the mystic—to live apart, to feed himself on communion with God, to be a son of God and to refuse to be a son of man. Jesus rejected this, saying that he lived by every word that proceeded out of the mouth of God, and that word for him was identification. "Then," said the Tempter, "if you must go back to men, do not take the position in relationship to men you began to take—stand on the pinnacle of the Temple. Be looked up to and honored—the symbol of greatness in religion. Don't stand down with men as one of them; stand lifted up above them—that is the way to influence them. You are the Son of God, cast yourself down from that pinnacle, and lo, the angels of God will bear you up and place you on the pinnacle again." This is the temptation of the leaders of organized religion—to stand on pinnacles of prestige and

53

power, to dress differently, to impress by ritual and splendor, to be looked up to and worshiped as different from ordinary men—to be a man of the pinnacle instead of a man of the people. Jesus rejected this too.

Then the third temptation came in which Jesus was shown the kingdoms of the world and the glory of them. Note that the issue at stake was the kingdoms of the world and the way to secure them. Securing worldly glory seemed to be the underlying problem running through the whole of the temptations. Jesus' thought was not merely to change a few hearts here and there but to project a Kingdom on a world scale. It was to be nothing less than a new Kingdom which would supplant all other kingdoms and be the final order for all men of all time. With what weapons would he conquer these kingdoms? The Tempter suggested that all of them could be had if Jesus would be advised by him: "Be the politician in religion, wangle men, manipulate them, use them—– you need not suffer for them—use them for your purposes." This is the third temptation in religion—the temptation to win by the politician's art, to climb on the backs of men to power, to use them but not to suffer for them. Jesus rejected this. He would identify himself with men and bear everything they bear and share everything they share. Of course this would mean a cross, for at the end he would gather it all up into his heart and let it break it—the identification would be complete. He was baptized between sinners, he would live out his life among them, and in the end he would be crucified between them—he would redeem from within, not from without. The Kingdom of God would come by a cross and not by a club. It was all clear now. He would be the Son of man, and anything that would hurt any man anywhere would be forced through his own heart. He would overcome evil with good, hate by love, and the world by a cross of suffering for the world.

Jesus went into the wilderness "full of the Spirit;" he came out of the wilderness "in the power of the Spirit." Mere fullness had turned to power, for that fullness had been linked to a program of world redemption, hence it was now power. He went straight to the synagogue and announced that program.

The Christian world has not taken this Kingdom announcement seriously. Perhaps it is because it was a quotation from an Old Testament scripture, hence not something firsthand and fresh and out of Jesus' own soul. But in this we miss the point. Jesus was revolutionary, but he was a constructive Revolutionary. He smashed nothing until he had rescued the good at the heart of that thing to be smashed. Therefore it was in the fitness of things that, as he announced the most revolutionary conception ever presented to the mind of man, namely, the Kingdom of God on earth, he should link it up with the finest in the Hebrew prophetic past. He smashed the priestly portion of that system. It died with his death. But the prophetic portion lives with his life. It resonates again in his program. It is easy to be an iconoclast, but it is difficult, supremely difficult, to gather up and preserve the good at the very moment of destroying. That takes insight and patience and courage and bigness.

> **Jesus went into the wilderness "full of the Spirit;" he came out of the wilderness "in the power of the Spirit." Mere fullness had turned to power, for that fullness had been linked to a program of world redemption, hence it was now power.**

The Communists of Russia intended at first to smash every sign and symbol of the old, including the old art which they dubbed "bourgeois art." But they paused in the midst of its destruction and made the wise decision to preserve it. Had they done this in regard to the best that is in religion, and even the best that is in capitalism, half the world would be at their feet today. Now we have to struggle past their ruthlessness to get at the core of their proposed good. That ruthlessness stops most people before they even get to that good. The Communists gained, by that ruthlessness, a quick and comparatively easy victory in the local Russian situation, and in doing so defeated their ends in the larger world situation. Depend on it, it is not sheer stubbornness against change that makes the world hesitate to change toward a regimented society, for we feel the precious gift of freedom and personal initiative and religion—values which we cannot and will not throw away lightly. That hesitation is not reaction, but realism.

Jesus did not make this mistake of ruthlessness. He was correct in launching this most radical of conceptions by launching it from the high plane of the noblest of the past. In the end the best thought of the race will approve his method and spirit, although in the present mood of radicalism he seems too evolutionary and constructive and therefore lacking in that drive that comes from a program of hate and ruthless iconoclasm. But the longest way round is sometimes the shortest way home. It is so here. Jesus came not to destroy any fine thing but to complete and fulfill.

But if Jesus was right in choosing this method of fulfillment, he did not stop there. He put such newness of content into old forms that at the very moment he fulfilled he killed. Nature kills the seed by selecting the life germ from it and making it grow into a tree. The tree lives, therefore the seed dies. Jesus' method is likewise destructively constructive and constructively destructive. While he chose this noble utterance of the past, he rejected portions of that utterance itself. He stopped before he finished the quotation and left out "the day of vengeance of our God." There was to be no "vengeance" in his program. The Communists of Russia have put it in their program. They have visited vengeance to all members of the bourgeoisie even to the next generation—the children of the bourgeoisie are excluded from the rights and privileges of the children of the proletariat, except as they renounce their parents. The children of the disfranchised classes are excluded from the playgrounds and from Pioneer organizations. In Turgenev's novel, *Fathers and Sons*, Bazarov, the nihilist who believed in nothing but science, scolds his kind-hearted friend thus: "You have no audacity and no malice." It is the malice side of the Communist program which has helped them swiftly to their goal by sweeping out all who differ. But while it has probably saved their lives in Russia, for the time being at least, it has lost them in the rest of the world. For like produces like: hate produces hate, vengeance produces vengeance. Jesus left out "vengeance," for he would win a world. The Communists have put it in, and have therefore tied around their necks the millstone of the constant necessity of using force. Jesus has audacity, but no malice. His program is audacious, but not malicious. Therefore in the end the universe will back it, and it will win, for love is stronger than hate, though hate seems to be initially the stronger. Jesus' method, then, would be that he would use the past and fulfill its best, but he would be free to reject things in that past incompatible with his movement. We must therefore be prepared to accept this statement in the synagogue as the deliberate announcement of his program even though he used ancient forms through which to make it. The fact that he did this fits in with the genius of his movement.

We must now look at that announcement to see what is involved in his program. The first item is "To preach good tidings to the poor." This is usually interpreted to mean "the spiritually poor." When we do not know what else to do with a thing, we spiritualize it. It is easier to spiritualize it than to face its plain implications. It raises no great issues to talk about good news to the spiritually poor, but it does raise the question of the whole economic order when you announce good news to the economically poor. Of course there are passages which are obviously to be used in a spiritual sense, but when we spiritualize such passages, it must be obvious that the writer intended them to be so used. The burden of proof is on the spiritualizer for words normally should be taken to mean exactly what they say unless otherwise indicated.

Spiritualization is usually the first refuge of the skeptical mind. When I was about to go to Manchuria, the Chinese pastors of Mukden wrote me, "Please do not preach to us to love our enemies, but preach to us spirituality." We smile at the naiveté of the Chinese pastors; but that is exactly what we have done with this passage—we have spiritualized it and have thus rendered it innocuous. I do not see why it shouldn't mean exactly what it says, namely, that the coming of this new Kingdom would mean good news to the poor, the economically disinherited. Everyone knew who "the poor" meant. Had they not looked into the face of poverty every day of their lives? When Jesus was presented to the Temple, did his parents not offer a pair of turtledoves, the offering which the poor offered, instead of the more costly offerings of the well-to-do? Did not he and his hearers both understand what he meant by "the poor"? Just what shall we understand by "good news to the poor"? Was it to preach contentment in their poverty by offering compensation in a future world? Was it to make bearable this poverty by its acceptance as the will of God? An ancient hymn suggests this:

> The rich man in his palace,
> The poor man at his gate—

God made the high and lowly
And ordered their estate.

Or did this movement come to strike at the root of the injustices between man and man which cause this poverty? Was the "good news," therefore, release from the poverty itself? Would this movement, if really accepted, mean a brotherhood of sharing in which the ghastly distinctions between rich and poor would fade out?

If the "good news" means the first—that is, contentment in poverty through the promise of a future reward—then religion does become, as the Communists say, "an opiate to the people." If this preaching of contentment is the attitude of religion, then no fairer— and no more terrible—dart has ever been aimed at the heart of religion than this saying that it is an opiate. That it has often been true through the centuries there is no doubt whatever. It was Charles Kingsley, the Christian Socialist, who said, "The Bible was turned into a mere constables handbook—an opium dose for keeping beasts of burden patient." But note that it was Charles Kingsley, the Christian, who first gave the world the idea that religion was an opiate, and not Karl Marx, the atheist, to whom credit usually goes. Did Kingsley use it because he saw that while it was true in great measure of the Christian Church through the centuries, it was not true when we faced the gospel as Jesus gave it? I noted that the sign, "Religion is the opiate of the people," placed opposite the shrine of the Iberian Virgin in Moscow, which now has some of its letters missing, some of them having dropped out during the passing years. Is this symbolic? Did the statement hold true as long as it was directed toward the organized church, especially as it existed in Russia, but is it now falling to pieces as men discover the meaning of the Kingdom of God on earth?

To answer that question we must turn to the New Testament to see what "good news to the poor" really meant. We shall look at the passages that have bearing on this matter just as they come in the account in order to see the general trend and purpose of their teaching.

The first passage is Mary's song, as she, with deep insight, saw what would happen to the structure of human society with the coming of this Kingdom, inaugurated by her coming Son. It seemed so vivid to her that it was already accomplished. She burst into these words:

> He hath scattered the proud in the imagination of their heart.
> He hath put down princes from their thrones,
> And hath exalted them of low degree.
> The hungry he hath filled with good things;
> And the rich he hath sent empty away.

Mary saw that this coming Kingdom was to be revolutionary—it was to precipitate revolution in the sum total of human living. Everything in every realm of human living that would not fit into this coming Kingdom was to be swept away.

First, there was to be the general revolution: "He has scattered the proud in the imagination of their heart." This new Kingdom would tolerate no lifting of anyone above his fellows by special privileges or unreal assumptions, for it is a Kingdom of Reality. In the atmosphere of its utter reality the fictitiousness of pride would break down and would expose its inner falseness. Historically this became true. Pharisaism, which, until Jesus came, was the model of religious propriety, broke down under the impact of this new Kingdom of Reality and is now the symbol of pride which has been scattered in the imagination of its heart.

The first note that was struck in this new Kingdom was a revolution against all falsehoods, all untruth, all unreality. This new Kingdom would sustain itself, not by capturing all means of propaganda and suppressing everything that would oppose it, but by its own inherent truth and soundness. This, by the way, is in deep contrast to the method of both Fascism and of Communism, which sustain themselves, in large measure, by capturing the means of propaganda and by suppressing all that would question their system. But this new Kingdom was to be the Kingdom of Truth.

Second, there was to be political revolution: "He hath put down princes from their thrones." And yet there are those who say that religion has nothing to do with politics! It has nothing to do with the kind of politics we now largely have—except to overthrow it! If the rule of the princes should cut across this new Kingdom, the rule would be terminated, and, further—exterminated!

But an objection arises. When Jesus said, "Render unto Caesar the things that are Caesar's, and unto God the things that are God's," did he not

In this new Kingdom all life was to be rendered to God. As Jesus went on enlarging the borders of life which were to be rendered to God soon there was no standing room for Caesar.

thereby put his stamp of approval on loyalty to Caesar, and did he not at the same time separate religion and politics? At first sight it would seem so. But only at first sight. For we forget the emphasis. It was placed on rendering "unto God the things that are God's." In this new Kingdom all life was to be rendered to God. As Jesus went on enlarging the borders of life which were to be rendered to God soon there was no standing room for Caesar. Caesar would not fit into this new Kingdom so out he would have to go. We have been getting rid of Caesars ever since. Instead of this passage being a reactionary approval of Caesarism, no matter who that Caesar may be and no matter how corrupt he may be, it makes the standing place of Caesar very precarious, for he must fit into rendering to God that which is God's. In the Kingdom of God, God is the sole ruler. And only as "princes" fit into and embody that rule are their thrones permanent. This new Kingdom has been and is now putting down princes from their thrones. When men rise up against injustice and selfishness in princes and oppose them, it is the working of the spirit of this new Kingdom.

Third, there was to be a social revolution: "He hath exalted them of low degree." This new Kingdom was to be a Kingdom of man as man. There would be a canceling of all privileges based on birth and property and social standing. It was to throw open the gates of life and opportunity to all.

Fourth, there was to be an economic revolution—

The hungry he hath filled with good things;
And the rich he hath sent empty away.

This proposal is astounding and far-reaching. We have lost its significance, because instead of taking it at its face value we have set it to music in our liturgies. A Hindu once told me that he had to read the sacred books of Hinduism in a foreign language to get their meaning, for the rhythm of the Sanskrit hid the meanings from him. That is what has happened here. We have put this verse into our services instead of putting it into service in the making of a just and equitable economic order. Its rhythm has put us to sleep when its righteousness should have stabbed us broad awake.

Translated into modern terms this verse would mean: Necessities should be provided for all before luxuries are provided for any. Economically the first concern for this new Kingdom is for the poor, not that they should be comforted by promises of future rewards to be content now, but that poverty should be banished by providing for the poor the good things which God has provided for all. When the laborer sings in irony that "Religion says that you will get pie in the sky, by and by, when you die," he may be rightly directing his thrust against a system of religion which sets this verse to music and refuses to set it to work, but he cannot rightly direct it against this new Kingdom.

Here, then, was a new Kingdom which was to precipitate a general revolution in scattering the proud, a political revolution in putting down princes from their thrones, a social revolution in exalting them of low degree, and an economic revolution in filling the hungry with good things and turning the rich empty away. No wonder Bernard Shaw said that "this song of Mary is the most revolutionary song that has ever been written in the history of Europe." It is.

Necessities should be provided for all before luxuries are provided for any.

But was it a chance note uttered in the ecstasy of a woman's song, or did she strike the keynote of the new Kingdom? Our study will show us, I think, that Mary, with deep insight, caught the meaning of what was going to happen. It was significant that a woman first caught the meaning of the new Kingdom, and that woman a mother. It was a woman who first conceived the idea of melting the cannon of Argentine and Chile, and erecting a statue, "The Christ of the Andes," cast out of the melted cannon, on the border between the two countries, as a symbol of perpetual peace between them. Here it was a woman who would set up this "Christ of All Races and Classes" on the border line of every single conflict between man and man. The fact that it was a woman who first did it begins to put new significance into the meaning of the Kingdom.

That same note sounded again in John as he came preaching and preparing the way for the Coming One and his Kingdom:

> Make ye ready the way of the Lord,
> Make his paths straight.
> Every valley shall be filled,
> And every mountain and hill shall be brought low;
> And the crooked shall become straight,
> And the rough places smooth;
> And all flesh shall see the salvation of God.
> (Luke 3: 4-6.)

The way of the Lord would mean moral straightness applied to the personal and collective order: human equality in that every valley would be filled and every mountain would be brought low; humaneness in human living in that the rough places would be made smooth, and universality in that all flesh would see the salvation of God. Note that Christ would not fit into human society as it now is—he would not conform to the exaltations and depressions of human organization and views. There would be radical change, and that change would be in the direction of human equality and the sharing on an equal basis of the rights and privileges of life for all. Note that "every valley shall be filled, and every mountain and hill shall be brought low"—the depressed portions of humanity shall be raised and the exalted portions shall be brought down.

Most of us would not mind the depressed portions of humanity being raised, but we would mind "the mountains" being brought low. We feel that would be unjust. But we must remember that mountains are made at the expense of the valleys. The valleys have become depressed because the mountains have gone up. That is the tragedy of any selfish order. At the foot of the mountains of financial success you find the valleys of financial depression. The creation of one over rich man usually means the sending of a whole host below the poverty line. The surplus of earnings from industry which should have gone to the raising of the level of the many goes into the making of a mountain of the one. Every over rich man becomes a magnet which draws around him the labor of the many to supply his luxuries, labor which should have been employed in supplying the necessities of the many. Then the vicious circle forms—labor is not able to purchase what it produces, industry suffers from overproduction, and depression sets in. As long as you have economically depressed portions of humanity you will have depressions. Then God stands in the shadows waiting—waiting to see if we shall learn the lesson from his inexorable laws and accept his Kingdom which would distribute the privileges of life.

> As long as you have economically depressed portions of humanity you will have depressions. Then God stands in the shadows ... his Kingdom ... would distribute the privileges of life.

When John, with this commission for a new order of equality ringing in his ears, met the multitudes who came to listen to his preaching, he began to apply the implications of this commission, "And the multitudes asked him, saying, What then must we do? And he answered and said to them, He that has two coats, let him impart to him that have none; and he that has food let him do likewise." The repentance that John demanded of the multitudes was important—they were not merely to give up individual sins, they were to share their material possessions; those who had a surplus were to share it with the underprivileged. This repentance, therefore, was deeply social. The Kingdom was to bring a brotherhood, but that brotherhood

CHRIST'S ALTERNATIVE TO COMMUNISM...

could not come as long as the material barriers existed. It is almost impossible to have fellowship across an economic chasm. You can have patronage on the one side and sycophancy on the other, but not real fellowship. So the economic barriers had to go down in order that the fellowship might be possible. But in insisting on this John did not proclaim a law, he asked them to give rein to an impulse, an impulse toward a brotherhood.

That we were not straining the meaning when we said that the valleys being filled and the mountains being brought low involved an economic sharing which would bring a closer approximation to equality, is to be seen in the fact that when John applied it to life, he called for a repentance which demanded that he who had two coats was to share one of them with the man who had none, and he that had food was to do likewise. This meant the mountains coming down and valleys coming up.

There is a difficulty raised at this point in connection with John's demand of the soldiers that they should "do violence to no man [a soldier who did violence to no man would cease to be a soldier!], neither exact anything wrongfully; and be content with your wages." Preaching to people to be content with their wages comes under the charge of Kingsley that religion is often used as "an opium dose for keeping beasts of burden patient." But note that this statement has no reference to the question of ordinary wages of ordinary workmen. It was a case where soldiers by oppressing the people in various ways exacted from them an addition to their wages. John was not preaching contentment with a wage scale, but against graft beyond the wage scale.

When Jesus came, he called only workers to bring in this new Kingdom. Not an idle person was ever called. It was to be a Kingdom of workers. He saw Matthew "sitting at the place of toll"—the place of taking in—and called him to the place of giving.

But at the very moment that he called them from their secular occupations he affirmed these very occupations. The last thing he did before calling them from their fishing boats was to fill these boats with fish (Luke 5. 1-11). In getting them to leave their occupations he might have cast a slur on these sources of livelihood, but he did not. He did say to one to "leave the dead to bury their own dead," and commanded another to "sell all thou hast," and said to another, "No man, having put his hand to the plow, and looking back, is fit for the kingdom of God." But in none of these cases was an occupation involved. Jesus in his amazing sanity loosed them from their daily labors, and yet approved of these vocations in the very moment of doing so.

On one of his journeys he set the physical hunger of men over against the religious law and said that the hunger and not the law was determinative. His disciples went through the fields on the Sabbath, and because "they were hungry " they began to pluck the ears of corn and eat. The law allowed them to pluck as much as they could take away in their hands, but they were not allowed to do it on the Sabbath. Jesus set aside the religious institution in behalf of addressing the physical hunger of men. This is important, and if applied to the world of today, would undoubtedly mean that if hunger could be met *in any real way* by the sacrifice of costly churches, then the churches should go.

To re-enforce what he was saying Jesus appealed to what David did "when he had need and was hungered," how he entered into the house of God and took the shew-bread, which it was not lawful for any except the priests to eat, and gave to them that were with him (Mark 2: 23-28). Here the central determining thing was not the sanctity of a place of worship, nor an article of worship, but "need." That is sacred which ministers to the *needs* of men. David voided the privilege only accorded to the priests and gave it to man, and Jesus cited it with approval. So here was the breaking down of privileged classes and privileged institutions in favor of humanity. But David did not take it from the priest to eat it himself. Had he done so, that would have been a king taking from a priest—a privileged class taking from a privileged class; but he gave it to the people—the common people.

That word "need" is the word around which modern Socialism and Communism propose to organize the new society— "to each according to his need." We must remember that Jesus anticipated that concept two thousand years ago. For the Christian Church to act as though it were startled by this modern demand that "need" be the determining factor in the organization of human society, and to allow itself to be maneuvered into a position of reaction at that point, is too absurd for words. But perhaps the Christian Church has a right to be startled at this point, for if "need" is the determining factor, then other things beside bread which are in the house of God for "shew" will have to be sacrificed and used to meet that need. We often cite with approval and admiration the sacrifice of the poor for the sake of the church as an institution. Jesus would probably approve the sacrifice of many a rich institution for the sake of the "need" of the poor.

An age which has built its laws and institutions around the idea of the sanctity of private property has difficulty with the interpretation of the account of Jesus healing the demoniacs at the expense of the sacrifice of the swine (Matthew 8: 28-34). The account says, "And they that fed them fled, and went away into the city, and told everything, and what was befallen to them that were possessed with devils."

Note: "Everything and"—everything to them was swine and the healing of the stricken man an afterthought. Property was everything and personality was a very secondary consideration. Jesus reversed this, for the account means that in his eyes, if to rescue a single human personality extensive private property has to be sacrificed, it is worth it and is justified. If Jesus had reported the account, he would have "gone into the city and told everything and what had befallen the swine"—"everything" to him would have been the rescued man, and the lost property an after-consideration. And the difference between the two is the difference between two types of civilization. We have produced a civilization where swine are first and men are second, and we have become like our ideals. Greed, not need, often determines our policies. In the age of chivalry men often put the lion in a prominent place on their coat of arms. For the coat of arms of an acquisitive society, whose one aim seems to be to get, could we not find in the Gadarene incident the animal best suited for the place of prominence? I saw a cross on a pastor's study table and admired it—at a distance; but when I came nearer, I saw that there was a slit in the top of it—the cross was a moneybox! The transformation was complete—a competitive age had made Christianity into its own image.

> We have produced a civilization where swine are first and men are second, and we have become like our ideals. Greed, not need, often determines our policies.

"And they come to Jesus, and behold him that was possessed with devils, sitting, clothed and in his right mind, even him that had the legion; and they were afraid." They were afraid—afraid of sanity! We are like those men. We have become so naturalized in our insanities of hate and competition and unbrotherliness and injustice that we are afraid of the sanity of love and co-operation and brotherliness and justice. Could anything be more insane than the spectacle of half the world overfed and the other half underfed with enough for everybody in our very hands? And yet we are afraid of the sanity of a just distribution! Is there anything more insane than the dog-eat-dog method of competition? And yet we are afraid of the sanity of co-operation! Is there anything more insane than destroying food in a world that is hungry? And yet we are afraid of the sanity of distributing food rather than destroying it! Can anything be more insane than the piling up of armaments, producing hate and fear and war? And yet we fear the sanity of a world of mutual trust and brotherhood!

The most insane thing in this insane world of ours is to be afraid of sanity!

CHAPTER 2

GOOD NEWS TO THE ECONOMICALLY DISINHERITED (CONTINUED)

When we are inclined to question whether the gospel has anything to do with the economic life of people, it would be well for us to hear again Jesus saying to the disciples in regard to the hungry multitudes, "They have no need to go away; give them something to eat." This in reference to the Jews. "I would not send them away fasting." This in reference to the Gentiles. Twice he fed the multitudes —once his own people, the Jews (Matthew 14: 13-23); and once across the lake in the parts of Tyre and Sidon Jesus fed the Gentiles (Matthew 15: 29-39). He said, "I would not send them away fasting"— most religions would. They would say, "We have fed you spiritually, the material doesn't matter; and, besides, it is not our province and concern." With Jesus it was a concern, and it must be to us; for he is saying to us, "They need not go away to atheistic Communism to find a social order in which their material wants will be met; give ye them to eat." And we must listen to him at that point—or abdicate; for the multitudes must be fed.

But Jesus fed the multitudes not merely to satisfy their hunger, but also to set up relationships of fellowship. For it is at the place of eating that we are exclusive. Castes in India have many relationships with each other, but they cease at the place of eating. Caste in America has many relationships with the African-American, but the line is drawn at eating with him. In India the caste man in eating is not only untouchable, but unapproachable and unseeable. A Hindu rationalized all of this for me in this way: "You see, we are told that different people emit different kinds of electricity from their persons, and where a person, who has a different kind of electricity from yours, sees you eat, it stops digestion." Another Hindu went to great lengths to explain to me the basis of caste. At the close I quietly remarked, "My brother, if you were as good in doing away with caste as you are in explaining it away, you would be a wonder." Jesus explained little, and explained away nothing in regard to human relationships, but went straight to the heart of the matter and ate with both Jew and Gentile. Jesus therefore taught us two things: First, that religion has a concern for the hunger of men. Second, that religion has a concern for the relationships of men. At one and the same time Jesus satisfied that hunger and set up relationships of fellowship with outsiders.

On one occasion the Pharisees and scribes asked Jesus why his disciples did not wash their hands ceremonially when they ate their bread. Jesus turns the whole thing from the ceremonial to the social. "Why," he asks, "do you transgress the commandment of God by the tradition which allows you to say that the thing which might have profited your parents is now *Korban*—sacrificed to God?" (Matthew 15. 1-6.) Here was a clash of religious interest with a social interest, and Jesus took the side of the social. Here he says that giving adequate support to those in economic need is a duty that transcends in importance giving to so-called religions objects. This is radical to the core, and if applied, would mean the transforming of religious institutions themselves. For, said Jesus, they have no claim to our support unless they have a social purpose and dedication at the basis of them. Jesus also says that no religious sanction makes a social evil right.

Closely akin to this is Jesus' reply to the lawyer who tempted him by asking him the question, "Master, what shall I do to inherit eternal life?" Jesus replied, "What is written in the law? How do you read it?" It was one thing to know what is written; it is another thing to ask the question, "How do you read what is written?" For we often read our own interests into what is written. For centuries we have read into the account of Jesus self-interested meanings which have bolstered up economic and social wrong. Many bolster up the whole exploitation of the East by the white man on the basis of the passage:

"God enlarge Japheth [the white man], And let him dwell in the tents of Shem" —the brown man. Religious explanations for racial exploitations!

The lawyer answered that we are to love God with all the heart, the soul, the mind, and the strength and the neighbor as ourselves. Jesus answered, "*Do* this and you shall live." "But the lawyer, desiring to justify himself, said to Jesus, And who is my neighbor?" "You shall live;" . . . "but the lawyer desiring to justify himself" preferred to justify himself before others rather than live.

The lawyer preferred to *seem* to live, rather than to live. To be smart and clever was more to him than to be really alive. He preferred tinsel to gold. "And who is my neighbor?" He knew that Judaism had broken the force of this passage by defining the neighbor as a Jew, a man of the same race, and he had the suspicion that Jesus would say something different. He did!

Jesus tells of a priest coming from the Temple worship of Jerusalem who was too busy with memories of the Temple to help a man in need lying by the roadside; a Levite, also a Temple officer, was going up to the Temple, too busy about going to the place of prayer to help this man. Coming and going religious people were too taken up with services to be of service. But a Samaritan did something the other two did not do—"he came where he was." The other two "saw" him, and "passed by on the other side." But the Samaritan went where he man lay —he exposed himself to this need. In the end "whatever gets your attention gets you."

Let the Christians expose themselves to the injustices which are at the heart of our economic order and the injustices will get them, impact them to the depths. But now the church is "socially illiterate." It doesn't see things except at a distance. Let the church do what Ezekiel did when he went to speak to the captives by the river. He went "in the heat and bitterness" of his spirit to tell the people their sins. But God said: "Wait, Ezekiel; you are not ready yet to speak to these people. Sit down." "So for seven days," Ezekiel said, "I sat where they sat." For seven days he learned sympathy. He let all that fell on them fall upon him. At the end of the seven days he could speak, for he knew now by experience. The church must do the same. When it sits down with the dispossessed and exposes itself to the central need of humanity to change the basis of life from competition to co-operation, it will arise with a mighty sense of mission and message.

The result of the parable of the good Samaritan is that religious people have ringing in their ears the words, "You must not pass by on the other side." No matter how urgent the temple business may be, the man in need has the first claim. Could specifications be more specific, could directions be more direct than this simple statement of Jesus?

But the church is often taken up with other things. Jesus said to the Pharisees, "You tithe mint and rue and every herb, and pass over judgment and the love of God" (Luke 11. 42). Here he asks men to do two things: Have love toward God and judgment toward men. This statement is a variation of Jesus' other statement that the two great commandments were love to God and love to man. But here he defines our love to man as "judgment," or justice in one's relationships to others. Love to man was not to be a sentimentality, but it was to work out fundamental justice in human relationships. But the Christian world has found it easier to be charitable than to be just. Justice would give labor a just share in the proceeds of industry; now we give wages and charity. At our best we play "brother bountiful" to the poor instead of being brothers in a world organized on the basis of brotherhood. It is fundamentally unjust that a man who has money has with it the right to hire and to fire and to decide in general the economic destiny of his fellow men who have brain and brawn to contribute. That relationship needs not charity to soften it but

> **The result of the parable of the good Samaritan is that religious people have ringing in their ears the words, "You must not pass by on the other side." No matter how urgent the temple business may be, the man in need has the first claim.**

judgment to change it. To do social service around that central injustice and leave it untouched is to sprinkle rose water on a cancer to cure it. A business man once said to me, "We are ready to do anything for the laboring man except to get off his back." Judgment would end this on-the-back-of-another relationship and would bring a face-to-face relationship— in other words, a brotherhood world.

Ruskin's little book, *Unto This Last* (1860), changed the whole course of Mahatma Gandhi's life and made him renounce all in favor of the poor. Ruskin calls our attention to the fact that in the passage, "Shall the sun of righteousness arise with healing in his wings," "righteousness" is "justness," and that there can be no healing to society without justice. "For truly this healing is only possible by means of justice; no love, no faith, no hope will do it; men will be unwisely fond—vainly faithful—unless they are primarily just, and the mistake of the best men through generation after generation has been that great one of thinking that they can help the poor by almsgiving, and by the preaching of patience and of hope and by every other means, emollient, or consolatory, except the one thing God orders for them—justice" (p. 72). In reference to Jesus it was said that he was "just and having salvation." There is no salvation to society unless there is a fundamental justice at the heart of our relationships.

Jesus said to the religious leaders, "You pass over judgment and the love of God." They did not despise these things, nor reject them—they would probably have said that both were very good things indeed— they simply "passed over" them and did something else: they tithed mint and rue. In the parable of the good Samaritan the priest and the Levite "passed by" the man in need; here the Pharisees "passed over" judgment and the love of God. In each case they did not reject so much as neglect "the weightier matters." It is here that the Communists have hold of fact when they say that religion is opium. Very often it has been. Again and again it sends people off at a tangent just when they are about to face human need. It sends people to "mint and rue" instead of analysis and response.

This fact is further revealed when Jesus was invited to eat with a Pharisee (Luke 14: 1-24). He noted how those who were invited chose the chief seats. It cut him to the quick to see religious men take that attitude. He therefore took this occasion to give these religious leaders a challenge and a call. He asked them to do nothing less than renounce all thought of prestige and place and to lose themselves in the service of the poor. It was the great call to organized religion to throw itself into his movement for the Kingdom of God on earth. Take the lowest place in life, Jesus said, and humble yourself, "for everyone that exalts himself shall be humbled, and he that humbles himself shall be exalted." . . . "And when you make a dinner or a supper, call not your friends, worthy kinsmen, nor rich neighbors; lest haply they also invite you back and as a recompense to you." "Lest haply"—be afraid of paybacks! Be afraid of receiving a recompense! Be afraid of the selfish motive! This cuts straight across all our thinking in modern life.

As Jesus made this supreme appeal to the religious leaders at this dinner party there was a tense silence. All the future of real religion among the Jews was in the balance. Which way would it go? In that tense silence a gentleman broke the awkwardness of the situation by this interjection, "Blessed is he that shall eat bread in the kingdom of God." This polite gentleman hated awkward pauses and disliked serious challenges at dinner parties, so he tried to turn the edge of the challenge by talking about how blessed it would be to eat bread in the Kingdom of God. He piously rolled his eyes and looked toward heaven when Jesus was directing his attention to earth! He talked about eating bread when Jesus was talking about giving it! He talked about the future when Jesus was talking about the present!

It is this disposition to glance off at a tangent toward "spirituality," when faced with a challenge to change human conditions, which has plagued religion through the years. The very life of religion depends on its power to divest itself of that tendency. For we are faced in Russia with what is called "scientific Socialism" in contrast with "utopian Socialism." They repudiate all idealism in behalf of all realism. That irreligious realism must be met by a religious realism that is direct and positive in its attitudes. We must cleanse our hearts from the remnants of this polite gentleman who loved smooth dinner parties rather than judgment and the love of God.

The fact is that Jesus, taught us that the possession of spirituality depends on right relationships with the material,— Jesus said in Luke 16. 10: "He that is faithful in a very little is faithful also in much: and he that is unrighteous in a very little is unrighteous in much. If therefore you have not been faithful in the unrighteous mammon, who will commit to your trust the true riches?" The "true riches" was evidently spirituality. And the possibility of the possession of it is rooted in the fact of being faithful in mammon. How can we as Christian people develop spirituality when at the heart of all our economic relationships is the unspiritual fact of the competitive attitude ? It poisons all our relationships, individual, group, and nation. If we are not faithful at that place, how can God trust to us the true riches?

> **It is this disposition to glance off at a tangent toward "spirituality," when faced with a challenge to change human conditions, which has plagued religion through the years.**

Today we are at an impasse in Christendom. We have gone as far in spirituality as we can under personal selfishness. We are blocked at every turn in further individual and collective spiritual development. Christianity under selfishness seems an absurdity and unworkable. But change the order to a co-operative one and Christianity will seem the only natural way to live. Anything else would be absurd and unworkable. So we have reached a spiritual stalemate. God is saying to us, "Right that economic relationship with each other and then I will entrust to you the true riches." A spiritual awakening, possibly on a world scale, awaits the righting of that relationship.

In the verses following these Jesus says that a choice must be made: "No servant can serve two masters ... You cannot serve God and mammon." Translated into modern terms it would read: "You cannot serve God and individual selfishness." This launches a dart straight at the heart of the competitive system, a system founded on the drive of the private-profit motive. To choose to serve God would mean that we should have to organize life on the co-operative plan, with mutual service as the incentive, rather than on a competitive basis with the self-seeking motive as the incentive. In order to do this Jesus gave us in two parables, two guiding principles.

In the parable of the workmen in the vineyard (Matthew 20: 1-16) Jesus tells of the master hiring men at the beginning and the middle of the day. At the eleventh hour he went out and found some standing idle and asked them why they were idle. "Because no one has hired us," they replied. So the master sent them to work. At pay time he began to pay them their wages, beginning with the last man hired and giving to each man the same amount of pay. Those hired at the beginning of the day objected. But the master replied, "It is my will to give unto this last man hired as much as to you." Four things strike us here: (1) The unemployed had more sympathy from the master than the employed. He paid them off first. For if the others had borne the burden and heat of the day, these men had inwardly sweated at the thought of nothing to eat for themselves and their families. Their needs went on even though they did not work. (2) A living wage was given to them without regard to the number of hours they worked, for the only reason they did not work was that no man had hired them. This points to the duty of society to provide work, or unemployment insurance. (3) The parable implies that God wills equality: "It is my will to give unto this last as much as unto thee." This fits in with the kind of God Jesus shows us in the Gospels. If God is love, and if every human personality is of infinite concern to him, then how can he be satisfied unless the goods which he has given for all are wisely and justly distributed to all? Could a human father be satisfied if on one side of his table the children are overfed and embarrassed with food and the children on the other side are underfed and gaunt with hunger? If a typical human father could not be satisfied with such a family, could God our Father be satisfied with such a world as this? If he were satisfied, then I should be dissatisfied with that kind of a God.

We call America "God's country," but will God own it as his country as long as one per cent of the people own thirty-three per cent of the wealth, ten per cent own two thirds of the wealth, while the poorest twenty-five per cent own only three and a half per cent of the total wealth?

But the objection is made that if there were an equalizing of material things, it would soon all be unequal again, for the cleverer type would soon get it all back again from the more improvident ones. True, if the competitive order is allowed to operate. But it would not happen if life were organized co-operatively. For in that instance two things would operate against it: the collective will would make this impossible through its laws and regulations, and the underlying spirit would make this socially bad form—in other words, social sin. Would a decent father allow each meal to be a scramble in which the stronger and the cleverer children would get possession of the food and leave the weaker ones to starve ? That is what a competitive order allows. A co-operative order would make this impossible. It would see that "each is given according to his need." This parable teaches that very thing, namely, that "each should be given according to his need." It teaches that God wills equality. (4) This parable reveals that other workers objected to this equality. This is the crux of the matter. These inequalities do not depend on the will of God, but on the will of man.

This attitude on the part of man the parable calls "the evil eye"— "Is your eye evil because I am good?" The East is afraid of what it calls "the evil eye," for that "eye" falling on a child causes the victim to pine away and die; its falling on a family causes disruption and unhappiness; if on a business enterprise, it comes to grief. This is superstition of course. But it is no superstition in modern society but a fact that the evil eye of selfishness does fall on children and make them pine and die; it does fall on a family and make it a feud instead of a family; it does fall on business and in the end paralyze it. This objection to other people sharing God's goods is, in fact, "the evil eye."

But another objection is made to this suggestion of equality: Some suggest that if the goods we now have were distributed to all, it would raise the general level very little indeed. A few shillings would be added to the income of each. But there is a mistake here in reasoning; the idea of redistribution is not that each would possess all these things so that families would duplicate the possessions of other families. Rather, the idea is that the goods redistributed would be used for collective projects. For instance, it would not be necessary that everyone should own a large private library, for a public library would satisfy that need with a much smaller expenditure. And so with many of the other amenities of life—one public thing could supply the need of many people who would not need to have these things privately. In this way the redistribution of the surplus which the over rich now have would raise the cultural level of the many by collective projects.

But the underlying thought still remains in many minds: There are inequalities of ability and endowment among men and we cannot get away from them. If there are these natural differences in men, why should there not be these differences in material accumulation? "In trying to make a more just distribution," they ask, "aren't you unjust to the man of superior abilities? Are these to be suppressed, or are they to have a normal outlet?" The answer is that we do not expect to accomplish an exact equality, but a rough equality. Plato says that no man should be allowed to be more than five times as rich as any other man. That would leave too wide a gap. The needs of men could be met within a much narrower range. But in thinking about equality we do not think about doing away with natural endowments but only of unnatural inequalities. Society is responsible for many of these inequalities, for it opens the gates to some and closes them to others. The inequalities which are inherent in the wrong organization of human society are to be done away with. Tawney says, "While natural endowments differ profoundly, it is the mark of a civilized society to aim at the elimination of such inequalities as have their source not in individual differences but in its own organization, and that individual differences which are the source of social energy, are more likely to ripen and find expression if social inequalities are, as far as practicable, diminished."[1]

We would have what Rashdall[2] calls "an equality of consideration." We want a society in which each child born into that society would have an equal opportunity with every other child born into that society to climb to the top if its inherent powers or abilities would allow it to do so. We would take away barriers which society has unfairly erected, and give everyone equal opportunities, but at the same time we would recognize these superior abilities and would provide for their outlet

---

1 R. H. Tawney, *Equality* (Harcourt, Brace and Company, publishers), p. 63. First edition of this book came out in 1931 as a Halley Steward Publication. Hereafter, *Equality*.

2 Hastings Rashdall FBA (24 June 1858– 9 February 1924) was an English philosopher, theologian, and historian.

and use. Now, these superior abilities are, for the most part, harnessed to selfishness. Under a co-operative order they would be harnessed to the collective good. Then they would be constructive. Now they can often be disruptive.

If the parable of the laborers teaches equality, the parable of the talents teaches differences (Matthew 25: 14-30). In this parable there is a difference in endowment and hence a difference in the return that was expected from that endowment. The five-talented man was supposed to produce as much again, likewise the two and the one. The parable could be summed up in the phrase, "From each according to his ability." There is to be room for development, for the expression of latent powers. There is to be no cramping of ability in behalf of uniformity.

Now, if we put together the teaching of the parables of the workmen in the vineyard and the talents, we arrive at this: To each according to his need, and from each according to his ability.

The Kingdom of God would provide in the new social order an approximate equality of economic goods according to "need," and at the same time would provide for an inequality in contribution to the collective good. The channels for the expression of superior ability would be turned no longer toward selfish acquisition but toward collective well-being. In doing so, man grows, not so much in material wealth (although the general level of well-being will be far higher under a co-operative order than under a competitive one, for it will eliminate wasted effort), but in inner strength and character— quality. Turning the superior ability toward selfish acquisition means deterioration in personal character and chaos in collective life, but turning it toward the good of all would mean that the individual's inner life would develop and the collective good be enhanced. The person who insists that the person of superior ability should have superior material recompense would hear Jesus saying, "Verily I say unto you that you have your reward"—you have money and nothing else. The real man deteriorates —he saves his life and he loses it. But the Kingdom of God is organized on the basis of the ordinary man and the superior man losing his life in the collective good and finding it again in fellowship, in knowing that his life is contributing, not destroying, and in his own personal growth in character and happiness.

The idea that a man would not work except for the profit motive is being disproved in Russia and around the world wherever it is tried. The fact is that the men who work the hardest are the men who work for a cause. A self-seeking order cannot provide a cause; an altruistic order would.

If there is still any question left in our minds as to whether religion has anything to do with the economic needs of man, let us look steadily at the verses where Jesus tells us that he is perpetually incarnated in human need: "I was hungry, and you gave me food." . . . "Lord, when did we see you hungry and fed you?" . . . "Inasmuch as you have done it unto one of the least of these my brethren, you have done it unto me" (Matthew 25:31-46). I do not see how words could bind up religion and human need more closely than do these words. If Christ is so bound up with human life that anything that falls on any man falls on him, if all the hungers of the world are his hungers, then the sufferings of the cross were but a paragraph in the book of his continued sufferings. A friend of mine saw silhouetted against the evening skyline a day laborer bearing his luggage suspended on two ends of a bamboo pole. The figure made a cross against the skyline. My friend saw his burden making a cross for a brother man. In that burdened toil the Son of man was toiling and suffering.

If religion has nothing to do with the physical hunger of man, it has nothing to do with Christ. For that hunger is his home until it is banished. What would it mean to feed Christ as he hungers in the hunger of the world? Give him charity and allow him to be subservient to our whims and impulses? Then that very charity would be his further and deeper crucifixion, for we would add humiliation and insult to hunger. As long as society is organized by the few in favor of the few their very charities to the dispossessed are an insult.

I looked on the Bambino, the child Christ in the Cathedral at Rome, laden with expensive jewels, and then walked out and looked upon the countenances of hungry children around the Cathedral and wondered whether Christ, in view of this hunger, was "enjoying" his jewels. And the thought persisted that if he did, then I could no longer enjoy the thought of Christ. That bejeweled Bambino and the hungry children are a symbol of what we have done in putting around Christ the expensive livery of stately cathedrals and churches while leaving untouched the fundamental wrongs in human society. In doing so, Christ is left hungry in the unemployed and the dispossessed. To feed him in modern society would mean to

> **If religion has nothing to do with the physical hunger of man, it has nothing to do with Christ.**

strike at the roots of the system which allows the few to gather and possess what is intended for all. Nothing less than that would satisfy the hunger and the self-respect of Christ.

In this parable religion and social reconstruction become one. Christ is incarnate perpetually in human need! Was there ever such an identification as this? It is stated that he was identified here with everything except sin. He could not *state* that he was identified with sin. He could only *show* that. Had he stated it, there would have been endless misunderstandings. We had to see it. The cross is the final word added to this identification, for here he was identified with our sin. Had we heard that only with our ears, we should have misunderstood. Now we stand at the cross and worship at the mystery and miracle of it all—he was one with our sins too! Society must take the same attitude of vicarious suffering: the sins and failings of the weakest member must be considered the sins and failings of us all, and we must suffer with those sins and failings. Now the attitude of society is largely punitive toward these sins and failings; when it becomes Christian—it will be vicarious. A co-operative society would send us in the direction of the vicarious; a competitive society now sends us in the direction of victimization.

But the moment we begin to worship at the shrine of that identification we are pierced by the fact that, if Jesus is identified with the hunger of the world, he is also identified with the sin of the rest of us who are responsible for that hunger. He is therefore doubly crucified—deeply in the hunger of the poor, and more deeply still in the sin of the rest of us who allow that hunger to remain.

In the Lord's Supper and the Agape, or Love Feast, there was the partaking of a common meal, symbolic of the fact that as they shared all things from Christ—the Lord's Supper—so they would share all things with each other—the Agape. How could they share a common meal with the Master and refuse to share their common meals with their brethren? They could not without betraying the meaning of the whole thing. Communion meant having in common, both at the Lord's Table and at their own. But we have dropped out the Agape and have retained the Lord's Supper. Is not this just what has happened in Christianity—we are ready to take from Christ, but are not ready to share with our brothers?

This teaching about sharing sank deeply into the minds of the disciples, so that when Jesus committed the organization of the new society to them after he left them, they made religion function toward the banishing of hunger. The impact of Jesus on this point produced the most remarkable society of that ancient world. When we turn to the Acts of the Apostles, we read: "All the believers kept together, and had everything in common. They sold their lands and other property, and distributed the proceeds among all, according to everyone's necessities. And, day by day, attending constantly in the Temple with one accord, and breaking bread in private houses, they took their meals with great happiness and single-heartedness, praising God and being regarded with favor by all the people" (Acts 2: 43-47, Weymouth trans.). "Among all those who embraced the faith there was but one heart and one soul, so that none of them claimed any of his possessions as his own, but everything they had was common property . . . And great grace was upon them all. And, in fact, there was not a needy man among them, for all who were possessors of lands or houses sold them, and brought the money which they realized, and gave it to the Apostles, and distribution was made to everyone according to his wants" (Acts 4: 32-35, Weymouth trans.).

> **Here is the most remarkable society that has as yet existed in our world: it was a miniature Kingdom of God on earth.**

Here is the most remarkable society that has as yet existed in our world: it was a miniature Kingdom of God on earth. These people had their inner lives fused into one by the Spirit of the living God at Pentecost. They became one in spirit, sharing the same life in Christ.

That inner oneness blossomed into its natural corollary, an outer oneness. That outer oneness knew no limitations, for it leaped across racial and economic boundaries and made them one there as well. This shows a unity of all life —they knew no distinction between the spiritual and the material, the sacred and the secular. Since they shared the same spiritual life they shared the same economic life too. A sort of "communism" resulted.

However, it was a communism that was different from Russian Communism in that (1) it was voluntary. There were no compulsions. Peter said to Ananias: "While the land remained unsold, was it not your own? And when sold, was it not at your own disposal?" The sin of Ananias was not that he did not give all the proceeds, but that he lied about it and acted as though he had. (2) It had a spiritual, not a materialistic basis. (3) The method by which it was brought into being was a classless love, and not a class war.

That kind of society persisted through the early Christian Church. The Epistle of Barnabas (70-110 A. D.) says, "Thou shall have all things in common with thy neighbor and not call them thy private property." Justin and Tertullian (110-180 A. D.) said, "We have everything in common except our wives." "The Preaching of Peter" (second century) says: "Understand then, you rich, that you are in duty bound to do service. Learn that to others is lacking that wherein you super abound. Be ashamed of holding fast that which belongs to others. Imitate God's equity and none shall be poor." And even in the fourth century Saint Augustine held that "Private property has no right in nature." ". . . Since the existence of private property, it has brought into the world, lawsuits, hostility, dissension, war, rebellion, sin, injustice, murder— evils that will disappear again by its abolition." Bishop Clement I said: "The use of all worldly things should be common to all. It is wrong to say, 'This is mine, this belongs to me, and that belongs to someone else.'

88

It is this which has caused dissensions among men." So this early spirit persisted far into the early Christian centuries.

But this early *communism* failed. It failed, first, because it was a *communism* of consumption only and not a communism of production as well. No Christian *communism* could succeed that did not take in both. Since the Christians at Jerusalem produced nothing, they were soon poor, and the other churches had to take collections for "the poor saints at Jerusalem." Second, it failed because it did not gain possession of the total social order. The total social order under which they were compelled to live was pagan and competitive. They remained a small group within that crushing order. It crushed them—at least as a Christian *communism*. By the time the Christians gained control of the social order, through the conversion of Constantine, they had changed Christianity out of recognition. It was now competitive, acquisitive, and fused with the war spirit. The church began to take the attitude of shearing rather than sharing. The medieval church seems to be among the last to look with favor upon the freeing of the serfs.

So that early Christian experiment failed, but it did not fail because its spirit was wrong. Its spirit was essentially right. It failed because it tried to apply it under impossible circumstances, with an inadequate application. As Pentecost died so the spirit of sharing died with it. Selfishness reasserted itself. We must regain that original spirit and profit by their failure. What the regaining of that spirit and the profiting by their failure would mean we must see when the total picture of the Christian program is complete.

All we can say now is that the first item of the program—good news to the poor—would mean, according to the total teachings of Jesus, and according to the results of that teaching and that spirit in the lives of the early Christians, the creation of a new kind of society, spiritual in its basis, but issuing in a collective economic sharing and cooperation in which each would have material goods according to his need—poverty would be banished.

The only good news to the poor that would be adequate would be that there are to be no poor.

CHAPTER 3

GOOD NEWS
TO THE SOCIALLY AND
POLITICALLY DISINHERITED

It is significant that Jesus made good news to the poor, the economically disinherited, the first item in his program. This item came before "release to the captive"—the socially and politically disinherited—and rightly so, for almost all our relationships depend upon the economic relationship. You cannot right the other relationships unless you right the economic.

Marx was so impressed that all human life rests upon the economic that he gave forth what is called economic determinism, or the economic interpretation of history. By this Marx meant that "the material productive forces and no other factors make up the objective conditions which give rise to the various forms of social life." Upon the basis of how a man's material needs are met is erected the sum total of the life of man—the social, the cultural, the political, and even the religious life. This Marx believed to be the key to history. "So they took the money and did as they were taught," is said of the soldiers after the resurrection of Jesus, but according to Marx, all life does the same —it obeys the sources of its economic life.

This is an exaggeration of a great truth, for it can be shown that you cannot interpret history by this one factor alone. It has been pointed out that there is no important difference in the economic circumstances and difficulties in the little kingdoms of Israel and Judah and those of their neighbors, Moab and Edom, Syria and Philistia. Their history is different because they dealt with the same situations and faced the same disasters in a different spirit, owing to prophet and lawgiver. It was chiefly the moral and religious factors and not the economic that made the different national history. The Hindu and the Muslim have faced the same economic conditions in India for centuries, and yet their spirit, their temper, their outlook, and their civilization are quite distinct and different. Again, it is the religious and not the economic factor that has made the difference. "At every turn man's dealings with wealth are influenced and modified by art, by politics, by religion, and by science."

Wood points out that the confusion within Marxism at this point comes from the use of the words "to condition" and "to determine" as interchangeable. To condition is not to determine. A condition is a limit within which and through which one must work, but one's activity is never determined by such conditions. A painter decides to paint in oils, or it may be that he has no other medium available. His work is thoroughly conditioned by his medium, but not in the least determined by it. Tools condition men's industrial activities and their social organization without in any real sense determining them.[1]

Fortunately, economic determinism is not true or else man would never rise. He can rise because he is not economically determined. Middleton Murry says: "What Marx saw was that the moment was approaching when oppressed humanity could stand erect. This is not

---

1 H. G. Wood, *Christianity and Communism* (1933), pp. 67, 68.

92

economics, it is vision; not theory but truth." Here Murry, the Communist, saw that Marx went beyond his theory of economic determinism and disproved it.

So while Marx's statement has to be qualified and therefore modified, nevertheless it contains the very challenging fact that at the root of most of our difficulties lies a wrong economic relationship. You cannot have a brotherhood in the social life unless you have a brotherhood in the economic. Doctor Chaffee tells of a college in the United States where the professors all received the same salary; the *esprit de corps* was remarkable, the fellowship very real. Another college president came and felt that this was not good business, so changed the basis, giving to each professor what his services would get in the competitive market. Immediately the spirit of the institution changed, instead of a brotherhood there was a struggle for position and consequent jealousy and strife. We missionaries all get the same salary and as a consequence there is a wonderful sense of brotherhood among us, but we find it difficult to extend that brotherhood to the indigenous workers, for there the salary scale is different. In our Ashram there is a wonderful brotherhood, which includes the indigenous workers, for there the economic level is the same.

Jesus, therefore, was right when he made the first item in his program good news to the economically disinherited, for he could then go on and announce "release to the captives," the socially and politically disinherited. You cannot free the social and political captives unless and until you free the poor from their poverty, for the whole superstructure of social slavery rests upon an economic slavery.

We usually take this statement of release to the captive to mean the spiritually captive. Again we resort to spiritualization in order to dodge the difficulties raised by taking the statement to mean what it says. For it does not shake the basis of our relationships throughout the world when we talk about freeing the spiritually captive, but it does disturb things to the very depths if this verse means that man is to be freed by the New Order from all things that suppress and repress him in all realms of life. This verse implies that man is not merely to be released inwardly from bondage and then await heaven for final release, but that the Kingdom undertakes to bring in a New Order where bondage would have no place.

> **You cannot free the social and political captives unless and until you free the poor from their poverty, for the whole superstructure of social slavery rests upon an economic slavery.**

This will be resisted on various grounds. Some people still think with Aristotle that "some men are born naturally rulers and some are born naturally slaves, as a dog is naturally a dog and a cat is naturally a cat." This thought in the mind of the philosopher became objectified in the facts of Grecian life: there were four slaves to every free man; in the Athenian state there were 12,000 urban citizens, 50,000 rural citizens and 430,000 slaves. The philosopher had time to philosophize because the slave did his work. But that brutal, underlying fact arose and upset his philosophy and his state. The state went to pieces on the rock of that inhumanity. India's philosophers rationalized the degradation of the sixty million outcastes of India, and are now suffering the penalty of having her political progress determined by the condition of these disinherited millions.

The Russian minister of education, Delyanov, announced in 1887 that "the children of coachmen, servants, laundresses, small

94

shopkeepers, and such like people should not be encouraged to rise above the sphere in which they were born." The children of "such like people" arose and smashed the old order which degraded them, and now rule Russia with a rod of iron.

Gopson, a priest, went to the Czar with a great crowd of people, bearing the picture of the Czar and chanting hymns. They were workmen going to petition for the improvement of their condition. They were met at the palace gates by troops who fired on the crowd, and on the ground were left five hundred dead and three thousand wounded. The Russian Revolution, culminating in 1917, began that day.

Nicholas II said that there were two black-letter days in his life. The first was May 25, 1905, the day of the defeat of the Russian fleet by Japan; and the second was October 17, 1906, marking the establishment of the Duma (a parliamentary body) and the proclamation of the bill of rights. Could he have told the third black-letter day, it would have been the day when he and his family were taken out by these "subjects" and shot. And all three black-letter days were connected as cause and effect.

Capitalism began as a revolutionary, radical movement. It was part of the French Revolution and stood in opposition to the vested interests and nobles with their numerous monopolies of rights to trade. It stood for a wider opportunity for the ordinary man. It was the Red Terror of those days, and the devotees of the status quo thought that the foundations of society would go to pieces with the rise of capitalism with its radicalism. R. H. Tawney says, "In France and Germany, civil, not to mention political, rights were not identical for all men but graded from class to class, and the demand of the reformers for their equalization was repudiated by conservative thinkers with the same confident anticipations of social dissolution, were it conceded, as were aroused in the nineteenth century by proposals for a more

95

equitable distribution of wealth."[2] Capitalism, it will be seen, while containing a demand for greater equality, brought over with its radicalism a wrong to man. The "surplus value" of the product of labor went to those who provided capital. Labor produced more than it received. It was therefore always behind in purchasing power. It could not buy back as much as it produced. Nor could the capitalist consume the surplus. He had to reinvest it in enterprises that produced more goods. But since the laborer was always behind in purchasing power there was overproduction, hence unemployment, hence depression—and hence this world-shaking upheaval on the edge of which we now stand.

We read a wrong into the constitution of our collective life, and now that wrong is standing up to judge us. The nemesis has now met us. The battering ram which is thundering at the gates of civilization is the class war. We created a class society and now we are on the verge of having to pay for it. Man "as a slave was property, as a serf semi-property, as a servant he was subservient to property, and as an employee he is under duress to the privileges and superior powers of property." If you take away an employer's property, the law will punish you; but if an employer discharges a man from his employ, the law will do nothing. In each case there is a cutting off of the means of subsistence. But the law is built around property rights and not around personal rights. That inequality is eating at the heart of civilization. Matthew Arnold said, "On the one side, in fact, inequality harms by pampering; on the other side by vulgarizing and depressing. A system founded on it is against nature, and in the long run breaks down." This system with an inequality at its heart is now being shaken. A classless society must be built.

---

2 *Equality*, p. 122.

Has the program of Jesus any decisive word in a world seeking to establish a society based on equal ability? What did Jesus mean by announcing "release to the captive"?

First of all, we must note what he did not mean. We can get an intimation of this by what he left out of the quotation from Isaiah. He left out not only "the day of vengeance of our God," but also the rest of the passage which promises to the Israelites that "strangers shall stand and feed your flocks, and the sons of the alien shall be your plowmen and your vine-dressers." In one breath the prophet says that with the coming of the new day there is to be "release to the captive," and in the next breath he says that "strangers" and "aliens" should be captive to the Israelites and do their work. In other words, the freedom promised was to be freedom to man as Israelite and not to man as man. Jesus left that out, for his Kingdom was to be founded on the worth of man as man, and not man as a member of a particular race or class.

Capitalism, it will be seen, while containing a demand for greater equality, brought over with its radicalism a wrong to man.

Engels, in *Anti-Duhring,* speaks of a parallel happening in American history: "It is significant of the specifically bourgeois character of these human rights that the American Constitution, the first to recognize the rights of man, in the same breath confirmed the slavery of the colored races then living in America."

The Hebrews felt that the new day would bring to them a dictatorship of God's chosen people, for they were the Messianic people. This is similar to the feeling of the Communists of Russia, who feel that the proletariat are the Messianic people of the new day. In both cases the promise is held out that society would pass through this stage of the dictatorship of a class to a classless society, but in the meantime they would hold the power as trustees of the future. Jesus rejected this by omitting it and by putting something else into his program.

The test of any civilization is its view of man. What does it think of a man apart from race and class and money? Religion too must pass this test, without subterfuges or attempts to explain away. A Hindu lawyer remarked to me after listening to a fellow Hindu trying to explain away some Hindu customs: "He who excuses accuses!"

When we turn to the Gospels to see what release to the captives would mean, we see Simeon taking the infant Jesus in his arms and exclaiming as he catches a vision of what is going to happen when the impact of this new Kingdom, represented in the person of this Child, comes upon life: "A light for revelation to the Gentiles [Marg., "For the unveiling of the Gentiles"], and the glory of thy people Israel" (Luke 2: 32). Note that the marginal reading says that Christ would be "a light for the unveiling of the Gentiles." He would unveil hidden possibilities, show the amazing wealth of contribution possible in every human personality. Now note that this was to be for "Gentiles," the lowest in the social scale according to Jewish belief. According to that belief society was blocked off into five classes: at the top the Pharisee, proud of his God-given position; below him "the common people" among the Jews, who, not knowing the law, were accursed; below them were the Galileans, who, being of mixed blood, were considered inferior; below them were the Samaritans. To call a man "a Samaritan" was to abuse him, for their blood had been mixed in captivity, hence they were not allowed to help in building the Temple; so they built a rival one of their own. Below them were the outsiders, the Gentiles— "the Gentile dogs."

Every day the pious Jew thanked God he was not born "a woman, a leper, or a Gentile."

Now note that Christ was going to unveil the possibilities of these Gentiles, possibilities which had been hidden by prejudice. And this has been fulfilled, gloriously fulfilled, for wherever Christ goes there is an unveiling of the possibilities of man: life that has been withered under suppression and stultification begins to lift up its head. Said a Brahmin policeman to a Christian from the out-castes, "What has your religion, Christianity, done for you?" And he said it with a sneer of contempt. "Well, for one thing," said the former outcaste, "I am no longer afraid of you." The fears, the inhibitions, the inferiority complexes which had lain across the souls of the outcastes for centuries had been lifted by the impact of Christ upon human life. A certain Brahmin city is now being ruled over by a former outcaste. The government of the city had broken down through corruption, and the British Government was forced to intervene. They needed a man of character and could find none better than this former outcaste, for Christianity had given him character and courage. An outcaste as the manager of the city from which he would formerly have been excluded is a divine joke!

> **The test of any civilization is its view of man. What does it think of a man apart from race and class and money? Religion too must pass this test, without subterfuges or attempts to explain away.**

I think this cannot be contradicted: To the degree that Christ has been given to and accepted by any people, to that degree has that people gone up. You can practically fix the scale of the different peoples of the earth—in civilization, in enlightenment, in character, in progress—by the one question of how pure a type of Christianity has been given to and accepted by and acted upon by that people. If Russia seems an exception to this, in that she is making more progress in every way since the repudiation of religion, my reply is that there is more genuine Christian spirit in the Communist demand for the rights and the opportunities of the common man than there was in the Russian Orthodox Church with its superstitions and with its alliance with inhuman Czarism. To the degree that Russia embodies that demand for justice and an equal opportunity to all men she will go up; to the degree that she mixes in with that justice and brotherhood a spirit of hate and revenge and a stifling of human liberties she will break herself.

Christ has come to unveil the Gentiles, to unveil man as well as to unveil God. He is thus the double revelation of what God is and what man may become.

This unveiling of the possibilities of the common man runs like a golden thread through the whole of the Gospels. In Luke 3: 1-2 it is said, "Now in the fifteenth year of the reign of Tiberius Caesar, Pontius Pilate being governor of Judaea, and Herod being tetrarch of Galilee, and his brother Philip tetrarch of the regions of Ituraea and Trachonitis, and Lysanias tetrarch of Abilene, in the high-priesthood of Annas and Caiaphas, the word of God came unto John." Now, note how God passes over Caesar, Pilate, Herod, Philip, Lysanias, Annas, and Caiaphas, men in government, in politics, and in religion, and gives his word to a common man—John. The writer notes these notables, but goes on and makes them only the framework of the central thing: the word of the Lord came unto John. What are offices in church or state compared to a man who has a message from God! And the common man was the vehicle of that message! It was to shepherds watching their flocks by night that the announcement of His birth was made—to shepherds, ordinary, unlettered, toiling people; toiling, for watching flocks day and night in an unfenced country is toil. Why were the religious leaders, the rabbis and the scribes, passed over in favor of these common people ? Well, for one reason the priests would probably have searched sacred texts to see whether these things were valid, while the shepherds arose and said, "Let us now go . . . and see this thing." They were less cluttered up with prejudices and inhibitions and more simple and direct. The Kingdom could use only the simple and the direct mind. Besides, Jesus was producing a classless society in the new Kingdom. He could only produce that society by beginning with those who had the least consciousness of class. The Communists are probably right in saying that they can produce a classless society by reducing all classes to one class—the class of the workers. They are probably wrong in saying that it is through the dictatorship of the proletariat that it will be done, for that dictatorship produces another class in the process of liquidating all classes, and that class which now has power will probably cling to it after liquidating all opposing elements. There is no sign that it is lessening its grip. On the contrary, it seems to be extending it, so the fading out of the state, to which they look forward, seems very remote. The tendency has been increasingly in the opposite direction. The state is becoming more and more powerful, and those directing it more and more dictatorial in spite of the fact that they have the most secure state in Europe at the present time. They have tried to produce a classless society by the creation of an all-powerful class which in the end may be its undoing. For their purposes, they were probably right in saying that all classes must be reduced to the class of the workers.

Jesus began with them. He called to his discipleship fishermen and the common, ordinary people. That fact has been repeated so often that we have forgotten its significance. A movement that was to replace the whole present world order was a movement headed by a Carpenter and a group of fishermen disciples! Jesus told a scribe who wanted to follow him to go home, as "the foxes have holes, and the birds of the heaven have nests; but the Son of man has nowhere to lay his head." This scribe wouldn't do. He who was a carpenter knew that you had to begin with raw materials to build a house, for wood that had been cut and planed and fitted for another structure would be difficult to fit into an entirely new structure. So he began with raw material. It was to be a Kingdom of Man. To get into it you had to reduce life to its simplicities —to become as a little child.

A child knows no distinction of color and race and money. All this is imposed later. So the child-mind was the only type he could use, for it was fresh and unprejudiced. Jesus told his disciples that the Kingdom which he was inaugurating was different from the ordinary kingdoms. "You know that they which are accounted to rule over the Gentiles lord it over them; and their great ones exercise authority over them. But it is not so among you: but whosoever would become great among you shall be your minister: and whosoever would be first among you, shall be servant [or bondservant] of all. For verily the Son of man came not to be ministered unto, but to minister, and to give his life a ransom for many" (Mark 10: 42-45). Jesus vividly contrasts his Kingdom with the older type. In these verses there is enough dynamite to blow to pieces most of our existing institutions, founded as they are upon lording it over others, and making them serve us instead of loving others and becoming their servants. Think of Jesus saying that Caesar with his mighty empire was only "accounted to rule"—it wasn't real ruling, it was wearing "a crown as it were" (Revelation 9: 7). He saw that it was all a tinseled, flimsy fabric founded on the exploitation of man and that it would go down into the dust. Today Jesus walks amid the mighty empires and governments and looks at them with an appraising eye and says, "Men say you rule, but my verdict is that you are only accounted to rule." These two phrases, "accounted to rule," and "they that have authority over them are called Benefactors" (Luke), have enough gentle irony in them to make ridiculous all our systems founded on the pomposity of authority which forces service from men instead of an authority won by service. In this new Kingdom the degrees among them were these: If you would be "great," become the "servant"; if you would be "first," then become "the bondservant of all." And then he says, very gently, "I am your Lord, because I give my life a ransom for many." The three degrees of greatness are these: the great who are the servants, the first who are the bondservants of all, and, as Lord of all, the Son of man, who gives his life for all. But there is only one class, the class of servants, varying in their degree of self-giving in the service, and that degree of service determines their authority. This is sound and will have to be adopted in any rational society.

Here, then, was the emergence of a new society, a classless society, the Society of Servants, the Contributors. The Communists are trying to produce a new society based on the workers. No one shall have the franchise who lives off others; he must work or have no part in the new society. Here the Kingdom of God includes this idea, but it goes beyond it and says that it is not only a Kingdom of workers, but a Kingdom of Contributors. This is greater, for one may work and not really contribute to the collective good, for he may work only for himself.

A Kingdom of Contributors—was there ever such a name and ever such an outlook?

We noted that the Jew thanked God every day that he was not born "a woman, or a leper, or a Gentile." In the very chapter in which Jesus makes his announcement of his program he emphasized the worthwhileness of all three: he cited with approval the fact that Elijah was sent unto a woman in the days of famine, Elisha was sent unto a leper, and they were both Gentiles (Luke 4. 25- 27). Jesus thus canceled their prayer and cut across the attitudes that religion had taken toward these three classes in society.

The account says that Jesus began his ministry in

> "Galilee of the Gentiles,
> The people which sat in darkness
> Saw a great light,
> And to them that sat in the region and shadow
> of death,
> To them did light spring up."
> (Matthew 4:12-17.)

Note that Jesus began his ministry in "Galilee of the Gentiles;" his ministry from the very beginning was identified with the despised. Among three classes he constantly lived—the publicans, disowned because of occupation; the sinners, disowned because of moral condition; the Gentiles, disowned because of birth. And note also that he "dwelt" among them—his was not a long-distance interest that cost little, but an everyday bearing of everything that fell upon them.

The very close connection of the inner life and the making of a just social order is seen in Matthew 12: 18, 19: "I will put my Spirit upon him, And he shall declare judgment to the Gentiles" —he shall give justice or a fair, equal opportunity to the Gentiles.

And he shall do this "until he had led on justice to victory"— justice shall be victoriously embodied in human affairs. Here was the Spirit-directed life focused on the giving of basic justice to the despised members of human society. No wonder the passage ends in these words, "And in his name shall the Gentiles hope." The only hope for the world is a spirituality directed toward basic justice in all human living.

One of the charges made against Jesus at the trial in Jerusalem was that "he stirs up the people, . . . beginning from Galilee" (Luke 23:5). The sting to his accusers, whose lives were founded on so-called God-given prestige, was that he had begun in Galilee. He had passed by the religious Brahmins and had begun with the outcastes. It was a sin against their station. It was a passing by the classes and a starting of a movement among the masses—the dangerous turbulent Galilean masses. It was dangerous. It was—and is! "He stirs up the people"—made them feel within them the stirrings of new aspirations and hopes, made them feel that the possibilities which before had been in reach of certain men of certain classes, made them feel that life belonged to them and that they could enter into it. Wherever Christ has gone he has stirred up the people. Lord Inchcape complained that it was the missionaries who were at the bottom of the trouble in China. He was right! For the "trouble" to men like Lord Inchcape was that the people were no longer willing to be exploited like dumb, driven cattle.

To tell a man that God is the Father of all, and that he can, if he but will, enter into the family, and that all men are brothers, is to lay the foundation of the greatest stirring up of the people that can be imagined. For this stirs to a deeper depth than Communism is able to do, for man is no mere economic animal—he is a child of God.

Perhaps the greatest distance between man and man is made by knowledge. Lord Haldane said that "class division in knowledge goes deeper than any other class division." But Jesus launched a Kingdom where this would not be: "I thank you, O Father, Lord of heaven and earth, that you hid these things from the wise and understanding, and did reveal them to babes; for so it was well-pleasing in your sight"

(Luke 10: 21). The only time that Jesus ever exclaimed about God's greatness—"Lord of heaven and earth"—was in connection with his founding a Kingdom in which the snobbery of superior knowledge was ended and the deepest and the fullest was open to "babes." God's greatness was in the fact that he takes account of littleness. No wonder Jesus exclaimed over such a God and over such a Kingdom!

When, in healing people, Jesus walked across religious laws, he justified it on the basis that man and his need have precedence over laws and customs. On two different occasions he used a similar reply: "But go and learn what this means, I desire mercy, and not sacrifice" (Matthew 9: 13). "But if you had known what this means, I desire mercy and not sacrifice, you would not have condemned the guiltless" (Matthew 12: 7).

Findlay translates, "I desire brotherly feeling and not sacrifice." Mercy, or brotherly feeling, is socialized, moralized religion; sacrifice is unsocial, ceremonial religion. Go learn the difference between the two, said Jesus. And when he said so, he gave religion its supreme lesson to learn. Had we learned it, the history of religion and the history of the world would have been different. "If you had known"! How little religion has known this desiring right relations to man instead of meaningless sacrifices! And "sacrifice" of those days would mean, translated into the terms of today, ornate ritual and elaborate church ceremony, which preoccupies men and makes them blind to the real issues regarding human injustices.

One of the most penetrating verses in the New Testament on the subject of the worth of human personality is this: "The sabbath was made for man, and not man for the sabbath: so that the Son of man is lord even of the sabbath" (Mark 2: 27, 28). Reduced to its essence this verse means that religious institutions are made for man and not man for them. But we have made religious institutions primary and secondary: man fits into them, instead of their fitting into man, after the manner of the celebrated bed, upon which if a man lay, and he were not long enough to fit the bed, he was stretched until he did; and if he were too long, his legs were chopped off—in any case he must fit the bed! But Jesus makes personality primary, and the right of governments, of industry, of social customs, and of religious institutions to exist is to be determined by the effect of these institutions upon human personality. When the Greeks said, "Man is the measure of the universe," they were thinking abstractly and philosophically, but when Jesus said the same thing, but in other words, he was thinking concretely and morally. Here is what Seeley calls "an enthusiasm for humanity."

> **One of the most penetrating verses in the New Testament on the subject of the worth of human personality is this: "The sabbath was made for man, and not man for the sabbath: so that the Son of man is lord even of the sabbath" (Mark 2:27, 28).**

At this point Jesus stands on higher ground than the Communist, who, while having a great human passion, is tending toward a Communist orthodoxy and is prepared to sacrifice man to the maintaining of that orthodoxy. One can see the hardening of the beliefs and institutions of Communism, and woe to you if you disagree with them. At the very point that the Communists have been light they are in danger of turning to darkness—they have established beliefs and institutions for man, and now those institutions and beliefs are becoming the end and man is sacrificed to them. The fallacy that these beliefs and institutions are good for man, and that therefore man must be sacrificed to them, is a fallacy into which religion and Communism have both fallen. Jesus holds the corrective. In the end he will judge both religion and Communism at this point.

Now note the significant word "so" in these verses— "the sabbath was made for man and not man for the sabbath: so that the Son of man is Lord of the sabbath." Does it mean that the Son of man is Lord of everything that stands for man? The Sabbath is for man, "so" the Son of man is Lord of that Sabbath. Then all the movements and institutions that stand for the betterment of humanity have Christ as their Lord. He sits as king wherever life stands for man. He may be unknown, even hated, but he is Lord of everything that tends to help man. This is an assumption of regal authority that is astounding. He says that he is Lord and king not in heaven, but in the midst of everything that moves toward man and the new humanity. Jesus establishes his throne not in the placid precincts of heaven, but in the turbulent places of earth. This means that his throne is also a cross, for he rules where to rule is to bleed. The fact is that he rules because he does bleed.

> Jesus establishes his throne not in the placid precincts of heaven, but in the turbulent places of earth. This means that his throne is also a cross, for he rules where to rule is to bleed.

The Son of man is Lord of the Sabbath, the Sabbath was for man; therefore the Son of man is for man. Man and he are made for each other as the eye is made for light. His Lordship is man's freedom. His

108

rule and man's nature coincide.

The Son of man is Lord in every movement that lifts the sons of men. Then it may be that he is as much at home in the movements for man as in the old cathedral. Perhaps more so.

So far the teachings of Jesus would make us not indifferent to the distinctions between man and man, but would do away with those distinctions. The Hindu quotes the passage from the Gita as the high-water mark of the right attitude toward man, "The wise look with equal eye on the Brahmin, adorned with learning and humility, a cow, an elephant, and even the dog and the outcaste." Equal eye on all! But I do not want to look with equal eye on the Brahmin and the outcaste, I want to do away with the outcaste. I do not want to look with equal eye on the rich and the poor, I want to do away with the poor. Religion should not make us indifferent to distinctions, but should do away with the distinctions themselves.

CHAPTER 4

GOOD NEWS TO THE SOCIALLY AND POLITICALLY DISINHERITED (CONTINUED)

As Jesus projects this new Kingdom into human life we see before our very eyes the changes which take place in the relationships between men and men, and between men and things. The Kingdom meant reversal—reversal of the most thoroughgoing kind. To see the process of reversal in actual operation let us take a passage where an ordinary cross-section of what Jesus was doing may be seen. In Luke 8: 1-3 we read, "It came to pass soon afterward that he went about through cities and villages, preaching and bringing the good tidings of the kingdom of God, and with him the twelve, and certain women which had been healed of evil spirits and infirmities, Mary that was called Magdalene, from whom seven devils had gone out, and Joanna, the wife of Chuza, Herod's steward, and Susanna, and many others which ministered unto them of their substance."

Here was an ordinary day, and yet if it was an ordinary day, how very extraordinary it was! For the whole of life was being quietly reversed. Let us begin at the end of the account and work back toward the center. This new power at work wrought the following reversals:

1. There was the mastery of the material by the spiritual—they "ministered unto them of their substance." Substance was no longer the master, it was the minister. But that is a real reversal, for in ordinary life material things master, determine, and decide the spiritual. Things are in the saddle. We decide life courses on the basis of the amount of the material involved. But here was a movement which was breaking the power of the material, breaking it in the only way that it can really be broken, namely, by the dedication of the material to spiritual ends. We cannot run away from the material in order to break its power; we can only take it into our hands and direct it toward the spiritual purposes for which we live. It is then no longer a material thing; it is the agent of the spiritual, and hence spiritual.

2. There was the mastery of the social by the spiritual. It is stated that Mary Magdalene, out of whom seven devils had gone—this woman and Joanna, the wife of Chuza, Herod's steward, were together in the same company. To be the wife of the steward of Herod the king was to be a woman of high social position at court. But this woman of high social position and an outcaste woman were brought together in a movement that wiped out social classes. Here was the mastery of the social by the spiritual.

3. There was the mastery of the sexual by the spiritual. Here were single and married men and women going throughout these cities and villages in the same company, a thing that was not done in that day. Did not the disciples marvel that Jesus talked with "a woman" as he sat near her by the well? Were not the holiest among the Pharisees called "the bleeding Pharisees," because they went around with their eyes on the

ground lest they look on a woman, hence constantly bumping their heads against trees and walls and thus making bloody their foreheads? Saint John of Lycopolis would boast that he had not seen a woman for forty-eight years. But in the company of Jesus men and women moved freely, and the amazing thing is that the breath of scandal never touched it. The disciples and Jesus were accused of many things, but never scandal. Here was a new kind of society based on the equal freedom of men and women. These people were pure, not because they had no opportunity to be impure, but because they had no disposition to be so. A new passion had taken hold of them that broke the tyranny of physical passions. They had gotten rid of a desire in the only possible way of getting rid of it, namely, by its replacement by a higher desire. Here was the mastery of sexuality by the spiritual.

4. There was the mastery of physical infirmity by the spiritual. These women had been healed of "infirmities." The whole burden of physical suffering was being lifted by this new redemptive movement.

5. There was the mastery of sin by the spiritual. They had been "healed of evil spirits." Whatever that means it certainly means that there was a mastery of sin and evil in human living. Sin and evil had met their match and a new and astonishing possibility had come into being—a man, no matter what he had been and done, could become good. Sin had met its master.

6. There was the mastery of the waste materials of life by the spiritual. "And with him the twelve." Now, the twelve were very ordinary representatives of humanity. Had they not come into contact with Christ they would probably have contributed little to their community. However, under the touch of his presence they were awakened and began to contribute. Here was the taking of the waste materials of life and the making of it into men who, by the very force of what they became, left an indelible mark on succeeding ages.

7. There was the mastery of the environment by the spiritual. They "went about through cities and villages." They were not afraid of the greatness of the city nor contemptuous of the smallness of the village. They were released from bondage to places. They felt that they were in the presence of greatness everywhere, namely in the presence of human beings with their infinite possibilities. Some of us are at the mercy of our environment—we are unhappy unless we get an environment great enough to fit our supposed greatness. All this matter of high and low, big and little, was canceled in their thinking and they were freed from the desire for particular places.

8. There was the mastery of themselves by the spiritual. They came "preaching and bringing the . . . kingdom of God." They did not merely preach the Kingdom of God—they brought it. They brought it as a living thing in their own lives. As people looked at them they saw in the joy and buoyancy and victory of their lives the fact of the Kingdom of God in actual operation. The people did not merely hear the good news—they saw it. At the very center of their beings these men and women were mastered by a new force, the reign of God. At the very center they had let go and God had the citadel. That mastery at the center of their being was the secret of the freedom which they had in all phases of their lives and relationships. They were freed from the tyranny of themselves, and hence from the tyranny of outside things.

Let us now step back and look at the picture of this mighty transformation and reversal as a whole. They were mastered at the center of their inmost being: the reign of God had begun in them. That central mastery had begun to register in relationships: there was the mastery of environment—they were freed from big and little places in their environment; there was non-contributive humanity now made contributive and creative; sin and evil had met their match; suffering was being faced and cured; physical drives were now sublimated into

113

creative activity and each was freed from its dominance; social distinctions were obliterated and a great brotherhood and sisterhood was formed; and substance was now the agent of the spiritual. Surely, there was never such a deep and thoroughgoing deliverance as this, for it reaches from the inmost depths of one's being clear out through every human and every material relationship. This was literally "a release to the captive," an entire and all-comprehending release.

> **Surely, there was never such a deep and thoroughgoing deliverance as this, for it reaches from the inmost depths of one's being clear out through every human and every material relationship.**

Now note that these verses were really the concrete expression of the program announced in the synagogue. So the new program was in actual operation. And that operation meant opportunity to man as man.

As we mark this passion for the freeing of man from all that binds, it is no wonder that this spirit blazes out against those who hurt human personality by contemptuous attitudes and words. This is a part of the life of Christ which the East finds difficult to understand. They see in his pronouncement of woes upon the Pharisees only a loss of temper and of poise. Neither Hinduism nor Buddhism has this passion for humanity, hence those who are imbued with the spirit of these faiths see in Jesus at this point a loss of detached aloofness. But Jesus never had aloofness, and he was never detached. He was identified so deeply with man that when any man was hurt he winced under that hurt. So when he lashes out against the Pharisees, it was not the cry of a personal, disappointed anger, but the manifestation of a wounded heart, a heart wounded in the wounds of others. But even in that pronouncement of woes upon the despoilers of others Jesus turns from woes to weeping —he wept over the city upon which he was pronouncing woes. Here was not anger, but a redemptive love. So he turned to those who were guilty of contempt and said, "You have heard that it was said, you shall not kill, but I say unto you, that whosoever should malign his brother by stating, *Raca* (which means, I spit on you), is guilty before the congregation, and whosoever curses his brother, is condemned to hell fire" (Matthew 5: 21, 22, Aramaic trans.). The old law said, "You shall not murder the body;" Jesus said, "You shall not murder the soul." To use contemptuous terms and to show contemptuous attitudes was to commit soul murder. To lower a man in his own estimation, to hurt his self-respect, is to degrade him at the very center of his being, and this, said Jesus, is to deserve the severest judgment of God and man.

When John in prison doubted whether this kind of a Kingdom was the kind that was wanted, for it seemed to lack smiting force and power, he sent messengers to ask whether Jesus was the one who was to come or must they look for another. Did Jesus in reply send an argument as to his credentials? No, in that hour he healed many, so he said to the disciples of John: "Go your way and tell John the things which you do hear and see: the blind receive their sight and the lame walk, the lepers are cleansed, and the deaf hear, and the dead are raised up, and the poor have good tidings preached to them. And blessed is he whosoever shall find none occasion of stumbling in me" (Matthew 11: 2-6). "My credentials," said Jesus, "are written in the healed bodies and souls of men. They are written in the new lives before me." For that day and for this the supreme test of religion is its effect upon human living. The God that answers by healed men, let him be God! Its vitality is its vitality!

115

Now note how this statement of Jesus as to what he was doing closely approximates the announcement of his program which he made in the synagogue at Nazareth. Practically all the items were seen in operation in actual fact. It shows that Jesus took the program seriously and pointed to its operation as proof for John.

What an amazing thing to say, "Blessed is he whosoever shall find none occasion of stumbling in me"! All of us would have been compelled to say, "Blessed am I if men find no occasion of stumbling in me." But Jesus said that the other man is blessed if he finds no occasion of stumbling in him. What an assumption! What an amazing thing to say, "Happy is that person, that society, that institution, that state which fits into me!" Here was a belief in himself that was astounding. "None occasion"—no situation, no outlook in thought, no spirit of life, no program for human living—never am I not right! This would sound like hollow boasting did not the ages attest the truth of every syllable of it. Never has Jesus been wrong on any issue, and we have the growing conviction that as we rebuild the world we must read his mind into its foundation or else the whole thing will tumble to pieces around us.

> **The supreme test of religion is its effect upon human living. The God that answers by healed persons, let him be God!**

As Jesus went in to eat with a Pharisee on the Sabbath "they were watching him" (Luke 14: 1-6). We are still watching him! The world's eyes are on this Man. And as we watch him we begin to feel that he is the one hope for a world floundering in its own follies and selfishness's. Jesus is the one way out!

On that occasion a man with dropsy (edema) was before him. And

116

Jesus said, "Is it lawful to heal on the sabbath, or not?" But they held their peace. And Jesus healed the man and let him go. And he said unto them, "Which of you shall have a donkey or an ox fallen into a well, and will not straightaway draw him up on the sabbath day?" And they could not answer again about these things." Of course "they could not answer again about these things," for there is no answer to controvert successfully the idea that a human personality is supreme over things and institutions and must be treated as supreme. But this was not a mere "idea." They could not answer again about these "things." They were things, and could not be answered by words but by better things. They had no better things. Nor have we.

In Matthew 13: 41 it is said that "they shall gather out of his kingdom all things that cause stumbling," all things that are in the way of the progress of humanity. That is the one task before the world now—to gather up the things that cause stumbling to the progress of man and banish them. There is an eternal growth before man and nothing must cause men to stumble on the way. "I am come that they might have life, and that they might have it more abundantly." He comes to root out what is anti-life. The self is to be expressed and completed, so nothing must hinder it. "Then shall the righteous shine forth as the sun in the kingdom of their Father." The Kingdom of God is the place where health reigns, and hence where human personality is expressed: they shall shine forth as the sun. The Kingdom of God is the great affirmation.

Jesus cried out against everything that hurt human personality. In Luke 17: 1-2 he said, "Woe unto him through whom they [offenses] come! It were well for him if a millstone were hanged about his neck, and he were thrown into the midst of the sea, rather than he should cause one of these little ones to stumble." In Matthew 18:7 Jesus cries, "Woe unto the world because of occasions of stumbling!" What a passion for people in that statement! It is the cry that no human personality is to be hurt by others. The worst physical calamity that can come to you, a millstone about your neck and you thrown into the midst of the sea, is preferable to your causing the slightest injury, physical or spiritual, to come to one of these little ones. Here is clear-sighted passion indeed!

As a blind man sat by the wayside begging (Mark 10: 48), he cried out, "Jesus, you son of David, have mercy on me." But "they that went before rebuked him" (Luke 18: 39). Those who head the procession of life try to keep the undesirables quiet. They are disturbing us. These people were not interested in blind people. But Jesus called to the blind man. Then the very people who had told him to keep quiet now ran to him and said, "Arise, be of good cheer; he calls you." They were not interested in blind persons until Jesus was. Then they began to follow his interests. On that day we began to follow his interests. And if we follow his interest far enough, we shall make a new world. We cannot be interested "in" Jesus without being interested in the people who are seated on the waysides of life, out of its central stream. We are more and more asking,

> "Who has given to me this sweet,
> And given my brother dust to eat?"[1]

The world is more and more following Jesus' interest in children, in the outcastes, in the sufferers, in the laborers, in the "impossible" people. For the "impossible" become the possible when touched by Jesus' possibilities.

Jesus became the Way, for one reason, because of the way he treated people by the wayside. As he was on the way to become the Way he was

---

1 William Vaughn Moody, "Gloucester Moors" (1909).

different. It is not merely that he had a wonderful goal; he was wonderful in his treatment of people on the way to that goal. Many people have wonderful goals ahead of them, but the decisive thing is what they do on the way to that goal. The Hindu sannyasi has what is to him a wonderful goal—union with God—but the point is, what does he do on the way to that goal? Usually nothing! Some have no goal, and treat well the people by the wayside (the humanists), and some have a great goal and do not treat well the people by the wayside (the mere religionists). Jesus had both—a great goal and a great goodness.

Of the many tyrannies that oppress humanity none is causing more havoc than the one based on so-called superior and inferior blood. It has made snobberies seem sacred, and slaveries seem destiny. Marcus Aurelius was an emperor, and Epictetus was a slave—both Stoics; however, each was to keep his station and be content with it, and not rebel against the destinies of life. Hinduism teaches the same. Do your duty—or

The world is more and more following Jesus' interest in children, in the outcastes, in the sufferers, in the laborers, in the "impossible" people. For the "impossible" become the possible when touched by Jesus' possibilities.

dharma—in the station in which you are born and all will be well. But Jesus canceled all these snobberies based on blood and station. When his mother and his family came to see him, Jesus announced a new kinship based not on blood but on belonging to the family of God. He looked on "them which sat around him" and said: "Behold, my mother and my brethren! For whosoever shall do the will of God, the same is

119

my brother, and sister, and mother." Here was a relationship that transcended birth and national relationships, and bound men and women together in a great fellowship of the doers of the will of God. This new relationship in the Kingdom of God was one that not only transcended human relationships, but one that gathered up all that was fine in them and added to them. A mother can be a mother to you, a sister a sister, a brother a brother, but the Kingdom of God relationship had the meaning of all three of these— and more! It is the sum total of human relationships, plus the divine relationship. It thus comprehends Life.

Jesus summed up these relationships in two glorious passages: "One is your Father" (Matthew 23: 9), "And all ye are brethren" (Matthew 23: 8). Here were the ideas of the Fatherhood of God and the Brotherhood of man—concepts so simple that we do not catch their significance—placed before us in two brief phrases. And this was spoken "to the multitude and to the disciples," not to the disciples alone. We have tried to make this mean "disciples" alone, thus narrowing the concept to fit our narrow minds, instead of broadening our minds to fit the concept.

Jesus reduced religion to love to God and love to man. In telling us what love to man meant Jesus said, "Thou shall love thy neighbor as thyself"—the self-interest and the other-interest were exactly balanced, giving a perfect code of ethical truth in a sentence. "To love our neighbor means that each shall count for one and no one for more than one." Love to God and love to man—was religion ever reduced to greater simplicity and to greater profundity than this? Men are trying to reduce it further—You shall love your neighbor! But to reduce it further is to divide the indivisible. It is the death of each. Humanism is dying because it is severed from that which gives it meaning, namely, God.

But to see the fusing of the religious and the social in an amazing blend we turn to the account of Jesus' saying on the last day, "I was in prison and you came unto me." Here he shows a perpetual incarnation in human need. He is bound with every prisoner, whether that man be a prisoner of the legal or the economic or the social system. If this be true, then Christ is being tortured on a thousand battlefields and exploited in a thousand mills. In Luke 9: 22 it is said, "The Son of man must suffer many things"— of course he must if he is the Son of man, for the sons of men suffer many things, and every one of their sufferings is his. If the Son of man enters into all of these things—as, indeed, he must if he is Love, for it is the nature of love to insinuate itself into the sorrows and pains of others— then it becomes a solemn fact that the "desperate tides of the world's great anguish are forced through the channel of a single heart."

> **Jesus reduced religion to love to God and love to man. In telling us what love to man meant Jesus said, "Thou shall love thy neighbor as thyself"— the self-interest and the other-interest were exactly balanced, giving a perfect code of ethical truth in a sentence.**

The Emperor of China was the Son of Heaven. Once a year he accounted before Heaven for all the people whom he had executed during the year. He justified himself as one who carried out the decrees of Heaven. Jesus came not to impose the decrees of Heaven, but to be Heaven entering into earth with its pangs and sorrows and sins. He was the Son of man. Touch humanity anywhere and you touch Jesus. This makes the cross not an accident at the end, but an inherent part of the process from the beginning. It was inevitable.

Jesus' last thought on that cross was of his enemies — "Father, forgive them, for they know not what they do." And his last deed was to release a captive— "Today you shall be with me in paradise." So this passion persisted amid the tortures of the cross. After he could do nothing else for anyone, "Jesus, knowing that all things were now finished," thought of himself— "I thirst." That was the summing up of his life: the needs of others were primary, and his own secondary.

This passion for man he compresses into one glorious sentence: "A new commandment I give unto you, that you love one another even as I have loved you" (John 13: 34). It is that last portion, "as I have loved you," that gives it content. Love for man is no longer merely love for man, it is love for man as Jesus loved men. That makes it different, forever different.

But not only did he give them a new commandment; he gave them a new conception of authority: "Even as you gave him authority over all flesh, that whatsoever you have given him, to them he should give eternal life" (John 17: 2). The "authority" of Jesus was not to rule men with a rod of iron, but to give them "eternal life"—authority not to take from but to give to—the authority of service! His Kingdom is a Kingdom of servers, ruled over by One who has authority to serve.

These are the fundamental ideas which Jesus implants in the minds of his disciples, ideas which were to form the foundation of the relationships which men were to take in the new world order.

After Jesus left them, his Spirit continued to move in the direction of a classless society. When Peter hesitated to go and associate with Gentiles, he tells us that "the Spirit told me to go with them making no distinction" (Acts 10: 20, R. V.). Here was the Divine Spirit urging men on toward a society in which no distinctions of race or class are made. This was based upon the fact, as Peter put it, "I clearly see that God makes no distinctions between one man and another" (Acts 10: 34, Weymouth trans.). If that is God's attitude, then it must be ours, for to be like God in spirit and action is the very center of the Christian ethic.

This was in line with what the enemies of Jesus saw at work in him: "Teacher, we know that you do not discriminate between man and man—is it lawful," etc. They tried to trap him and only succeeded in revealing what was obvious, namely, that he treated persons without discrimination. How different has been the Christianity built up around him!

Of all the phrases that had to come into being to express the Christian attitude toward man, there is none that has such depth of meaning as the one that Paul uses— "a man (or woman) for whom Christ died." A man is no longer a mere man; he is a person for whom Christ died. I can no longer see the coolie on the street; he is a man for whom Christ died. This is a glorious phrase representing a more glorious fact!

> **Of all the phrases that had to come into being to express the Christian attitude toward man, there is none that has such depth of meaning as the one that Paul uses— "a man (or woman) for whom Christ died."**

Paul stood on Mars' Hill, the place dedicated to Mars, the god of war, and announced, he "has made of one blood all nations of men for to dwell on all the face of the earth" (Acts 17: 26). The oneness of our common humanity may be a commonplace now as sociologists are making the discovery that we *are* one, but it was not commonplace at the time this was uttered. Nor is this a commonplace everywhere even today. The fact is that most of our divisions are based upon the fact that we believe that this statement of Paul is not true. But in the end we shall find that basically and fundamentally we are one, but that differing social heredities which are imposed upon us have made and are still making many of the differences. They are not inherent but are socially imposed. A British judge of distinction told me that he had discovered that the brain of East and West is the same, for he found that lawyers in England and Burma came out at the same fallacies in their arguing. Scratch beneath the surface and you find just a fundamental, common humanity in East and West. A person is a person.

When Paul would unfold the doctrine of the "one blood," he sums it up in one glorious sentence: "In that new creation there can be neither Greek nor Jew—racial distinction; circumcision nor uncircumcision—religious denominational distinction; Barbarian nor Scythian—cultural distinction; slave nor free man—social distinction; male nor female —gender distinction" (See Colossians 3: 11; Galatians 3: 28). There could not be put into words a clearer affirmation of the oneness of humanity, and the solidarity of the race and the emergence of a new brotherhood based on that fact. No, this brotherhood is not entirely based on that fact, for it is really based on the fact that we are following One who is the Son of man, and in him *cannot* be these distinctions. If we still have these distinctions, then we are driven to the conclusion that he is not in us, however much we may name him. When we isolate ourselves from our brothers, we do one thing—we isolate ourselves from Christ.

But not to have these distinctions is not sufficient. The attitude of the Gospels is positive and can be summed up in these great words, "Bear you one another's burdens, and so fulfill the law of Christ" (Galatians 6: 2). A society based on these words could not be competitive, it could only be co-operative and based on mutual assistance. "The commonwealth of Christ is a mutual aid society." Instead of "the struggle for existence" which we have in lower nature we have in this *new Commonwealth* what Drummond called "the struggle for the existence of others."

These underlying attitudes toward "the captive" work themselves out in the attitude that Paul states in regard to Onesimus, the slave, when he wrote to his owner, "You might receive him back, ... no longer as a slave, but as something better than a slave—a brother" (Philemon 16, Weymouth trans.). This passing from slavehood to brotherhood was a direct result of the impact of the spirit of the Gospel. Had we given it full rein in society today, we should have had a brotherhood world instead of chaos. Whenever this spirit was allowed to operate there was a freeing from slavery. Lecky reminds us that with the coming of Christianity a great moral movement passed through the servile classes. Slave birth was no disqualification for entering into the priesthood. The wealthiest and the most influential often knelt at the feet of former slaves to receive absolution or benedictions. The first and grandest edifice of Byzantine architecture in Italy, the noble Church of Saint Vital in Ravenna, was dedicated by Justinian to the memory of a martyred slave. Christians emancipated their slaves. Saint Malinia was said to have liberated eight thousand; Saint Ovidius, a rich martyr of Gaul, freed five thousand. In the thirteenth century, when there were no slaves to emancipate in France, it was usual in many churches to release caged pigeons on the ecclesiastical festivals in memory of the ancient charity, and that prisoners might be freed in the name of Christ. This impulse, which is integral in the Christian spirit, must now be set to work to free men who are in social and economic servitude.

For this spirit of freeing the captive is inherent in the new Kingdom. Nietzsche saw this and raved against it, "The poison of the teaching of equal rights for all has been spread abroad by Christianity more than by anything else. As a matter of principle Christianity from the inmost recesses of bad instincts has waged a deadly war against every instinct of reverence and distance between man and man. Let us not underestimate the calamity, which, proceeding from Christianity, has insinuated itself even into politics ... And if this belief of the privileges of the many makes revolutions and continues to make them, it is Christianity which is responsible. Christianity is the revolt of all that creeps on the ground against all that is elevated." We plead guilty to that charge and glory in it, and have only one regret, namely, that it has not been operative on a world scale. We have blocked this impulse again and again.

Who will doubt the truth of that last statement when he is reminded that even after 1861, a certain great church declared "its deep conviction of the divine appointment of domestic servitude," and of "the peculiar mission of the _____ Church to conserve the institution of slavery"? On this question this particular church was on the wrong side and against its own gospel. That is past and gone, but the question arises as to what will be the position of the church as a whole as the battle line moves on and closes in on the question of economic slavery. Wilberforce found the bishops of the House of Lords voting to a man against his endeavors to free the slaves. When Lord Shaftesbury introduced legislation regulating factories and mines, preventing exploitation of women and children, the whole bench of bishops voted against him in the House of Lords. But even Wilberforce, who labored so earnestly to free the African slaves, opposed every attempt to free the white slaves of British industry. Will the church continue to be blind in spots? If so, then in this coming crisis she will lose her eyesight entirely, and possibly her very life.

There is a central contradiction in the heart of our life today. Sherwood Eddy says, "On its social side religion is founded on

126

reverence for personality, equal brotherhood, and love as implying practically equal sharing with all. Our present economic order is founded on the profit motive, monopolistic ownership and consequent class inequality, injustice, and strife. Here is a flat contradiction." It is.

There is only one side of that contradiction which we as followers of Christ can take—we must throw ourselves out on the side of freedom, freedom for every man and woman in every realm of life. Only thus can we ourselves remain free. Revelation 13: 9 says, "If anyone is eager to lead others into captivity, he must himself go into captivity" (Weymouth trans.). Where there is a conflict between persons and property, the Christian has only one side he can take and remain Christian. A missionary lady gave minute instructions to the contractor about putting on a concrete roof. But to save money he disregarded her instructions; the roof collapsed, injuring a coolie boy and causing great loss to the missionary. When she was told of the calamity, she came and, without paying any attention to the loss, went at once to attend to the coolie boy. Some of the Hindu workmen were talking about the matter and were wondering why the memsahib had paid so little attention to the loss and had given such immediate and genuine attention to the injured boy. "Don't you understand?" said another coolie boy. "She is a Christian, and Christians always think more of persons than things."

> **There is only one side of that contradiction which we as followers of Christ can take—we must throw ourselves out on the side of freedom, freedom for every man and woman in every realm of life. Only thus can we ourselves remain free.**

Would that the statement of the coolie boy had been and were true of us today! Were it so, our world would be entirely different. We must make it so. In religion we have given man equality before God; in democracy we have given him equality before the law; in social relationships we have yet to give him equality in spite of differences of color and race; in economic relationships we have yet to give him equality at the place of the central bondage, namely, the bondage through the power that the possession of things gives over persons.

The second item in the Christian alternative to Communism is the release of the captive from bondage of every type and kind, to let him stand forth God's free man in a world of brothers. This brotherhood would smash all snobberies based on color or lack of color, on class or lack of class, on money or lack of money, on personal gifts or lack of personal gifts; and greatness would consist in none of these extraneous things; but in the service we render to the common good—the greatness of those who greatly give.

If we should do this, the world would be drawn to this brotherhood. "If there had been a real brotherhood within Christianity, the whole of the sixty million untouchables of India would have been in it by now," said a professor of a law college, himself an untouchable. Had there been a brotherhood within Christianity which would have included not only the spiritual, but the social and the economic as well, then by now the whole world would have been in it. In idea, in teaching, in impulse it is within Christianity. In actual realized fact this brotherhood still awaits embodiment. The place which Christianity will have in the future will be determined by its power to embody it.

CHAPTER 5

GOOD NEWS TO THE PHYSICALLY DISINHERITED

We sat in the early morning on the ridge at our prayer hour in the Ashram at Sat Tal in quiet meditation. In the midst of our communion with God two sounds broke in upon us, one from the one side of the ridge far below, and the other from the other side. One was the song of a Christian singing, "O happy day"— and how beautiful it was! The other was the sound of a hacking cough coming from an Indian hut—and how distressing it was! Into religious meditation these two voices intrude —one the voice of a soul released and happy, and the other the voice of physical distress. Shall religion deliberately turn its back on and refuse to listen to the sound of the hacking cough, and give itself to producing souls that can sing their "O happy day"? Or shall religion do something about that hacking cough? Has religion anything to do with physical suffering? Has it any program at that place?

Jesus announced that he had a program to address physical suffering: "And recovering of sight to the blind," the physically disinherited. As in the other cases we usually spiritualize this passage and make it mean the spiritually blind, but I cannot see why it should not mean exactly what it says. The program of Jesus would banish physical suffering.

In a very real sense Christianity is the most materialistic of religions. Its central thesis is that God was made man—that he meets us in a physical body, speaks to us in a human language, and shows us how to live in a human environment with all the limitations of physical embodiment. The gospel is not a philosophy about life, which would of necessity make it abstract, but it is a Fact working itself out through the material. A Hindu once said to me, "The soul is entangled with matter through the mind. We must break that entanglement by getting rid of the mind; then the soul will be freed from its fetters, the body." There is nothing of that in Jesus. He works his program in and through the material. A Hindu ascetic was so spiritual that he shivered at the touch of money. The Buddhist monks of Burma keep their money in handkerchiefs, but never touch it with their hands, lest they be polluted. The whole outlook of asceticism is founded on the idea that the material is evil and must be reduced to a minimum. But Jesus had none of this: "A body thou hast prepared me, ... lo, I am come to do thy will." That will was to be wrought out through the body.

He came to give men life and to give it abundantly, and that included the physical. Jesus gave a strange, new definition of salvation. He calls it "health" or "wholeness." Wherever he used the word "Be saved," it is literally "Be whole." This meant that he would get rid of everything that was unhealth. Sin is unhealth. It causes disruption, unrest, discord, uneasiness, and anemia in the soul. This is not merely a doctrine, it is a fact. Jesus would free men from sin so that they might live an adjusted, harmonious, rhythmical, integrated life.

Physical disease is also unhealth. It too keeps us from wholeness, from being at our best. Jesus therefore made the banishing of physical suffering an integral part of his program. He would agree with Paul when he says that "we wait and long for open recognition as sons through the deliverance of our bodies" (Romans 8: 23, Weymouth trans.). The full sonship would be realized only when there was the redemption of the whole man, and that included the body.

The resurrection of Jesus is in line with this materialism in Christianity and completes it. To make it only a spiritual resurrection is to give up the battle at the place where it becomes acute, namely, can the victory be wrought out in and through the physical? Jesus' incarnation attempts it and the resurrection completes it. If he did not rise from the dead, he ought to have done so! The whole story would come out wrong if he had failed to bring the victory to a completion at the place of the physical. The early church brethren experienced the glow of this, for they felt that life had been met in all of its phases and had been conquered.

> **In a very real sense Christianity is the most materialistic of religions. Its central thesis is that God was made man—that he meets us in a physical body, speaks to us in a human language, and shows us how to live in a human environment with all the limitations of physical embodiment.**

The four enemies of the human personality were to be banished: sin, error, sickness, and death. The evil of the will is sin, the evil of the mind is error, the evil of the body is sickness, and the evil of the whole man is death. Jesus confronted these with life, life. He did not hesitate to confront sickness and suffering with power which we call miraculous, but that power was never exercised to show mere power. It was exercised to meet a human need. There was a time when we were accustomed to cite the miracles of Jesus as the method Jesus used to prove his divinity. We do not do that now. We see how unworthy it was. He never prostituted miracle in that way. He used that power because men had need, and he had come to meet that need. His miracles were sincere, for they had no extraneous purpose in them.

Moreover, he never used healing as a bait to get men to listen to his spiritual message. He healed men and then seemed content to let that stand as an integral part of the coming of the Kingdom. When he called back to life the dead son of the widow of Nain, he restored him to his mother, and went on his way, apparently not attempting to convert either the mother or the son or the mourners at the funeral. He had banished death, and that was a part, a real part of the coming of the Kingdom. When he raised the daughter of Jairus, he did not preach to her about being good in the future. He commanded them "to give her something to eat," content that the dead had been raised and the emaciated fed. Jesus healed men whether or not they believed on him, and whether or not they listened to his spiritual teaching. The healing stood in its own right as an integral part of the Kingdom.

In addition, his miracles did not mean the introduction of the unnatural into the natural. They were a calling back from the unnatural to the truly natural. Which was the truly natural, blindness or sight? Obviously, sight is the truly natural, so when Jesus restored sight he was substituting the natural for the unnatural. The man decaying with leprosy and segregated from his fellows was not the natural, but the man healed and going back to his home with joy was the natural. The healing of disease was thus not something extraneous and out of side-line compassion, but agreed with his definition of salvation as health, and that health meant the health of the total person, including the physical.

God does not send sickness, nor is sickness the will of God. He would banish it. The Kingdom of God is an offensive against it. Jesus did not teach submission to sickness and suffering—he cured them both. His was no fatalistic acceptance of conditions, but the impact of a redemptive movement that changed conditions. His movement was not an opiate that made men content, but an operation that made men well. It was not something that weakened the fiber of men's thinking by preaching contentment, but something that gave men the courage to believe that sin and suffering had met their match and could be conquered. "So you are a religious man," said an actress to me in Russia, with a look of incredulity in her face. "You are weak; therefore you are religious. You are the kind that wants somebody to hold your hand, and give you comfort. So you want God to be to you the Great Comforter and to hold your hand. You cannot stand alone."

> Jesus healed men whether or not they believed on him, and whether or not they listened to his spiritual teaching. The healing stood in its own right as an integral part of the Kingdom.

"You have missed it," I replied, "for the kind of faith I hold doesn't so much seek for someone to hold its hand for comfort; rather, it stretches forth its own hand to others and says, 'I say unto you, Arise!'"

Jesus never comforted the sick—he healed them. If Krishna had met the widow of Nain taking her dead son to burial, he would have said, according to the Bhagvad Geeta, "Weep not, for the Self has not died, for it is deathless." Buddha would have said, "Weep not, for existence and evil are one. Cut the root of desire, even for the dead, and you will enter Nirvana, the place of the desireless." Mohammed would have said, "It is the will of Allah, submit to it." Jesus said, "Young man, I say unto you, Arise." The philosophers of India would have explained how it all happened and why, and would have left things as they were before. Jesus explained nothing, but told the dead to arise! Jesus would have agreed with Marx when he said, "Philosophers have explained the world in various ways; the task is now to change it."

Jesus looked on sin, error, sickness, and death as hindrances and enemies. When he was about to heal the dumb man, he sighed in spirit, as much as to say, "When shall we get rid of this burden of suffering resting on men?" When he went to the tomb of Lazarus, "he was moved with indignation in the spirit" (margin) that death was still the oppressor. When the Kingdom of God fully comes, these four enemies will be banished. Life will reign.

The evangelism of Jesus was an evangelism to the total person. He did not love people's souls alone — Jesus loved people. A Hindu student came back from the West and said, "If those people had loved me a little bit more and my soul a little bit less, I might have become a Christian." Jesus did not go around loving people's souls—he loved people, and would lift everything that cramped body, soul, or mind. This is expressly stated, "Jesus went about in all Galilee, teaching in their synagogues, and preaching the gospel of the kingdom, and healing all manner of disease and all manner of sickness among the people" (Matthew 4: 23). The gospel of the Kingdom has in it three things— redemption for the mind ("teaching"), redemption for the soul ("preaching"), redemption for the body ("healing"), and its very nature is social ("among the people"). Here was a whole program for the whole person for the whole of society.

134

Incidentally, let it be said that as there was no asceticism of the body, there was no asceticism of the mind in the new Kingdom. When Jesus quoted the greatest commandment of the Law, he added something that was not in the original quotation in Deuteronomy, "Thou shall love the Lord thy God . . . with all thy mind." The Kingdom of God would employ all the best thinking, all the best methods that human intelligence, illuminated by the love of God, can devise. A tribe in Burma puts a metal band around the head of the newborn child to keep the brain from expanding. Some religions have done that too. But the gospel of Jesus has nothing to do with that spirit. When Jesus said, "Why even of yourselves judge you not what is right?"Jesus untied religion from ancient bondages and gave men the charter of liberty of mind. This insured that the Kingdom could keep abreast of and guide the intellectual movements of the ages. "This school is on the site of a former church, and it is well that the church has been supplanted by a school, for the church has done little for education," said

> **The evangelism of Jesus was an evangelism to the total man. He did not love people's souls alone — He loved people.**

a youth to me in a classroom in Russia. It may have been true of the church in Russia that it specialized in gorgeous ceremonies and did comparatively little for education; and yet even that is an exaggeration, for the Russian Church found the Russian people a nation of the uncultured, and gave them light and civilization and culture, before it became congealed and hardened and superstitious. But this objection of the Russian boy cannot be made of the gospel of Christ in general, for wherever it has gone the school has followed as effect follows cause. The mental eyes of humanity have been opened by Christ.

135

Moreover, there has been this impulse to heal wherever Christ brings his impact upon men. It is no chance that even now in this age of science half of the general hospitals of the United States are in the hands of religious bodies. Professor Robert Millikan says, that in his judgment, "ninety-five per cent of all altruistic and humanitarian work in the world has come and is directly or indirectly from the influence of organized religion." Science may give the technique of healing, but religion gives the impulse. In the bringing in of the Kingdom of God there must be a closer yoking of science and religion in the service of the suffering. Then we shall have "a union of all who love, in the service of all who suffer." A missionary contracts tuberculosis and out of that disability he inspires the setting up of the greatest tuberculosis sanatorium in India. Another missionary loses a daughter from leprosy and comes back to India to establish what is perhaps the greatest leper sanatorium of the world. "When the people knew him they brought unto him their sick," says the New Testament chronicle. Yes, and when the people know him, they go out and in his name heal the sick. "How did you get started?" I asked a doctor who had performed a hundred thousand operations on the eye, by actual count of hospital records. "Well," he replied, "I was mad after eyes. As a young doctor when I could get no patients I used to sit in my office and wait till a blind beggar would go by and then I would rush out and pull him into my office and operate on him before he would have time to protest, for I was mad after eyes." Beautiful madness! There is that same tender passion running through the pages of the New Testament—and beyond.

I was speaking in the theater of an Indian state with the Hindu prime minister in the chair. At the close of the address he arose and said: "I could not help contrasting this meeting tonight with the ones I used to attend as a boy. Then the missionaries preached on the streets and often had vegetables or stones thrown at them. But here tonight this great audience has sat so silent that you could hear a pin drop as the speaker has interpreted his Christian message. What has made the difference? The difference has been in this: in the meantime missionary doctors have lived among us in Miraj, and have given themselves unstintingly to the healing of the people for these years. It is the influence of the lives of these devoted doctors which has changed the atmosphere and has made possible this meeting tonight." It was a tribute which was more than well deserved, a tribute which was added to when the government of that Hindu state posted notices that all the wells and roads should be thrown open to all castes and ended with these words: "Just as the doctors of Miraj tend to everybody, rich and poor, high caste and low caste, without distinction, so must all the privileges of the state be thrown open to everyone." These men healed, but they also taught the meaning of the Kingdom as they healed.

One of the most beautiful touches in history is that scene in the Temple. It had been cleansed of money-changing and greed by the righteous fury of Jesus, and then after the storm had passed, "the blind and the lame came to him in the temple: and he healed them." These unfortunates sensed the quality of his fury—it was healing even where it was cutting. Those in greed were afraid of it, those in need were not. This scene is both a parable and a fact: we shall never be able to lift the burden of suffering from the body of humanity until we cast out greed from the center of life. The blind and the lame will never have a real chance, unless and until we overthrow money-changing for private profit in the temple of humanity, for it is greed at the center that keeps them on the edges. If we do not overthrow this greed, how can they get healing? —for only those who can pay for it can get it. It was no mere chance that in London a "gentleman" in 1884 lived on the average twice as long as a laborer; in Leeds the figures were forty-four years for "gentlemen" and nineteen years for laborers; for Liverpool, thirty-five and fifteen years respectively. The length of physical life can be greatly influenced by the economic realities of the individual. The poor are compelled to live in unsanitary and squalid surroundings, and when they die young, it is not the will of God, but the will of society which prefers to cater to the greed of the few rather than to the need of the many.

Russia, under a co-operative order, has plans whereby every person will be assigned to a hospital nearby, where beginning before birth, and on through childhood clear up to old age, the person's physical wants will be attended to free of charge. Here the science of healing is harnessed to the needs of all instead of the greed of a few. So far they are behind us in actual results, but they are ahead of us in plans and principles (a hundred years ahead, says one observer), and in the long run they will continue to forge ahead of us in actual results, unless we change and cast greed out of the center of the temple of humanity so that the blind and the lame can come for healing.

If we change from the present unchristian basis, to the basis of the Kingdom of God, what would it mean?

1. It would mean that the passion of Jesus to lift the burden of physical suffering would be an integral part of our religious outlook, and would be embodied in our working program. Healing would again be a living part of our commission to humanity. This healing program would lay hold on resources from many directions, for God heals in various ways—by climate, by medicine, by surgery, by mental suggestion, and by the direct touch of the Spirit of God upon the body. The skill of the physician and the surgeon, the penetrative insights of the psychiatrist, the loving, healing faith of the man of prayer—all of these would be, not rivals, but co-operators in the work of lifting the burden of suffering from the race. Many would leave out the prayer contribution to human healing, to their impoverishment. Eighteen years ago I had tried the resources of doctors and of climate

to regain my health, and for a year and a half sought in vain. Then in a quiet moment of prayer I was touched into health. Whatever the future may have in store for me in the shape of physical suffering, for eighteen years the difficulty has never returned, and I have never had such health. An article in the *Boston Transcript,* entitled "Professor Leuba Examines Stanley Jones," has this in it:

"Did Stanley Jones change his habits at the time of the supposed healing?

"The answer is, 'No.'

"Did he slow down and take things more calmly?

"The answer is, 'I have worked much harder than before.'"

Professor Leuba, standing as a spectator, says, "Merely psychological," while I, as a participant, say, "God." While I am grateful beyond words for this direct "touch," I am also grateful for what skilled Christian surgery did for me on one special occasion in my life. In both cases I say, "God." We should be prepared to use both science and psychology and pervade them with prayer, at the same time recognizing that God can and does give his touch of healing upon the physical frame.

> **Eighteen years ago I had tried the resources of doctors and of climate to regain my health, and for a year and a half sought in vain. Then in a quiet moment of prayer I was touched into health.**

Beatrice Plumb tells of being in the Physicians Church, built by Canon Twells, and of seeing a man come into the deserted church and go to the chancel. "I recognized the face as that of a distinguished surgeon whose operations were modern miracles. Why was the great man there? ... I saw him lay his fine surgeon hands on the altar rail, his face uplifted as if in silent urgent prayer ... I stared at those strong, white hands upturned in silent supplication. Was he pleading for Christ's touch, with its ancient power to come to them? I didn't know. But a few days later I read that he had successfully performed a surgical operation which would go down in surgical annals as the first decisive victory over a horrible disease before which earth's best doctors had until then stood powerless. 'I dressed him and God healed him,' I said to myself in the words of the Parisian Ambrose Pare. That surgeon with the touch of God upon his skilled fingers is the symbol of the meeting place of the scientific and the religious and both dedicated to the sacred task of banishing suffering.

> Today men perish for no other reason than that they have no silver or gold. In this matter we must reorganize society so that all shall bear the burden of the weak— all shall co-operate in the employing of the doctor who shall then be at the service of the afflicted, with no motive of turning people's pain into gain.

2. The possibility of obtaining healing would not rest upon the power of the individual to buy it. It would be free. Jesus charged nothing for his healing. He commissioned his disciples thus: "Heal the sick, raise the dead, cleanse the lepers, cast out devils: freely ye received, freely give." One Christian cult which specializes in healing has adopted the first portion of that commission as its motto, but has left out the last portion— "Freely you received,

freely give." We must not blame them too much for this, for life is organized as a whole on a competitive and profit-motive basis. But we Christians must reorganize life so that both sides of the commission shall be operative. When Simon Magus thought that the gift of God could be purchased with money, Peter said, "Thy silver perish with thee." Today men perish for no other reason than that they have no silver or gold. In this matter we must reorganize society so that all shall bear the burden of the weak—all shall co-operate in the employing of the doctor who shall then be at the service of the afflicted, with no motive of turning people's pain into gain.

3. In order to prevent many of the physical diseases which are now rooted in economic inequality we should distribute the goods which God has given for all in a more just and equitable way. The absence of wealth in ancient usage was called "ill-th." The fact is that the absence of material resources does often mean illness. This illness is preventable. To take from some who have an over plus and use it in the collective good would mean no more hardship to the possessors than the removal of a goiter which is about to strangle its possessor to death. For wealth is like manure: refuse to spread it and you have only a manure heap, but spread it and you have the waving grain and a fed people.

The third item in the Christian program would be "the opening of the eyes of the blind"—the physically disinherited. A great specialist of world fame in foot-surgery said to a friend of mine, "I have a passion to make men walk." In this he echoed the passion that runs through the Christian gospel. We must now take that passion and turn it into a program.

141

CHAPTER 6

GOOD NEWS TO THE MORALLY AND SPIRITUALLY DISINHERITED

The first three items in the program of Jesus refer to items other than the spiritual. The fourth refers to the spiritual: "To set at liberty them that are bruised."

Now, bruises may come from being trampled on by others or they may come from one's own falls. This item would seem to point to bruises that are the result of one's own falls, and those falls would seem to be moral and spiritual. The Aramaic translation by Lamsa bears this out when it says, "to strengthen with forgiveness them that are bruised."[1] If forgiveness is necessary in regard to these bruises, then it implies that they were received in connection with wrong moral and spiritual choices, in other words through moral and spiritual falls. Through these moral and spiritual falls we get into bondages and

---

1 The Holy Bible from Ancient Eastern Manuscripts (commonly called the Lamsa Bible) was published by George M. Lamsa in 1933. It was derived, both Old and New Testaments, from the Syriac Peshitta, the Bible used by the Assyrian Church of the East and other Syriac Christian traditions. (https://en.wikipedia.org/wiki/Lamsa_Bible Accessed April 20, 2019).

entanglements from which we have to be set at liberty by forgiveness and restoration. Jesus, therefore, included in his program an item which meets this very definite need of humanity, namely, to set at liberty them that are bruised—the morally and spiritually disinherited.

Many bondages come as the result of wrong economic relationships imposed on us, and may not be the result of our own choices at all. Other bondages come as the result of wrong social and political relationships for which we are not directly responsible. Others come as the result of physical disabilities and may have nothing to do with our wills. But these three kinds of bondages do not cover the sum total of things that bind us. If we were freed from all the bondages in all the realms just mentioned, we might nevertheless be in very serious bondage still. You do not settle all the questions of life when you settle the economic, the social, the political, and the physical. Give a man all he wants in these four realms and yet you leave untouched a very central need of his life. That need concerns the inner life. There are some bondages which come from within and can only be classed as moral and spiritual. And we feel very definitely that we are responsible for them, responsible for them and yet unable to undo them. We stand guilty before a moral law which judges us relentlessly, and there seems to be no appeal from its decisions.

This view is attacked from several sides. The Vedantist of India would say that we are a part of the Divine and that therefore moral evil is an illusion. "Ye divinities on earth," cried Swami Vivekananda at the Chicago Parliament of Religions, "it is a sin to call you sinners." But the Vedanta is being moralized more and more by the sheer pressure of the facts, so that the issue of good and evil put out at the door of theory is coming back through the window of necessity.

Modern dilettantism dismisses this sense of moral evil as an impertinence. But it registers itself in the sense of tiredness and boredom which is creeping over the world of the dilettante. Something seems wrong at the center of life. "Hell," cries the dilettante, and he thinks he is using an expletive, when he is simply describing where he is. Again the moral law put out as an impertinence comes back as an imperative.

The Communists would say that we are a part of a material process in which there are no supernatural sanctions of morality. There is only expediency in regard to ends in view. Lenin says: "We repudiate all morality which proceeds from supernatural ideas, or ideas that are outside class conceptions. In our opinion morality is entirely subservient to the interests of the class war; everything is moral that is necessary for the annihilation of the old exploiting social order. We do not believe in eternal principles of morality and we

> You do not settle all the questions of life when you settle the economic, the social, the political, and the physical. Give a man all he wants in these four realms and yet you leave untouched a very central need of his life. That need concerns the inner life.

will oppose this deception. Communistic morality is identical with the fight for the consolidation of the dictatorship of the proletariat." Here is the doctrine that everything is right which helps toward the ends of the class war and the dictatorship of the proletariat. Lenin could say again: "I love music and poetry and art, but I cannot give myself to them, for it interferes with my business of breaking heads." As he put aside poetry and music and art so he put aside all ideas of eternal moral sanctions, since it interfered with the business of breaking heads in behalf of the class war and the dictatorship of the proletariat.

But this is not the whole story of Communistic morality. They say that they are materialists and that they interpret history by the economic interpretation, and by that alone. But they also interpret it by the dialectic of Hegel, with this difference, that they reject his idealism and apply it to the realistic processes of history. Every thesis produces its antithesis, which results in the gathering up of these opposites in a higher form, the synthesis. Capitalism is the thesis, and it creates conditions which result in an antithesis, the decay of the condition of the workers, which in turn results in a synthesis, Communism. This dialectical process moves on to its destined end in Communism. It is to be noted that here materialism has been endowed with properties which are spiritual, for it seems to move on to moral ends. A process which works toward moral ends may be called material, but when it thus partakes of the properties of the spiritual, it has lost its merely material character. The moral and spiritual put out at the door of theory again comes back through the window of fact.

The truth is that we are not parts of an Impersonal Essence called Brahma, nor parts of an impersonal process called materialism—we are not God and we are not matter. We are men, moral and spiritual beings, embodied in a world of matter, but confronted with a moral universe that sides with good and against evil.

We were having a communion service in a student camp out under the trees. The ever-present and daring Indian crow was in the branches overhead, waiting for a chance to swoop down and take the bread from the communion plate. Two groups looked at the communion bread with different viewpoints: the students, who looked up through it as a symbol to a world which was spiritual and which had at its heart love and self-sacrifice—a cross; the crows, which looked on it as food to satisfy hunger and as nothing else. Now, who would say that the student view was superstitious and the crow view was science? Take the crow view of life if you will. I prefer the other. Even the most materialistic of modern movements, Communism, has been compelled to bring back the moral and spiritual, though in a disguised form. For the moral is written within the constitution of the universe and confronts us at every turn. And we must come to terms with it.

> The truth is that we are not parts of an Impersonal Essence called Brahma, nor parts of an impersonal process called materialism—we are not God and we are not matter. We are men, moral and spiritual beings, embodied in a world of matter, but confronted with a moral universe that sides with good and against evil.

We may repudiate morality, as one prominent humanist does, when he preaches to youth the right to taste all sexual experience apart from the conventions of morality, but it will come back to us to haunt us as it haunted him. According to first-hand information when he was in a delirium of illness he cried out, "Oh,____ this is not right; we shall have to right this relationship before the world!" That relationship with a woman had been rationalized into seeming rightness, but, however he might try to rationalize it in his more conscious moments, there the depths of his being were speaking, and they sided with moral law.

Wrote a Hindu nationalist to me, "I came back from committing adultery, trembling from head to foot." Why was he trembling from head to foot? Would the law punish adultery? No. Had anyone seen him and would he be punished by society? No, for no one had seen him in the dead of night as he made his way back to his home. But he had seen himself—had seen himself in the light of a moral law and he loathed himself. He was in the hell of not being able to respect himself—in that worst of all hells—the hell of being bad.

Even if every outer liberty in the economic, the social and the political should be granted to that man, he is no longer at liberty; he has forged his own inner fetters. He has driven his soul underground, for he can no longer be open and frank and free. He has dug for himself a cell of solitary confinement, where he wears his self-wrought chains in the darkness of concealment.

But the bruises from which we need release are not merely the result of lapses on the side of our physical appetites; they may come as the result of wrong dispositions. Sins may be of the flesh, they may also be of the disposition. The younger brother in the parable of the prodigal son sinned in his flesh, but the elder brother sinned in his disposition, in his lack of love, his smallness of soul, his selfishness, his bad temper. The sins of the disposition do as much harm to the Kingdom of God as the sins of the flesh—probably more. The soul of the world is being bruised as much by bad temper as by almost any other thing. The intolerances, the Pharisaisms, the narrow nationalisms, the racial hates—these are leaving great bruises on the soul of the world.

Jesus said, "What is a man profited if he gain the whole world and receive damage [margin] in his own soul?" In gaining the world he may not be damned, only damaged, but that loss to one's inner self is too costly even if the whole world be gained. The slightest vulgarizing of the soul, the lowering of the tone of the inner life, the loss of inner integrity, constitute too costly a price to pay, even if a universe of outer gain is thrown into the scale. The fact is that in a competitive order many have gained a world of material goods at the expense of their fellows, only to find that something has snapped on the inside. The Western world is troubled. Much of this is the result of fears of what may happen to the structure of society as impending changes draw near. But a great deal of it is just the sheer feeling of wrongness, of having missed the way, of the consciousness that life is running into dead ends. Many honest men in the West view with uneasiness of heart the fact of luxury and grinding poverty side by side, of a world half-starved and half overfed. And they feel that they are individually and corporately responsible for it. The conscience of the Western world is troubled. It may rationalize its errancy, but that very rationalization is proof of its smarting soul. We have exploited others and we know it. The palliatives we propose—a modification here and a tinkering there—are pathetic attempts at half-way repentances. We are bruised and we know it. The soul of Western civilization is a damaged soul. On Indian railways I have seen trucks labeled "Damaged," but they were still running. Western civilization is still running, but it knows that the warning label, "Damaged," is upon it, and that it should put in for radical repairs. But why do I say "Western civilization" only, for Eastern civilization too is at the breaking point everywhere. The fact is that there is no Western need, and no Eastern need, but just one great human need.

Jesus defined repentance as *metanoia*—a complete change of mind and attitude and direction. Will our world civilization repent in this thoroughgoing way? Will it change at the place of the central and basic injustice, namely, at the place of a change from competition to cooperation? If so, it can be saved. But before we do it we will try halfway repentances. When John spoke before Herod, he put his finger on the sore spot in Herod's life— he must give up the woman: "It is not lawful for you to have her." Herod winced. The account says that

"Herod did many things." Yes, he did everything except the one thing necessary—the giving up of the woman. As the more modern prophets put their finger on the central wound on the body of the world, a personal self-seeking, we shall wince and offer to do many things—

everything except the one thing troubling us. But nothing that we can do will atone for the lack of doing that one thing. Half repentances are not enough.

What does the program of Jesus offer to those who are bruised and who know it and want healing? It promises "liberty"—a fresh start, a new beginning, a new birth. This is an astounding offer. Its very commonplaceness in our thought has taken away the profundity of its significance. "Can a man be born

The conscience of the Western world is troubled. It may rationalize its errancy, but that very rationalization is proof of its smarting soul. We have exploited others and we know it.

again when he is old?" asked the anxious Nicodemus. "Yes," said Jesus, "He can. I offer him the gospel of a second chance, a new beginning, a clean slate. I will lift all that inner bondage of inhibitions, of complexes, of loathing, of fears. I will cleanse the springs of character and will sweeten the inner life. I will set at liberty them that are bruised."

Jesus did that very thing while on earth and he does that same thing still. A man was let down in his presence through the hole in the roof; Jesus saw at a glance the connection between the man's physical sickness and his soul-sickness. Physical sickness was the fruit, but sin was the root. He was physically helpless because he was spiritually collapsed. The weight of inner guilt was the heavier burden. Jesus struck at the inner shackles first of all: "Son, your sins are forgiven you." He then lifted the physical ailment. It may be that God is proposing that very thing to humanity today: the burden of physical suffering would be lifted if we were willing to have our sin hurt healed—to take basically new attitudes, in other words, to individually and co-operatively repent.

A woman, who had been promiscuous, lay crumpled at the feet of Jesus. Jesus, not willing to further shame her, wrote upon the ground. What he wrote upon the ground we shall never know, but we do know what he wrote upon the hearts of two types of participants that day, upon the hearts of her accusers a stinging condemnation for their self-righteous hypocrisy, and upon the heart of the poor troubled woman the word of forgiving release: "Neither do I condemn you; go, and sin no more." In one act he bruised the self-righteous and set at liberty the bruised soul of the woman.

The dying thief looked beyond the shame and the spittle and the blood of the crucifixion and saw the regality of the soul of Jesus amid the tragedy of things, saw that he was really a King in spite of it all and cried, "Remember me when you come into your kingdom." The prompt and healing words of Jesus answer that cry, "Today you shall be with me in paradise." A King in the realm of healing bruised spirits! A King who restores men to the paradise of forgiven sin and loosed burdens of guilt!

No wonder that a new sense of hope went across that despondent ancient world. It was a world that had lost its nerve. As Glover said, "It was suffering from failure of nerve." And then a new sense of hope came. As Dean Church says: "Through the early history of Christianity there is running a solemn joy. The routine of sin and vice had at last met its match. Men, not only here and there, but on a wide scale could attain to that hitherto impossible thing for the multitudes—goodness."

Christ had set at liberty them that were bruised. A friend of mine, an Indian official, held a garden party every year to celebrate his birthday. He invited all his friends, Christian and non-Christian, to celebrate a new kind of birthday—the birthday of his soul. At this party he recounted to his guests his gratitude for the inner birth of his spirit.

It was said in the beginning of this chapter that this is a world of moral law. It is. We reap what we sow. We are free to choose our actions, but we are not free to choose the results of those actions. The deeds we do are not done when we do them; they come back and register themselves in result. We do not break the laws of God, we break ourselves upon them. We break them seemingly, but they throw us back quivering, bleeding, blighted things. I saw an accident happen to a taxi, and almost immediately a large canvas sheet was thrown over it and it was hauled away. They did not want the world to see the battered thing beneath. So we throw sheets of outer calm over our bruised spirits and act as though nothing had happened, but the heart knows and we know. "The man who thinks he can cheat a moral God in a moral universe is a moral imbecile."

In such a world of law is not the idea of "strengthening with forgiveness them that are bruised" a contradiction and an absurdity? Can there be forgiveness in a world of iron law? The reply is that the iron side of nature is only one side. There is the urge for healing forgiveness running through nature. The bone is broken and the rest of the body marshals the healing materials and rushes them to mend the break. An infection attacks a wound and the corpuscles of healing hasten to throw themselves into the fray in order to ward off the attack. And many die that the rest might live. The hillside is scarred by the rains and nature proceeds to cover the scars with flowers. There is this healing urge all through nature, so that nature had her own Red Cross Society long before we thought of one. This healing urge comes to

151

fruition and completeness in a cross. There the universe crimsons into sacrifice in order to heal earth's many bruises.

The cross is God's redemptive word spelled out in living fact. I looked out of my window in Holland and saw against the skyline the radio antennae and noted that they were in the form of a cross. The cross of Calvary is the antenna, lifted on the skyline of the world, that catches the deepest notes of this universe. It tells us that back of things is the redemptive purpose of God, that God is going the full way to heal our bruises, that he was literally bruised for our iniquities and by his stripes (wounds) we are healed. So his bruises answer our bruises.

> **There is this healing urge all through nature, so that nature had her own Red Cross Society long before we thought of one. This healing urge comes to fruition and completeness in a cross.**

A brilliant young woman in Russia told me of a professor who had lectured learnedly on philosophy to his classes and then had walked out and paused before a crucifix to cross himself. A workman on a building nearby noticing it, turned to his companion and said one word in comment, "Darkness." Which was true if the professor looked at the cross as magic protection, or the crossing of himself as a talisman; in that case it was superstition and hence darkness. But if he saw through these symbols the fact of redemptive love meeting him in Christ and the crossing of himself was the throwing open of his inmost being to that seeking, redemptive love, then it was not darkness—it was LIGHT.

Christian orthodoxy is often embarrassed about the Judgment

scene, where Christ says that "I was hungry and you fed me," etc. And yet that is the very cross itself in operation—a continuing Calvary. For if everyman's hunger is his hunger, then everyman's sin is his sin. All of our divisions and strife rend his body again. The cross is not an accident on a Judean hill, it is "the very ground plan of the universe."

This is God's method of producing change in men. The Communists also believe in human change. Marx says that man works upon his environment and changes it, and that in changing his environment he changes himself. As someone else put it, "The dyer's hand is colored by the color in which he works."[2] We agree. We would therefore expose man to the highest conceivable environment—the Kingdom of God, the ultimate social and spiritual order. When he responds to that order, gives himself to the task of bringing that order into actual operation within himself and the order around him, he is changed and made into the moral and spiritual image of that new Kingdom. But that Kingdom is personalized in Christ—he is that Kingdom meeting us, so that all this is intensely personal and not vaguely impersonal.

But before we can respond to that Environment, the Kingdom of God, we must have inner freedom from that which keeps us from responding, namely, the sense of moral wrongness. Forgiveness offered to us by God in Christ lifts that sense of inner guilt, thus setting "at liberty them that are bruised."

Communism takes no cognizance of that necessity. It would lift the outer burdens from man's shoulders, but leave these inner burdens untouched. In this it heals the hurt of the world lightly. Too lightly, I believe. It says that there are no eternal moral laws, hence none are broken and hence there are no bruises. The only morality is the

---

2 William Shakespeare, *Sonnet 111*.

CHRIST'S ALTERNATIVE TO COMMUNISM...

morality of the class war, the dictatorship of the proletariat and the establishment of the Communistic state. Marx outlines this state and the steps leading to it and the morality inherent in it. He therefore takes the place of God as the author of morality. There is no God and Marx is his prophet. A new Trinity is growing up in Russia. I saw on the lowest landing of the steps of a school a huge picture of Marx, on the next floor, immediately above, a similar picture of Lenin, and on the next a picture of Stalin—all of equal size and impressiveness. Marx, the author of the scheme and the layer down of its moralities; Lenin, the interpreter of Marx and the one who establishes his kingdom; Stalin, the one who applies that interpretation and carries it on: the Father, Son, and Holy Ghost of atheistic Communism—these three, and these three are one. In the Anti-Religious Museum in Leningrad, at the foot of the statue of Lenin, are the words, "Ten years after Lenin, and his spirit is still with us." It is here that we find a new system of religion with its rites and its orthodoxies.

> On the contrary, into the Kingdom of God has gone the Spirit of Christ, which is synonymous with the spirit of love and self-sacrifice.

But into this new Communist system of morality has been injected a bitterness and hate and revenge from the spirit of its founder, Marx. He was quarrelsome and bitter, though very sacrificial. This spirit of the founder has run through the system, and the poison of it has formed great blood clots of hate and revenge under the skin of Communism, which look like bruises, and to all intents and purposes are bruises. And they still remain unhealed.

On the contrary, into the Kingdom of God has gone the Spirit of Christ, which is synonymous with the spirit of love and self-sacrifice. When we open our lives to the warm, rich, redemptive tides of his life, we find health and healing going through every fiber of our being. The bruises disappear and we find ourselves healthy—in other words, saved. At this place Communism has no message. After the wiping out of the class enemies, what about the personal bruises? Here they are silent.

Man as man needs nothing so much as he needs conversion, the change of the Master sentiment of his life. If, as the psychiatrist Alfred Adler says, the most dominant instinct is the ego instinct, then it is a fundamental necessity for world reconstruction that this instinct be turned from selfish, destructive ends to the ends of construction and brotherhood. Said a leading Hindu statesman to me: "I see what I need, I need conversion. Either I must be converted myself or else I must warm up my heart against someone's heart who has been converted." In saying this he revealed the heart, not of one man, but of every man.

Any program for world reconstruction that leaves out this basic necessity of conversion is leaving untouched a fundamental need of human nature, and is thereby truncated, partial, and inadequate. Communism leaves it out; Christ puts it in. I therefore choose Christ.

CHAPTER 7

A NEW BEGINNING—ON A WORLD SCALE

When we talk about changing individuals as the basis for the changing of the social order, a feeling of hopelessness and futility comes over many. They feel that results are too slow, too uncertain, and at their best end only in mitigation. The method has been tried for two thousand years, and while the indirect results have been great, the basic evils persist in spite of individual change. When individual slave owners were converted, it made for better relationships between the slave owner and the slave; it softened the harshness, but it did not change the fundamentally unjust relationship of owner and slave. There are Christian capitalists who soften the system and make it more tolerable, but that does not touch the fact that a relationship exists at the heart of society as now organized, whereby some people will not starve if they do not work, and some people will starve if they do not work. No amount of softening will atone for that central injustice. So individual change seems too slow and futile.

The Marxist Communists working at the other end, the social end, start by smashing the old order, and on the ruins of it impose a new order by force through which they hope to change the individual. His habits, his outlook, his spirit will gradually fit into the new order, and as he fits into it he becomes a changed person. The change comes from the outside in and not from the inside out. They claim for this quicker and more certain results. The claim that the results are quicker seems valid, but that they are more certain and lasting has yet to be proved.

But is the Christian program confined to the working from the individual out to the social order? Has it a program of working from the social order to the individual as well? I am persuaded that it works from both directions. The fact is that the gospel of the Kingdom was presented as a new order, breaking into the lower order, and it stood at the door of the nation as well as of the individual. There is no doubt that Jesus hoped that the Jewish nation, as a nation, would accept and embody the new Kingdom with its new order. "The Kingdom of God will be taken away from you, and given to a nation producing the fruits of it" (Matthew 21: 43, Weymouth trans., margin). John the Baptist called the nation to a national repentance in preparation for the advent of the Coming One and his new Kingdom. Jesus took up the same note and made his appeal to the nation. When he went to the mount to give the Sermon on the Mount and in it laid down the principles of the new Kingdom, it stood as a national counterpart of Moses going to the mount to get the laws for the formation of the Jewish race. Moses gave the laws for the formation of a theocratic state, and Jesus gave the laws for the reformation of that state and of the world. When the nation through its leaders refused that Kingdom, Jesus turned to the people. But even then, in the midst of his ministry he appealed with tears to the nation, saying, "O Jerusalem, Jerusalem, you that kill the prophets," etc. In his last command he reiterated the national purpose and said, "Go you into all the world and teach all nations"—he would keep before them the idea that the group, the nation, might accept and embody the program of the Kingdom.

This attitude of working from the social order to the individual, as well as from the individual to the social order, fits in with the next part of his program: "To proclaim the Lord's year of favor," or "the acceptable year of the Lord," or "the Lord's year of Jubilee." The last seems to be the correct meaning. This item undoubtedly points back to the Year of Jubilee as described in Leviticus 25:10: "You shall hallow the fiftieth year, and proclaim liberty throughout the land." At that time all slaves were freed and all land went back to the original owners, which meant that it went back to everybody, for God originally had given the land to everybody. This Year of Jubilee was intended to keep the land from getting into the hands of the few by its periodic redistribution. The Year of Jubilee was intended to right the relationships between man and man, and man and the land, and man and money. It was all in the direction of an approximate equality. It kept individuals from accumulating from generation to generation and thus gaining control over others by economic means. A brotherhood could only be produced and maintained as gulfs between the individuals were not allowed to form and widen because of economic inequality. The Year of Jubilee was intended to bring men back to equality and hence to brotherhood.

Jesus took this conception and set it as the climax of his own program. As the Year of Jubilee meant a fresh national beginning based on justice and equality and brotherhood, so his Kingdom would mean a fresh world beginning based on justice, equality, and brotherhood. The Year of Jubilee had become "The Lord's Year of Jubilee." Jesus enlarged it and applied it to a world. He expected a collective awakening and rebirth as well as an individual awakening and rebirth. He would work from the individual to the social order, but he would also work from the social order to the individual. His program provided for a collective revival and regeneration—a fresh world beginning.

There are two possible ways to look at human nature. One is to believe that there are permanent differences between man and man, and race and race, and that these differences are in the innate heredity, so that the destiny of a man or of a race is written in our biology. On this basis there are certain permanently inferior people, and there are certain permanently superior people. From this point of view the only way to get a better race is to breed one. Obviously, that will take a long, long time.

The other way is to look on the differences between man and man as being founded not so much in the innate heredity as in the social heredity. By the social heredity we mean the sum total of influences that play upon the person from without—the climatic, the economic, the social, the political, the moral, and the spiritual. This social heredity is unequal. Society is organized in favor of some, and against others. We must equalize the social heredity. That will leave unequal endowments, but the inequalities which come from the unequal social heredities will be done away. When this is done, we shall discover an amazing sameness in human nature. We shall discover that many of the things we thought were inherent have come to us through the social heredity. We shall discover that there are no permanently inferior peoples and there are no permanently superior peoples. There are undeveloped nations, but no permanently superior or inferior. We of the Anglo-Saxon descent should of all peoples insist upon this, for of us Servius, a Roman, once said, "The stupidest and the ugliest slaves in the market are those from Britain."

Change the social heredity and let the individual or the group respond and almost complete changes can be made in individuals and in groups. But let it be noted that this response to the social heredity has to be insisted on. Professor Macmurray is right when he says that only that part of the environment to which you respond really changes

159

you. That response may be the deciding factor. Today I met one of five brothers—one of them a minister in a prominent church, another a teacher, another a Y.M.C.A. secretary, another a college student, and one the physical director of a large college. The father of these five intelligent, useful, and honored sons was an outcaste of India, the lowest of the low. In one generation the father came from that depth to the moderatorship of a great denomination, and of him one missionary said, "We could better afford to lose any five missionaries from our ranks than that one man." For twenty years he was the honored chairman of the municipality where he had been an outcaste boy. Several times he tried to resign, but they would not let him go, saying, "You are the only man in this city that both the Hindus and Muslims can trust." Had he stayed in the social heredity in which he was born, he would have partaken of the mentality, the spirit, and the character of the outcaste. He was taken out of that and subjected to a new social heredity, the Kingdom of God, to which he responded, and the consequence was that he rose to be the intellectual and moral and spiritual peer of any of us, and did it in one generation.

Many of the things which we think are inherent are only socially conditioned. Two children of Scottish parents were left orphans in India. One was adopted by Indian Christians, who lived to all intents and purposes as Brahmins, so that the boy grew up with the speech, the mentality, and the spirit of the Brahmin. The other boy was adopted by an English family and was brought up with the speech, the mentality, and the spirit of the English. Later these boys met, but they would have nothing to do with each other, for each considered himself superior to the other. But the one little boy wasn't Brahmin, and the other little boy wasn't English— they were both from Scotland! What had been changed? Not the innate heredity, but the social heredity, and they were thereby profoundly changed.

If this principle is true—and after watching it work in the East for twenty-seven years I am persuaded that it is true—then it has profound possibilities for humanity. The social heredity is of our own making. We can provide for humanity any social heredity we desire. It is all in our hands. Suppose we provide a new social heredity on a large scale, and suppose people respond to it on a large scale, then we could remake humanity in a short space of time. Benjamin Kidd, the sociologist, who first called our attention to this principle in modern times, says that you can remake a nation in one generation by the change of the social heredity. He says that out of this social heredity "the emotion of the ideal" is created, and by the change of "the emotion of the ideal" the life of a whole people can be changed.

> The social heredity is of our own making. We can provide for humanity any social heredity we desire. It is all in our hands.

Look at this principle in operation. Take Japan for example. Had you looked at the Japanese people fifty years ago, steeped as they were in the customs and lore of the past, you would have said: "These people are unchangeable. They are a part of the unchanging East." But they have been changed, and profoundly so. They have learned the arts and sciences of the West—plus! What has changed them? Certainly not a change in their biology, for that remains the same. But the change has been in the social heredity, out of which a new "emotion of the ideal" has been created, and to which the nation has responded, and that response has changed the nation profoundly, for good or ill. Practically in one generation the whole nation has been made over.

Take Turkey. Had you looked at the Turkey of 1920, you would have felt that you were looking at an unchanging people—they were caught and grooved in an Islamic past. But look at the Turkey of fourteen years later, and it is an entirely new Turkey, a new mentality, a new tempo, and a new goal. What has done it? Hear the minister of education speaking to a group of us: "Hitherto the roots of our life have been in Asia; now frankly we put them into Europe. All the gods of the East are sitting gods, and all the gods of the West are standing gods. We frankly turn our backs upon the sitting gods of the East and follow the standing gods of the West. We will no longer be a passive, acquiescing civilization; we will be a positive people." They are. They are different. The biology is the same, but by the change of "the emotion of the ideal," through a new social heredity, the Turkish people have been changed. I do not say whether it is good or ill, I only say that there is change. "The sick man of Europe" has become youthful and vigorous.

But the place to see this principle at work in a very vivid fashion is Russia. Had you looked at the Russia of 1917 and then fallen asleep and awakened to see the Russia of 1934, you would have felt that you were looking at an entirely different people. You are. But it is not in the outer structure of the life alone that the greatest changes have taken place; the whole life has been changed—its tempo, its temper, its spirit, and its goal. For good or ill they are a different people. The biology is exactly the same, but they are a different people. Why ? Because of the changed emotion of the ideal. This has subjected them to a new social heredity to which they have responded amazingly, and which has changed them—one tenth of the human race— and it has done it in the incredibly short space of fifteen years.

Here we have hold of an important principle, fraught with amazing possibilities. Mankind can be changed on a wide scale in an incredibly short time. If we can get men to respond to the emotion of the ideal of the Kingdom of God on earth, then vast changes could be made in the total life of humanity, and they could be made in one generation.

The world ground is being laid for it. Up to this time men were segregated; now they are being thrown together by the amazing growth of communications. Ideas can and do spread with rapidity. A world mind is being evolved. It is now quite possible that we may act on a world scale.

> **If we can get men to respond to the emotion of the ideal of the Kingdom of God on earth, then vast changes could be made in the total life of humanity, and they could be made in one generation.**

Up to this time Christianity has been merely a tolerated sect in the Western world. It has been surrounded by a vast paganism which has controlled the political and economic life. The major decisions of life have been made for the most part on the basis of pagan ideals and procedures. I pick up my morning paper and read in it this debate in the British House of Commons:

Mr. Bevan: If I say that it is an unchristian act to bomb defenseless villages in India, is that seducing the forces from their allegiance?

Sir Thomas Inskip: Yes, under this bill, as under the present law.

Mr. Bevan: Then we have it now that it is illegal to call upon soldiers to be Christians.

This can be counterparted in the United States, where Professor Macintosh was refused citizenship on the basis that he would not bear arms. On that basis Christ could never become a citizen.

The fact is that Christianity has been looked on as an impracticable thing which might work in heaven, but not on earth. When it was acted on in the medieval ages, it was something other than Christianity that was acted on. It was a hybrid thing. For some centuries it has occupied the same position that Lenin and his followers occupied in Russia—on the edges or driven into exile or into hiding. But it looks as though Christianity may be presented with exactly the same opportunity that came to Lenin and the Communists during the hesitancies of the Kerensky regime.

The world situation today is confused, hesitant, and lacking confidence because of a lack of inner surety; that there is a possible way out. The hour for Christianity to assume control of the thoughts and the emotions and the directions of men has now come. Everything else has broken down or is breaking down, and has shown or is showing its bankruptcy. Everything seems to be breaking itself upon the moral facts of the universe. The universe won't back these unchristian ways. It may be that men, chastened and taught by bitter experience, may yet turn to Christ's program as the only sensible proposal in a world of chaos, brought on by our own follies. It is possible that there is enough disillusionment concerning the ways which have led to this world impasse to make men seriously turn to Christ and his program as the only way out.

In other words, there may be the possibility of "the Lord's Year of Jubilee"—a fresh world beginning. If we could get men to respond to the emotion of the ideal of the Kingdom of God as we can get them to respond to the emotion of the national ideal; if we could get men to have a patriotism to the Kingdom comparable to what they give to a national patriotism, then a new social heredity would be brought to bear upon the world and the world could be changed in an incredibly short time.

What would be involved in this new world beginning, the Lord's Year of Jubilee? Essentially what was involved in the Old Testament Year of Jubilee, namely, freedom—all slaves were freed; equality— the land went back to its original owners, all the people; brotherhood— there could be no brotherhood unless the slaves were freed and the land redistributed, for the social and economic cleavages divided man and made a brotherhood impossible.

We have proposed to God a world awakening on other terms, terms which would leave the basic relationships in the social and the economic spheres unchanged. And God has not accepted them. We have cried in vain for a world revival and it has not come. Had it come on our terms, it would have meant disaster, for it would fix unjust relationships by religious sanctions. So God stands aloof—waiting. The Year of Jubilee we propose is not "the acceptable year of the Lord." He cannot accept it, for it does not fit into the Kingdom of God. How can God apply power behind the Christian movement if it is turned in the direction of the ditch of selfish profit, social bondages, and ghastly inequalities? God waits for us to turn it in the direction of the freeing of the slaves of every type and kind, of the redistribution of the land and of the goods which God has given for all, of a brotherhood based on sharing with all men

> **The world situation today is confused, hesitant, and lacking confidence because of a lack of inner surety; that there is a possible way out. The hour for Christianity to assume control of the thoughts and the emotions and the directions of men has now come.**

165

of all classes and all races. He waits for us to set the Christian movement in that direction, and when we do, then unlimited power will be behind it. The resources of God will be at our disposal.

"But," someone objects, "to talk of freeing the slaves and redistributing land and goods sounds like Communism." I grant it. And I cannot soften it. The fact is that Christianity in its earliest manifestation did issue in a sort of "communism" by its own inherent nature. The "communism" of the Acts of the Apostles was not an accidental and marginal thing; it was the result of the very nature and genius of the gospel. It was not founded on some text of the Scripture, but on the very texture of its own thinking and attitudes. The fact is that Jesus and his disciples practiced such sharing before the Acts of the Apostles. They did it so unobtrusively that it is scarcely noticed. They had a common purse because they shared a common life. I am persuaded that if Christianity were really applied again, it would result in some form of collective sharing closely akin to the book of the Acts of the Apostles. Closely akin, but minus Communism's class war, minus its ruthlessness and compulsions, minus its denial of liberty and materialistic atheism. I grant that there are a good many minuses there! But there are also some pluses in the Kingdom of God which make Marxist Communism look like a reaction, for the Kingdom of God is the most astoundingly radical proposition ever presented to the mind of man. Communism would alter the economic relationships of man, this new Kingdom would alter every single relationship of man, including the radical altering of the man himself. The Kingdom of God is not a mere fold into which we run and are safe, but a new order breaking into and regenerating the total old order. We have become so used to a comparatively innocuous conception that the real thing seems alien to us.

Just what form that collective sharing would take I am not certain.

That it would include everything good in Communism is certain. But that it would not be synonymous with Communism is equally certain. After the Communists have founded a Communist state—so far they have only founded State Socialized Capitalism, and are only on the way to Communism—even after it has been founded, the Kingdom of God will judge it and call for something better. In other words, Communism is not the goal, but the Kingdom of God is. If you had said to the early Christians that the accomplishing of the fact of Communism was the accomplishing of the Kingdom of God, they would have smiled, for they saw that, while the Kingdom of God included a corporate sharing, it broke out beyond and was far greater than that corporate sharing. The Russians date everything from the Revolution, but the Revolution is not the same as the Lord's Year of Jubilee.

I am equally certain that it would not be a competitive order where the weakest go to the wall and the devil takes the hindmost. Christianity must, on no account, be considered bound up with capitalism or any other selfish order, for it was here long before capitalism arose, and it will be here long after it has been changed; or, if it cannot be changed, then supplanted by a better social order. I am persuaded that Christianity cannot fit into a self-seeking order. It is not its genius. In a competitive order it is gasping for breath, for it is not its native air. Its native air is love and brotherhood and sharing, therefore it would fit into and come to its own in a co-operative order. Christianity is now looked on as an impossible, unworkable method. It must be confessed that it is—under selfishness. When you think of society organized on the basis of exploitation of the weak by the strong, and of the elimination of competitors by whatever means possible, then, of course, Christianity seems quixotic and impossible. Oh, business is business, and Christianity is Christianity, and never the twain shall meet. Of course, as business now is. But visualize a cooperative order and then anything but Christianity seems absurd. The moment humanity

167

decides to base its future on co-operation instead of on competition—and the hard facts seem to be driving men in that direction for sheer survival—that moment will it have to turn to Christianity as the only possible spirit and temper to make it work. As long as we believe that the present order is workable, so long will we exile Christianity into cloisters and churches and take it up only on days we are not in business, namely, on Sundays! But when once the world comes to the conclusion that the present self-seeking order is impossible and is breaking down—and we are fast approaching that point now—then to turn to the gospel of the Kingdom would be as normal as for the needle to turn to the pole.

When in the early days of the Revolution some of our missionaries showed Lenin the Social Creed of the Churches of America, he replied, "Well, if this is what you stand for, then go on." But when he saw about him in the organized church, not the embodiment of the social creed of the churches, but the embodiment of reaction and special privilege and Czarism, then he hardened to his former attitude against all religion. In the next world crisis, for which we are definitely headed, will the leaders of thought and action see in Christianity the Christianity of the Kingdom of God on earth? If so, then they may feel that this is the normal and legitimate and only instrument that can bring into being the new order.

Men will try to bring in that new order by the processes of the Revolution or by the Lord's Year of Jubilee. Each marks the transition from the old to the new. But each brings up an entirely different picture to the mind. The Revolution!—blood and fear and compulsion and hate, the Red Terror! The Lord's Year of Jubilee!—men sensibly deciding that it is the only way out, catching the thrill of the new emerging brotherhood, willing to sacrifice to bring it to pass as men were willing to sacrifice during the last war, marching into that day with a strange new joy, a joy which cannot be had either from the thought of competition, or the thought of bringing the new day into being by hate and compulsion, humanity at last jubilant, for it sees an open road for all men, a world of brothers, the Lord's Year of Jubilee!

Lyrical and impossible? My answer is that the present order is anything but lyrical. It is a discord with notes in it that seem nothing less than a wail, and it is anything but possible, for it is breaking down before our very eyes by its own weight of injustice. Listen to Bernard Shaw, a cynic, Socialist and a critic of organized Christianity: "After reviewing the world of human events for sixty years I am prepared to state that I see no way out of the world's misery except the way that Christ would take were he to undertake the work of a modern statesman." In other words, if he should usher in the Lord's Year of Jubilee.

> **Listen to Bernard Shaw, a cynic, Socialist and a critic of organized Christianity: "After reviewing the world of human events for sixty years I am prepared to state that I see no way out of the world's misery except the way that Christ would take were he to undertake the work of a modern statesman."**

The possibility of a world awakening taking place through the Lord's Year of Jubilee gives hope that Christianity will not be looked on only as a means of personal conversion, but as a possible and workable program for world reconstruction. The Lord's Year of Jubilee is the acceptable year of the Lord—the only year that God will accept, for it is the year of reconstruction and regeneration. And, depend upon it, if it is the only year that God will accept, then we must accept it, or perish by our own confusion and strife.

But will men accept it? Yes, I think they will. For two reasons or pressures: disillusionment and desire. In regard to the first we find men slowly, but surely, realizing that the old ways are closing up as unworkable and impossible. It is true that we committed these follies in the past, but never have they become so patent to us as now; never before has there been so much intelligence brought to bear upon human affairs. Hitherto our follies have been more or less hidden follies—they are now more and more disclosed to us; our selfishness's were, in large measure, hidden from ourselves—now we are stripping off illusions. The mind of man is becoming more and more latently Christian, perhaps unconsciously so, because of the application of the method of trial and error—other ways have proved that they invariably end in chaos. So the facts are pushing man to the only open door—the Kingdom of God.

But disillusionment is not the only working force. There is desire. I am persuaded that there is more hidden desire for the New Day than most of us realize. Men now often suppress that desire, not because they want the old, but because they see no better alternative. But let men see the Kingdom of God as a really possible way, the only possible way, and this latent Christianity will burst into flame. The Lord's Year of Jubilee may be nearer than we suppose.

CHAPTER 8

THE DYNAMIC

The motive power behind any movement is an all-important matter. You may have a perfectly good end in view and that end may be spoiled by wrong means. That spoiling may be permanent, because you cannot stop the wrong means as means, for they pass on into the end and corrupt it. We must therefore inquire as to what is the motive force behind the program of Jesus.

We have seen the items in the program: (1) Good news to the poor—the economically disinherited; (2) Release to the captives—the socially and politically disinherited; (3) Opening of the eyes of the blind—the physically disinherited; (4) Setting at liberty them that are bruised—the morally and spiritually disinherited; (5) A new beginning on a world scale—the Lord's Year of Jubilee. But all this is useless except as an ideal, unless there is a working force behind it to put it into operation. That working force is the first item, "The Spirit of the Lord is upon me." The dynamic is the resources of the living God. His mind is behind the conception of the Kingdom, his power is behind the completion of that Kingdom.

We have left the discussion of the dynamic until the program is clearly before us, for had we taken it up at the place where it appears in the program, many would have stopped at that and would have left untouched the practical issues. It is a fact that talk of spiritual power makes many minds glance off at a tangent. It keeps them from coming to grips with essential problems. But now having laid the foundations of that program, we turn to the power that will make it work. For obviously, if the program is what we have outlined it to be, then only God working in partnership with man can make it work.

There are these possible attitudes toward the new order and the ways of its realization:

Marxist Communism	=	All human effort.
Apocalypticism	=	All God's gift.
Mysticism	=	Emphasis upon the inner.
Asceticism	=	Suppression of earthly desires.
Interim-ethicism	=	Sell all you have—the Lord is nigh.
Barthianism	=	Belief in social progress, man helpless—God speaks.

The nearest to a Christian position would seem to be—a belief in social progress, and that one must work as if the whole thing depended on man, and trust as if the whole thing depended on God.

Two sets of Christians come to this whole matter. One set, modern in mind and approach, takes the program and pays little or no attention to the dynamic behind the program. They are interested in good news

172

to the poor, the release of captives, and so on. They feel desperately that these things are the important things and that all talk of spiritual power is spiritual moonshine. These are the humanists in our midst. They are usually sincere and desperately in earnest. But most of them grow tired. There is nothing more obvious on the horizon than the tired humanists. They lack inner resources, and hence life becomes too much for them. John Dewey voices this when he says: "The chief characteristic of the present age is its despair of any constructive philosophy, not just in its technical meaning, but in the sense of an integrated outlook and attitude. The result is disillusionment." Theodore Dreiser says: "I find life to be a complete illusion or mirage ... in the wholly inexplicable world. The best I can say is that I haven't the faintest notion of what it is all about, unless it is for self-satisfaction... I catch no meaning from what I have seen, and pass quite as I came, confused and dismayed." James Truslow Adams puts it in this way: "We are floundering in a morass. The present situation cries aloud for some code. We are bewildered." Bertrand Russell writes that "we must build the future on the firm foundations of unyielding despair ... Brief and powerless is man's life; on him and on his race the slow sure doom falls pitiless and dark." Joseph Krutch says: "A color has faded from our palette; a whole range of effects has dropped out of a symphony... We are carried nearer to that state in which existence is a vast emptiness... We have grown used to a Godless universe, but we are not yet accustomed to one which is loveless as well, and only then when we have so become will we realize what atheism really means." Irving Babbitt, a religious humanist, sums up the demand in these words: "Unless there is a reaffirmation of the truths of the inner life in some form—religious or humanistic—civilization is threatened at the base."[1]

---

1 Irving Babbitt, *Living Philosophies* (New York: Simon and Schuster, 1931).

A modern woman put it to me in a letter in this way: "We are like very sick children. We need something."

Most of these are the voices of the nonreligious humanists and they are, on the whole, very, very tired. They have run through their human resources and don't know where to go next. But there is also a strain of tiredness in those who, while taking the Christian program, neglect to get hold of the Christian dynamic behind it all. After all, the Christian gospel is not merely a demand, it is an offer as well. If we do not take that offer, we will find that the demand is too much for us. Many who do not take that offer of victorious vitality become cynical and question whether the Christian way is really workable. They feel that they must turn to the Marxist dynamic of force to bring in the new day. The humanists lack a sense of adequate inner resources.

On the other hand there are those who come to this and take the power without the program. They are very eager for the power and very easy on the program. They joyfully say: "The Spirit of the Lord is upon me. I am very happy, and, thank God, heaven is my home." And they often leave it at that. For a great deal of our spiritual life is like the fire in the grate—too much of the heat goes up the chimney and too little goes to the social use of warming the people in the room. The unrelated power on the part of the Christian ends in sterility, unless it be the dynamic behind an adequate program of reconstruction.

But the cynical humanist endeavoring to put into effect the Christian program without the Christian power, and the ardent seeker for Christian power without the Christian program, are alike ending in sterility and paralysis. Each has thrown stones at the other for worshiping half-gods. There has been truth in the contention of each, also error. We must now put them together. Each must give to the other his truth. The half-gods must go. The program without the power is pretense, the power without the program is piffle (nonsense); the two put together is a new world.

The clash between the social and the individual gospel is a phase of this taking one or the other. The clash must end in a co-operation. We need each other. Even the Russian Communists, who are social emphasizers par excellence, now say that, having laid the foundations of social attitudes in the minds of the people, their next step is to emphasize individual culture and development. We Christians swing from one emphasis to the other, for we are not big enough to hold them both in a living blend within us. The significance of Kagawa[2] is that he is big enough to hold them in an amazing balance in his own life and work. He believes in individual conversion and yet it is all harnessed to social reconstruction. As a French philosopher said, "No man is strong unless he bears within his character antitheses strongly marked." Christianity will never be strong unless it bears within its character these antitheses of the individual and the social gospel very strongly marked.

We must not lose sight of the fact that this is God's Kingdom. His resources are behind it, if his Spirit directs in the establishing of it. Unless we keep the movement for the remaking of the world under his guidance and empowering, we shall muddle it, as Russia seems to be muddling a good end by incongruous means. The kingdoms of man are usually muddled by man. We must have our insights heightened, our perceptions deepened, and our vagrant wills steadied by the impact of the Spirit of God.

---

2 Kagawa Toyohiko (10 July 1888 – 23 April 1960) was a Japanese Christian pacifist, Christian reformer, and labour activist. Kagawa wrote, spoke, and worked at length on ways to employ Christian principles in the ordering of society and in cooperatives. His vocation to help the poor led him to live among them. He established schools, hospitals, and churches. (Source: https://en.wikipedia.org/wiki/Toyohiko_Kagawa Accessed May 25, 2019).

Just what would it mean to have the Spirit of the Lord upon us as the dynamic behind the movement for reconstruction? Jesus used "the Spirit of the Lord;" we would use "the Spirit of Christ." For Christ has interpreted God to us. He has made definite the character of the indefinite God. The character of Christ unlocks for us the secret of the character of God, and lets us see what God is like in the only place where we could understand it, namely, in the stream of human history. The character of God determines the character of the goal and the character of the advance as we move on to that goal. The Christian program is not opportunist; it gets its starting point and its inspiration from the very character of the God behind everything. We have seen his character in the face of Jesus Christ. "Amid the turmoil of things a Christlike God holds my heart," said a thoughtful young teacher in

> "Behold, I stand at the door and knock," is an astounding statement in a world in which doors are now battered down without ceremony and human personality is invaded and compelled to accept the will of a dictatorship. God is not the supreme dictator, but the supreme Father.

one of our Round Table Conferences. He does. And more! He holds the movement for world-reconstruction from the vagaries of passing theories and keeps it consistent and consonant with the character of God.

This determines the weapons by which the new order is to be brought into being. It rules out force and compulsion at once, for the very essence of the Spirit of Christ is reverence for personality.

"Behold, I stand at the door and knock," is an astounding statement in a world in which doors are now battered down without ceremony and human personality is invaded and compelled to accept the will of a dictatorship. God is not the supreme dictator, but the supreme Father. He does not say, "I will conquer that child no matter what it costs him," but he does say, "I will help that child to conquer himself, no matter what it costs me." There is a difference there, and the difference between the two is essentially the difference between the Marxist and the Christian method.

When Dr. Reinhold Niebuhr says that the new day cannot be accomplished except by force—and by force he must mean military force—he definitely throws away the Christian weapons and takes the Marxian. When you take the Marxist weapons, you must take something other than the Christian goal, for the Christian goal can only be attained by the Christian method. To talk about getting to the Christian goal by the Marxist method is absurd, for the Christian goal is lost by the very method used. The spirit that is used in the means will pass into the end. When the Crusaders waded through blood to capture the holy city of Jerusalem from the Moslems, they found that Christ was not there. He had been lost in the very weapons used.

The Marxist method gets quicker results, quicker but questionable. Stalin exults, "Russia will soon be one vast factory, and one great machine," which is true, and it may include man in its mechanization. To put up the robot as the ideal and say, "Behold the man," may satisfy some, but some of us prefer to look at Christ, even in his rejection, and say, "Behold the Man." You cannot make free men out of compulsions any more than you can make silk purses out of swine's ears. The Marxian say that these compulsions are only temporary and will pass away with the passing of the state. But you cannot drop the means with their use, they pass on into and become a part of the end. It is no chance that the Russian state is becoming more and more ubiquitous and more and more dictatorial. It is probably the most firmly established state in Europe, and yet instead of loosening its grip upon the liberties of the people, it tightens it. It is true that if you fit into the system, there is a sense of freedom. But it is a freedom to fit into, not to differ from it, nor to get out of it. Freedom to act in one direction, however much it may be said to be for your good, is bondage. You cannot change the system, nor get away from it, but you can fit in—or perish. The means have passed into the end and seem to have become a permanent part of it.

Europe, in the person of Napoleon, made this ghastly mistake at the time of the birth of democracy. Democracy was such a boon to humanity that men must take it whether they want it or not. So Napoleon took up the sword to make men love democracy. He would teach fraternity by fratricide. The result? Napoleon fastened upon Europe a legacy of militarism which is now about to destroy it. He put a dictatorship at the heart of European thinking, and that dictatorship is now in the process of ruling over the ruins of democracy. The Estonians were conquered by the Danes and forced to be Christians. The Germans came along and hanged some of the village elders for not waiting for them to baptize them. The Germans rebaptized the Estonians. The Estonians went to the river and washed off this baptism! Europe is now in the process of washing off a democracy imposed in great measure by force and compulsion. Russia in the end must face this same inevitability. For the time being it succeeds, but in the end a Saint Helena awaits the system imposed and the imposers. "They that take the sword shall perish with the sword," said Jesus, and the whole of history is a comment on that statement.

Professor Macmurray says: "Dictatorship, so far from being a part of communistic society, is incompatible with it. This is the essential difference between Fascism and Communism." True. But whether compatible or incompatible with Communism, they have adopted it in Russia, and that adoption may mean its ultimate destruction. "Great problems in the lives of nations are solved only by force," says Lenin. Yes, for the time being, but in the end the problem is back again, namely, how to get rid of the force used in solving the great problem. "Master," said the sorcerer's apprentice, "I am in great distress. I have called up a spirit and now I do not know how to rid myself of him." If you call things in to help you out of your difficulties, you may have to pay the supreme price for the compromise. Some kings in Ceylon were warring against each other. The Portuguese came with their firearms and one of the kings invited them to come and help him. They did— and took possession of the country. The Dutch came to help one of the kings against the Portuguese. They came to help, and they stayed to possess the country. One of the kings at Pudukottah, South India, called in the Kallars, the robber caste, to help him against his enemies. They did, but took over the government and have it to this day.

All these illustrate the danger of calling in to help you a force which you do not want when that help is no longer necessary. Will Russia again illustrate it?

Jesus refused to entangle his Kingdom with force. "My kingdom is not of this world, else would my servants fight." This is the distinguishing mark of the kingdoms of this world—the servants of them fight to establish them, and then have to fight to hold them. "My kingdom is not of this world," its genesis is not in the processes of nature and history. It is a new Kingdom breaking into the processes of nature and of history from above, therefore using weapons that are different. But we have tried to survive by using the weapons of lower nature. The tragedy of the West is that when Darwin discovered the laws of survival of the fittest in lower nature, men felt that it was a gospel and immediately made them the method of survival on the human level. It led us to the brink of the abyss in the last war and is leading us to it again. We looked to the kingdom below instead of the Kingdom above for our code of survival. The lower kingdom of the animal stands for self against the rest, the higher Kingdom stands for self for the sake of the rest; the lower for the survival of the fittest, in terms of cunning or of physical strength, the higher stands for the revival of the unfit in terms of redemption; the lower is red in tooth and claw, the higher is red with the blood of its own sacrifice; the lower stands for mutual annihilation, the higher for mutual aid; the lower ends in war, the higher in brotherhood.

> **Jesus refused to entangle his Kingdom with force. "My kingdom is not of this world, else would my servants fight." This is the distinguishing mark of the kingdoms of this world—the servants of them fight to establish them, and then have to fight to hold them.**

"My kingdom is not of this world" does not mean that it belongs to another world entirely, and has nothing to do with the affairs of this one, for Jesus said, "When you pray say, Our Father, . . . may your kingdom come, and may your will be done on earth as it is in heaven." "Of this world" is the genitive of genesis, its source is not here, but its establishment is to be here. Its nature is different, therefore the method and the weapons for establishing it are also different.

There are three passages which seem to imply the possible use of force on the part of the Christian movement. "Think not that I am come to send peace on the earth: I came not to send peace, but a sword." Luke puts it in a parallel passage: "I came to cast fire upon the earth; and what will I, if it is already kindled? But I have a baptism to be baptized with; and how am I straitened till it be accomplished! Think you that I am come to give peace in the earth? I tell you, No, but rather division." Now note that the "sword" of Matthew (Matthew 10: 34) is interpreted by Luke as "division" (Luke 12: 51), and hence was not intended to be a literal sword. The gospel has not come to bring a sword, but it has come to bring division, and rightly so. It does not cry "Peace!" with a basis of injustice underlying that peace. There must be a separation on questions when the world is so badly mixed with justice and injustice. The gospel is not a peace-at-any-price namby-pambyism. It stands for certain things and will stand for them to the death. But note the place of "division." The context shows us what it is. He came to cast "fire" on the earth, and the "fire" was what? A "Baptism." And the "baptism" was what? A cross! The place of division was, therefore, a cross. It was then, and it is today. It was a division based upon the question of whether men will be ruled by a cross. The cross stands for overcoming evil with good, hate by love, darkness by light, the world by suffering for the world. It is God's method of compulsion. But that very method of compulsion becomes an impulsion. He helps us to conquer ourselves no matter how much it costs him. This is the method of God's omnipotence. But that omnipotence does not result in our impotence. He saves the world, but in doing so he saves his own character and our liberties at the same time.

This is literally the dividing line of the world. The Marxians take one side of that issue and the Christians the other. It is Caesar or Christ again. This time Caesar stands not as the dictator of an empire, but as a dictatorship of the proletariat, the cause a better one this time; but still Caesar with the same weapons of force and compulsion. In the battle between unselfishness and selfishness the unselfish principle will win, for it is a higher principle. In the battle between the method of Caesar and the method of Christ, Christ will win, for his method is higher.

To force ideals by compulsion is a ghastly mistake. In doing so the ideals become less than ideals. In a city in India I saw a sign over a Y.M.C.A. which read, "The Y.M.C.A. is an ideal with a club." They didn't mean to say that, but the Communists mean to say it, for Communism is literally an ideal with a club. Fascism is too. Christianity is an ideal with a cross. Communism and Fascism produce slaves, and Christianity produces freemen. They are bound to, by the very nature of the case.

I stood in the square in Leningrad and watched a parable unfolding before me. On the veranda of the great cathedral was a factory machine of no apparent use, but parked there as a symbol of the fact that in this new civilization the machine was to take the place of the cathedral. It barred the entrance to the cathedral. The figure of Christ on his cross, with his feet almost touching the sidewalk, hung alongside of the cathedral. Some passers-by stopped and kissed his feet. On the opposite side of the street, exactly parallel with Christ, stood a group of Communist recruits drilling, or, rather, they were going through a bayonet practice, jabbing at a dummy, one after the other. The drillmaster earnestly shouted instructions for getting better results in disemboweling. Two ideas had come together there. The belly-piercing bayonet or the nail-pierced Christ. Which is the stronger? For the time being the bayonet holds the field. But only for the time being, for the issue is not a fair one. For it wasn't the Christ of the New Testament whom I saw hanging against the background of an Orthodox cathedral which was wedded to an old order. It was a caricature. But Christ has a way of surviving caricatures as he survived the mock-crown and the reed-scepter and the purple robe. The real Christ, which the Marxians and all others will have to deal with in the end, will not be a Christ with the background of a decadent cathedral, but with the background of his new Kingdom, which stands for the new and ultimate order. When that issue becomes clear, then the cross will seem to be befitting and the bayonet an incongruity. For you cannot put truth into a man's heart by ripping open his belly, nor can you create a brotherhood by dismembering man. I cannot visualize the bayonet pointing the way to the new day. But I can look up through those open wounds and see a universe of love and self-giving and brotherhood breaking into and healing this world of strife and hate and injustice. As love will outlast hate, so the cross will outlast the bayonet. It has survival value. When the conscience of the world, in a moment of deep insight, signed the Kellogg Pact,[3] it judged the use of the bayonet to be a felony; it has yet to gain a deeper insight and see in the cross a fellowship.

If I seem to be overstating the motive behind the Communists, then let Zinovieff, an able interpreter of Communism, tell us what it is. "The hate-laden cry of rage is our delight," he says, and then he adds, "The whole of the essence of Lenin's teaching is contained in these words." Or Lenin's own words reveal the method, "In order to bring in peace you must split open men's skulls."

When Jesus chose the cross instead of the bayonet as the method of the Kingdom, he chose a longer road, and a costlier one for him, but in the end the longest way round will be the shortest way home. "God led them not by the way of the land of the Philistines, although this was near" (Exodus 13: 17). That near-cut was not God's cut, for in that near-cut a fatal corruption would have corrupted the whole. The

---

3 The Kellogg-Briand Pact is a 1928 international agreement in which signatory states promised not to use war to resolve "disputes or conflicts of whatever nature or of whatever origin they may be, which may arise among them." (Source: https://en.wikipedia.org/wiki/kellogg-Briand_pact Accessed May 25, 2019).

Norwegians were made Christian in large part by the king and the bishops going round to preach the gospel to the pagans. If they listened and accepted, then well and good; but if they hesitated in their decision, a pan of live coals was placed upon their abdomens to help them come to it. It did help make a decision, but in the process the Christian gospel was more deeply seared than the abdomen of the hesitator. Europe is still suffering from the unhealed wounds of force inflicted in the propagation of the gospel. Let those who are tempted to lay aside the Christian weapons and adopt those of force to get quick results remember that in trying to bring in that Kingdom by force, you may have something entirely other than the Kingdom if you succeed by that method. "German barons Christianized and took over lands in Courland and Livonia," blandly remarks the historian, and yet real Christianity received enough wounds in that process to make it bleed to death. Its power to survive the wounds of its friends is astonishing. Its power to continue in spite of perversion is an index of its vitality. What would the real thing do!

> When you divide by the sword, you permanently divide; when you divide by a cross, you temporarily divide on a lower level to meet on a higher level, minus the evils that caused the division.

Christ did send the sword of division, but it is not a permanent division. He divides men at the lower level that they may meet on a higher level. To talk of unity is maudlin and dangerous sentimentality when that unity would be on the lower level, where untruths and injustices would be part of it. Christ would divide men, for life is now tangled up with injustices and wrongs, but in the very dividing he appeals to men to meet together again on a higher level, for he divides by a cross. When you divide by the sword, you permanently divide; when you divide by a cross, you temporarily divide on a lower level to meet on a higher level, minus the evils that caused the division.

Men have divided the world at the place of their authority, but has anyone ever divided the world at the place of Jesus' self-sacrifice? This is a new way to divide. He divides to deliver and to unite on a higher level. The end is not division, but a higher unity.

The second passage that is used to put the authority of Jesus behind force is the incident of the cleansing of the Temple with the whipcords. But this is a slender basis for the use of force, for the fact is that he did not use the whipcords on human beings, but only on sheep and oxen, "And he made a whip of small cords, and cast all out of the temple, both the sheep and the oxen." This defines the "all" as "both the sheep and the oxen." Had he used physical force on that crowd of men, they would have torn him to pieces. It was the terror of his eyes before which they slunk away. Whip cords for dumb animals, but the lash of his righteous indignation for the men. He will use those same weapons today in the cleansing of the Temple of Man.

The third passage used to defend force is the statement of Jesus to his disciples: "But now he that . . . has none, let him sell his cloak, and buy a sword. . . . And they said, Lord, behold, here are two swords. And he said unto them, It is enough" (Luke 22: 36-38). This too is a slender foundation for the use of force, for, on the face of it, it would seem that two swords which Jesus said were "enough" would hardly be adequate military preparation against a multitude! We must look for some other explanation. Jesus had just asked them whether they lacked anything when they went out without scrip or purse, and they replied that they had not. The multitudes were friendly. But now the atmosphere had changed. They would go into an atmosphere of hostility, and they would not be supported as they had been. That the disciples had missed his point is shown by the impatience of Jesus, for he replied to their statement that they had two swords, "It is enough, it is enough" (Moffatt), as much as to say, "Don't you see I am not talking about swords literally?" It was gentle irony. That this is the interpretation is seen by the fact that when Peter did use one of these swords and cut off the ear of the servant of the high priest, Jesus rebuked him and said, "Put up thy sword, for they that take the sword shall perish with the sword," and he stooped down, picked up the severed ear and said, "Let me do this at least" (Moffatt), and Jesus healed the servant of the high priest.

A pamphlet of the War Department of the United States says, "Jesus gave his apostles the authority of the sword and the gift of the Holy Ghost in token that he can safely trust the sword to the Christian conscience illuminated by the light of the Holy Ghost." But this pamphlet fails to note that when Peter used the sword, Jesus said to him, "Put up again thy sword into his place; for all they that take the sword shall perish with the sword." The authors of this pamphlet failed to note that the last and final word of Jesus about the sword was to put it up. Let militarism listen to Jesus at that place or cease to quote him at all. All militarism does is to cut off the ears of people. Thereafter they hear nothing; they are deaf to reason and sense.

The fact of the matter is that the two things that have deeply prejudiced the world against Bolshevism are its doctrines of the class war and world revolution. This two-edged sword has simply cut off the ear of the world. The world has no ear to listen to the other side of the Communistic program. This has resulted in the failure of Communism to spread. The Communists have seen this and have ousted Trotsky with his world-revolution insistence and are now confining themselves, for the most part, to the creation of a successful Socialist state in

Russia itself. The militaristic part of their program is hobbling the whole experiment. Russian Communism will be as disillusioned of the method of war as we have become since the last war. But to have said that we would be disillusioned concerning the methods of war while the war was going on would have brought down on us wrath. It was only after it was all over that we saw the bankruptcy of the method. The Communists are now in the war and have the war fever, and hence to say that force won't work seems absurd to them. It always does work—for a while. A South-Indian proverb says that "a lie is like a waning moon and the truth is like a waxing moon." Militarism is a waning moon and will always end in night and darkness. The method of Jesus is very small and despised in the beginning, but it waxes into perfect light. For the fact of the matter is that hate produces hate, force produces force. Two hates never made a love affair. They never have and they never will. Jesus said, "How can Satan cast out Satan?" Can you, by acting like the devil, get the devil out of people? The Communists have not hesitated to try it. Again and again in its persecution of its supposed and real enemies it has acted like the devil to get the devil out of people. It won't work. You cannot produce free human personalities out of compulsions.

> **Jesus repudiated the weapons of force and substituted the weapons of good will. The world must follow him at this point or perish.**

Jesus repudiated the weapons of force and substituted the weapons of good will. The world must follow him at this point or perish. The Spirit of Christ as the dynamic of this new Kingdom repudiates force and uses the healing forces of love. But that does not mean

187

acquiescence to evil. Evil is resisted from a higher level. Mahatma Gandhi gave the world a glimpse of the possibilities of this weapon which would have been amazingly effective had it not been compromised and confused by his personal vagaries which concealed from many the tremendous reality behind it all. In spite of all that he has shown us a technique by which evil may be resisted and how a group or a nation may attain its objectives without recourse to the barbarities of war. It will yet be intelligently applied, stripped of the Mahatma's vagaries, and will yet show the way out. The thousand miners starving down in the mines of Hungary for five days in order to call attention to the slow starvation of their low wages brought a pressure to bear upon the situation and led to the settlement of the strike in a far more effective way than if they had used force and destroyed property. They let us see the possibilities of the power of taking suffering rather than giving it. The capacity to take suffering rather than give it is closely akin to the spirit and method of the cross, and that spirit and method are as much higher than the method of force as the method of co-operation is higher than the method of competition, and at the last will win. It has higher survival value and in the end it will wear down all lesser methods.

The fact is that even Marx believed that there were two countries in which these changes could take place without military force and armed revolution, England and America. Marx here sensed a possibility which we must actualize throughout the world.

But the Spirit of the Lord, or the Spirit of Christ behind the movement as its dynamic, not only saves the movement from wrong methods and weapons, but it also saves the movement from becoming static and fixed and authoritarian. Maurice Hindus says that one of the charges brought by the Bolsheviks against the Protestant movement in Russia is that "it is rooted in dogma. The fixity of purpose which such dogmatism implies they consider to be incompatible with both the practice and the principles of the Revolution." This may be a valid objection against Russian Protestantism, and against many other forms of Christianity built up in the West, but it certainly cannot be valid against the original spirit of the Gospels. Jesus never formulated a fixed creed, nor did his immediate disciples. Paul says in 2 Corinthians 3: 6, 17, "He also who has made us competent to serve him in connection with the new Covenant, which is not a written code, but a Spirit. . . . Now by 'the Lord' is meant the Spirit; and where the Spirit of the Lord is, freedom is enjoyed" (Weymouth trans.).

> **It is true that the ideas underlying the Christian movement are fixed in an historical Person. They are not philosophies, but facts meeting us in a Person. That truth saves us from the vagaries of theosophical speculation and gives us a touchstone in history itself.**

It is true that the ideas underlying the Christian movement are fixed in an historical Person. They are not philosophies, but facts meeting us in a Person. That truth saves us from the vagaries of theosophical speculation and gives us a touchstone in history itself. It keeps the feet of Christianity upon the ground, that it may not vanish into mists and into mysteries. It steadies the movement and gives it a starting point. But note that it is only a starting point. "I have yet many things to say unto you, but ye cannot hear them now. How be it when he, the Spirit of truth, is come, he will guide you into all truth; for he shall take of mine and shall show it unto you." Note that phrase, "the Spirit of truth." "Truth"—how fixed and unchanging it seems,

CHRIST'S ALTERNATIVE TO COMMUNISM...

written into the very nature of things! "The Spirit of"—how fluid and unfolding it seems, writing itself in the unfolding of advancing events! Could any phrase of four words sum up in itself a more complete blend of the static and the unfolding?

Jesus is "the incarnation of universals." He therefore says, "I am the truth." He is God's final Word, but he is also God's unfolding Word. The Spirit of God is constantly bringing out fresh implications of the meaning of Christ. This age is on the verge of the discovery of the meaning of the Kingdom of God. Anyone who is in it can feel the very illumination of the Spirit, unfolding, revealing, urging to acceptance. Static? The Word smashes all my words like the growing seed smashes the preserving shell. I weave my web of words around him, and say that I have caught him at last, but he steps out beyond my words—the Living Word!

So when the Communists hurl at us the charge of being fixed creedalists and dogmatists, we smile, for the Spirit of Truth within us tells us it simply isn't so. We smile, moreover, as we watch "Marxism and Leninism become just as rigid as anything to be found in religious dogmatism." We note that every school of Marxism tries to prove itself orthodox according to the gospel of Marx. "Un-Marxian" is as condemnatory and decisive when pronounced by the votaries of Marx upon any person or position, as any papal bull of excommunication ever was. Lenin said, "Marxism is a final truth; no historical development can ever shake it or alter it." At the center of that system they have not what the Kingdom of God has, namely, the Spirit of Christ, which is the Spirit of Truth. So it shall be that long after Marxism has hardened into an orthodox system the Christian movement will be unfolding its redemptive purpose in wider and wider and deeper and deeper areas of human life. The story is told that when the Pilgrim Fathers set out from the church at Leyden, Holland, to sail to America, John Robinson preached to them saying, "Fresh light shall yet break out from God's Word." Whether the story is true or not, light did break out then and it is doing so today. We are pilgrims of the Infinite. The next bit of light that seems to be breaking out from God's Word is a discovery of the meaning of the Kingdom of God on earth.

But the dynamic of the Spirit is not only unfolding; it is untiring. It is said that Christianity conquered the world of Greece and Rome because the Christians "out-thought, out-lived and out-died the pagans." In the present struggle we think the followers of Christ will conquer not only because they out-think, out-live and out-die the pagans, but because they out-experience them, and will therefore out-wear them. I have found in my Round Table Conferences that those in fellowship with Christ have a better way to live than those not in fellowship with him. They have inner resources that seem to save them from cynicism, from failure of nerve, from curdling of spirit—from themselves.

> I have found in my Round Table Conferences that those in fellowship with Christ have a better way to live than those not in fellowship with him.

This has worked out with an almost mathematical precision. Others were fumbling with fitful and uncertain insights but with a certain fundamental lack at the center of life. They seemed to be living on marginal resources, but with the center empty, or at least shaky. As we sat in the Round Table Conference in Nanking, China, and went around the circle and listened to what the leading men of that city and of that country were saying about the inner resources by which they lived, we passed from spiritual deserts to spiritual oases, and it was

191

always the Christian, limited though his life may be in many ways, who gave you the sense that at the center of his life was a spring and therefore growing life and hope. Had this worked in isolated cases, I might be charged with picking facts and therefore conclusions, but when it has worked precisely the same for fourteen years and in hundreds of Round Table Conferences, then I feel that I have a right to announce results, and the results would be as thoroughly tested, and therefore as sound, as most scientific conclusions.

"You Christians began this Student Center, didn't you ?" asked a Hindu when invited to become a member of the governing board along with the Christians. "Then you had better continue it, for whatever you take up you carry on; you have a strange power of persistence; but whatever we take hold of we let wane and die." The Christian has a power of persistence because he believes that, in spite of present appearances, the universe is with him ultimately. He has gained his optimisms, not out of a Pollyanna, smiling, surface view of life, but out of a cross. There he has seen life speak its cruelest and most unjust word, and then at that very moment speak its most glorious word of victory. A Hindu proverb says that "he who is born in the fire will not fade in the sun." The Christian's optimism is born in the fire of the cross and will not fade in the sun of lesser difficulties.

> The Christian has a power of persistence because he believes that, in spite of present appearances, the universe is with him ultimately. He has gained his optimisms, not out of a Pollyanna, smiling, surface view of life, but out of a cross.

We expect Christianity to outlast atheistic Communism because it has a deeper and a more meaningful universe, and a firmer ground for believing in man. There is a haunting sense of melancholy running through Greek literature. The Greeks professed a glorious faith in man, but gave no ultimate grounds for putting it into practice. Of that central skepticism these civilizations collapsed. Ultimately Communism will collapse of that same inner skepticism, unless it is renewed at the heart by a religious reason for believing in the ultimate worth of man. Now it seems to need no such inner renewal, for its enthusiasms seem to be carrying it on. They are doing just that. But they are now flushed with the wine of war, a war on many social and economic fronts, a good war compared to the war of ruthless competition, and hence giving them the sense of being based on ultimates. But wait till the effects of the wine of war fade out and the duller, more drab moments of ordinary life lay bare the ultimate foundations upon which the system rests, and then the testing moment will come. It will then be the moment when the tortoise of Christianity may surpass the hare of Marxist Communism. "An age of social creativeness never flowered on the stalk of cynicism," and this will hold true ultimately in Communism, for while it has temporary optimisms it has within it an ultimate cynicism. For within it there is no ultimate reason for believing in life and in man. God must be at the basis of life or the sod will be its ultimate goal. God or sod is the ultimate issue.

The knowledge exists, lack of love prevents it from being applied. In the end it will be the Christian dynamic which will make it work. Glenn Frank, a modern educator, says, "This dynamic will be found only in some fresh manifestation of the religious impulse." Strangled as it has been by its own devotees, crippled by its perversions, and nearly paralyzed by overlaid superstitions, nevertheless Christianity, in spite of all, has filled the world with schools, orphan asylums, hospitals, leper asylums, and other institutions of various kinds for the uplifting of humanity, until there is not an island of the sea, nor a place anywhere where this has not happened. The Christian Church, with all its faults, is the best serving institution on earth. It has many critics, but no rivals in the work of human redemption. If it has done this in a semi-crippled state, what will it not do when the Kingdom of God is rediscovered and fully applied in its full implications and power? Its greatest moments are ahead. In the early days when it was fresh and living, the Christians did so much for prisoners that Licinius passed a law that "no one was to show kindness to sufferers in prison by supplying them with food," and that "no one was to show mercy to those who are starving in prison." In the same way the Communists forbid any social work to the churches, instinctively fearing that dynamic of love in Christianity which lies hidden is ready to burst into world-manifestation and world-redemption.

> **The Christian Church, with all its faults, is the best serving institution on earth. It has many critics, but no rivals in the work of human redemption.**

A Hindu said to me recently: "Christianity has done ten times as much for India as the British Government. It has washed the inner thinking of India. Mahatma Gandhi could do no greater service to India than to say to India, 'Become Christian.' Although I am not a Christian, I can say that if any country needs to become Christian for its own sake, it is India." Yes, India does need to become Christian for its own sake, but these words would apply just as well to the world situation: if there ever was a world that needed to be Christian for its own sake, it is this world of ours. I see nothing else on the horizon that can give us the program and the dynamic except the Spirit of Christ.

Materialism in the end will lack dynamic. A man in Glasgow, Kentucky, cranked his car, and finding it wouldn't start, opened the hood and found that someone had stolen his engine! Cynicism will in the end steal the engine of every human system and leave only a body of social ideas and principles. Joseph Krutch saw very clearly that if you let God go, then you would have to let love go too, and if you let love go, where is the dynamic? A very thoughtful member of one of our Round Table Conferences said, "After I let God go I found that I was compelled to let one thing after another go, until I have now come to the place where I am about to be compelled to let myself go, for I see no meaning or purpose in myself." When God went, then the bottom dropped out of life, and if the bottom drops out of life itself, then it drops out of any plans for the remaking of life. When the root is cut, the fruit withers.

Education apart from God cannot give that dynamic. The elder Bentham said in 1840: "If we can get universal and compulsory education, then by the end of the century all our social and political and moral problems shall be solved." The end of that century came and there was universal and compulsory education, but had all the problems become solved? They had become more acute. President Glenn Frank, of the University of Wisconsin, again says: "I do not believe, however, that the future of the West lies exclusively upon the laps of the educators. I cannot share the confidence of the social analysts who think that education is likely to provide compelling impulses that will prompt a whole generation consciously to embark on the noble enterprise of social renascence through scientific humanism. If, as H.G. Wells says, 'it is a race between education and catastrophe,' then my guess is that catastrophe will win, for I do not believe that existing education of our schools has in it to salvage our civilization." Nor has the highly propagandized education of Russian Communism a sufficient dynamic to make it work in the end, for the cancer at the heart of the whole system will be the fact that there is no ultimate reason for changing life, since there is no ultimate reason for believing in life. It is working now—amazingly so, for the cancer has been rendered quiescent by the fierce rays of the light of the Revolution, but when the light fades, will not the cancer begin to eat? You cannot long believe in man unless you believe in something more than man. The Christians will believe in man long after others have lost their faith in man. Their "Yes" will outwear the skeptics' "No." In the end most humanists will have to agree with Joseph Krutch when he says, "Ours is a lost cause, and there is no place for us in the natural universe, but we are not for that reason sorry to be human. We would rather die as men than live as animals." The Christian will outlast that, for he believes in man because he believes in God, for to him a man is no longer a man— he is "a man for whom Christ died."

It is significant that the power Christ announced was bound up with the program. This fact insures that direction should be given to spiritual impulses. They are not to be vagrant and vague and ingrown, but linked with a program of human redemption. This actually happened when the Spirit of the Lord was released upon the disciples at Pentecost. The disciples could say, "The Spirit of the Lord is upon us, therefore there is good news to the poor." A voluntary "communism" resulted, and there was none among them that had need; "there is the proclaiming of release to the captives"—a classless society resulted; "there is the opening of the eyes of the blind"—a passion to heal disease was in the movement; "there is a setting at liberty the bruised"— men who had been morally hurt found forgiveness and joyous release; "the Lord's Year of Jubilee has come"—there was a fresh hope given to a morally jaded world. The germs of a new order were there. But that life was smothered by creeds and ceremonies and ecclesiasticisms. A new world would come into being if we today should rediscover that program and that power.

I asked Professor Harnack once what the Christian solution was to a certain question. He replied, "Christianity gives no solutions, but it gives a goal and power to move on to that goal." He was right. The Christian movement has in it those two things: it offers the most glorious goal ever offered to humanity—the Kingdom of God on earth—a Kingdom in which there would be no poverty, no classes, no sickness, and no sin, which would, in fact, be the Lord's Year of Jubilee, a new world beginning. That is the goal. Then there is the power to move on to that goal, with the resources of the Spirit of God.

With that program and that power we confidently expect to outlast humanistic Communism. But if we do, then we must sincerely and without equivocation or compromise adopt that program and then lay hold of that Power. The lines of that program are being laid in the minds of men, the channels are being dug, and when they are sufficiently ready God will release his power upon us. I am persuaded that we stand on the verge of a spiritual world awakening. We sat in a Round Table with the leading Christians and non-Christians, and when it came the turn of the Christian Chief Judge to speak, this is what he said: "I haven't much to say now, for I feel like a man standing before a button, ready to touch it. The wires are all laid, the lamps are all ready to be lit, the dynamo is throbbing with energy. But I hesitate to press it. I feel that something tremendous would happen if I do, but I stand hesitant." That judge is the Christian world —we stand before a world situation which is being prepared for world changes, God is laying in our minds and spirits the wires along which the redemptive movement will run, his dynamo is throbbing with redemptive energy. It all awaits our touching the button, our appropriating the power. If we do this, something tremendous will happen. That something tremendous will be nothing less than the emergence of a new world.

CHAPTER 9

WHO WILL BRING IT IN?

As Jesus announced his program the people in the synagogue were astounded beyond measure. They "wondered at the words of grace which proceeded out of his mouth." Here was something new in religion—it was not lawgiving, but lifegiving, not a set of commandments but the unfolding of a conception, a conception which was to issue in a world-conversion. The disinherited in all realms were at last to find equality and freedom and brotherhood and moral health in a new unfolding society. They felt as men who stood on the verge of some new dawning era: something new was at their doors. How could they but wonder "at the words of grace which fell from his lips?"

But he sensed that underneath that wonder was an illusion, an illusion which he would have to destroy at once. He saw shining in their eyes, not the light of a new dawning brotherhood of all men of all races, but the fierce glow of a racial patriotism and pride. "At last," they were evidently thinking, "the moment of our racial triumph has come. A new kingdom is here which will triumph over all kingdoms, and we, the chosen people, will be the center of that triumph." To them the words of grace were words of race. Had the nation not prayed for many a year, "O God, thou hast made us for thyself. As for the rest of the nations they are but spittle"? This prayer was the expression of an inner attitude. Jesus saw that attitude on the faces of the people that morning as they sat before him. Religious fervor was there, but racial egotism was at its heart. And that racial egotism could not be at the heart of the new Kingdom, or else it would not be a new Kingdom at all, but the old one dressed up now in the more flowing garments of world brotherhood. So Jesus would have to dispel the illusion, decisively and at once. He would not let them go on under a misunderstanding. Nor would he accept a popularity with a misconception underlying it. He was realistic and relentless. He would let them know at once the full implications of the new Kingdom. He would let them see how far he meant to go. So he struck at the illusion with these words: "There were many widows in Israel in the days of Elijah; . . . and unto none of them was Elijah sent, but only unto Zarephath, in the land of Sidon, unto a woman that was a widow. And there were many lepers in Israel in the time of Elisha the prophet; and none of them was cleansed, but only Naaman the Syrian."

What was he saying? That God cared specially for people outside their race? And he cared for "Gentile dogs" at that? Did he mean to say that all special privileges were to be canceled, that all barriers of race and class were put down in the coming of the new Kingdom? Did he mean to say that Israel as a race was not necessarily going to be the center of that triumph ? That the new Kingdom was going to be for man as man and not man as a member of a special race or class? That is precisely what he was saying.

They saw at once the implications of this conception and purpose. They felt that these implications struck at the foundations of their racial and religious history. It was subversive. "Instead of leading us into a racial triumph through religion he is leading into the disintegration of our race and religion through this movement"—so they felt. The atmosphere in the synagogue changed immediately. "And they were all filled with wrath in the synagogue, as they heard these things; and they rose up, and cast him forth out of the city, and led him unto the brow of the hill whereon their city was built, that they might throw him down headlong." If this was to be the meaning of religion, they would have none of it. They listened to truth until it cut across their race and class prejudice, and then they closed up.

The issue was joined: a Kingdom which stood for man as man and would be directed by man as man, or a Kingdom which would help man as man, but would be directed by man as Jew.

This issue is modern. It is emerging throughout the world. Everywhere we find movements launched with the idea of helping

Religious fervor was there, but racial egotism was at its heart. And that racial egotism could not be at the heart of the new Kingdom, or else it would not be a new Kingdom at all...

humanity, but always with a messianic class or race as the center of those movements. Men are quite prepared to see the world saved, provided it be through them, for in the end that would mean their supremacy, however altruistic it may all seem.

The Communists have as their goal a classless society. They have succeeded marvelously in wiping out distinctions. A Jewish lady said to me in Russia: "I prefer to stay in Russia, although I was well treated in England, for here I have no consciousness of being a Jew. No one ever reminds me of it." Under the old Czarist regime every Jew was made to

201

feel conscious of being a Jew, so much so that he could not go beyond the Pale. All that has now been wiped out. It is now a criminal offense to speak offensively to a Jew. The Communists allow every nationality within the U.S.S.R. to develop its nationality and culture and language. There is no distinction made on account of race and color. Everything is open on equal terms. But having acknowledged all this, one is bound to note that it is one particular class that is doing all this, a class which regards itself as a messianic class—the proletariat. In all their plays and cinemas and posters the proletariat is the hero and the bourgeoisie is the villain. All the virtues reside in one class and all the vices in the other. If Jesus should stand in Russia today as he stood in the synagogue and should announce that the new day of equality was at hand, that man should be treated as man, that all classes should be wiped out, and that this new day should be brought in by man as man, and not man as a member of a particular class, he would probably be acclaimed until he reached that last phrase. At the mention of that last phrase the same thing would happen as happened then—they would all be filled with wrath. For they hold that this classless society is to come only through one class, the proletariat, and until it comes there shall be a dictatorship of that class. There is a snag there, however logical it may seem, just as there is a snag in the statement of the Theosophists and the Bahais that all religions are basically one and the same and are equally good, therefore join the Theosophical Society or the Bahais on that basis! If they are all the same, why another? Jesus put his finger on that particular snag at the very outset. This new Kingdom would not mean a new messianic race or class. The Messiah was the Son of man, and the sons of men would be the medium through which this new Kingdom would come.

As this would knock on the head all talk of messianic classes such as the proletariat, so it would just as decisively knock on the head all talk of "Aryan superiority." Between the assertion of the Jewish messianic race and the Aryan messianic race there is nothing to choose. Nothing except that the Jews have had a greater history and have contributed more than the Aryan. The moment we begin to talk of being a messianic race that moment we are eliminated as being the instrument of the coming of the new Kingdom. It is the old mentality and nothing new can come out of it.

Nor can the white race act as though they are a messianic color. The new Kingdom is color blind. It sees man and not the tincture of his skin. In a Round Table with ministers in America a Black woman arose and said: "I am Black. When I sat down here, a man got up and sat down over there. And he was a minister. How do you fit that in with Christianity?" The only answer is that it can be fitted in with the kind of thing we call Christianity, but with the Christianity of Christ it

> **The Messiah was the Son of man, and the sons of men would be the medium through which this new Kingdom would come.**

cannot be fitted in. When that Christian minister got up, Christ came and took his place, and he went and sat down where Christ was not sitting. He had isolated himself—from Christ. To the degree that the white race takes this attitude it renders itself unfit to be the instrument of the coming of this new classless society. You cannot bring in a brotherhood through snobberies.

I asked a Pullman porter on the train one day what he was reading and he replied, "A book on Bahaism."

"Why are you interested in Bahaism?" I asked.

"Because it teaches me brotherhood," was the answer.

"But doesn't Christianity teach you brotherhood?"

"Yes," he said, very slowly, "but not this kind, for this kind transcends race and color."

Inwardly I felt staggered as by a blow. The brotherhood of Christ turned into a racialism!

This is what we have reduced it to!

"These people won't listen to me anymore," complained a sweating Westerner as he had tried in vain to manage some workers. Of course not! He was talking the language of fifty years ago, and his speech was now growing unintelligible to self-respecting men. The only language that will command a hearing in the future is the language that speaks of and means brotherhood and equality for all. I saw a sign in a railway station in America which read,

Exit, White Only,
To Universal Cab Co.

But someone must have seen the incongruity of putting "universal" on that sign, which showed the way out to whites only, for he had partly painted it out. If we look on our gospel as a way out for whites only, then we must cross out of our gospel the word "universal." And if we cross out the word "universal," then we must leave out the word "true," for that which is not universal is not true, because truth by its very nature is universal. The moment you discover truth it rises above local and national boundaries and belongs to man as a man. Error by its nature is local. So when we make our gospel less than universal, we make it less than true.

Moreover, this new day will be brought in not by the bounty of the white man, but by the brotherhood of endeavor of all men. All people must not only benefit by this new day, they must also have a share in

204

bringing it in. Many of us are willing as white people to work on behalf of people of another race, but not with them. We are willing to be paternal but not fraternal. For Christian work on that basis satisfies a superiority complex. Someone asked a Black man about the possibility of the Black and the White man co-operating, to which he replied, "It's all right, but the white man does most of the 'operating' and we do the most of the 'co'-ing."

That sign in America is very like the one in Indian railway stations—"The Way Out for First and Second Class Passengers Only." There is no way out in the world situation for the upper and middle classes only. It leaves out the third class—the laborer. And without him there is no way out. Our present mess is the result of trying to find a way out for first and second classes only. The Communists have replied with a sign, "The Way Out for Third Class Only." They have answered an upper snobbery by a lower one. But in both cases it is a snobbery. The children of the intellectuals cannot get into the schools until the quota of the laborers' children has been filled. The Kingdom of God is different. Its sign is, "The Way Out for Humanity."

In Shanghai there used to be a sign on the Bund, put up by Western snobbery, "Chinese and dogs not allowed." It has now been removed. But a sign on a South Indian temple still exists, "Europeans and dogs not allowed." Between the white Brahmin and the brown Brahmin who would put up such signs there is nothing to choose. They both have eliminated themselves as far as having any real part in this new day is concerned. They are out of it— self-eliminated. Two sets of people are losing their prestige in the East: the Europeans and the Brahmins, who, in fact or in attitude, put up such signs. They are slipping. But the servants of all in both races are becoming the greatest of all. They are not slipping. They are rising.

A Hindu professor of a college told me he wanted to become a

Christian, and then added, "I was helped to this decision by listening to His Holiness, the Shankaracharya of Puri. He said in his lecture that 'it had been proved by microscopic examination that the blood of the Brahmin is different from the blood of the non-Brahmin; that the blood of the non-Brahmin is polluted and the blood of the Brahmin is pure.' This was in such contrast to what you said about God making of one blood all nations that dwell upon the face of the earth, and the insistence upon the worth of a man as a man, that I knew that the future belonged to your gospel and not to his." Trying to prove one's superiorities ends in one thing, namely, our elimination from further consideration. The future belongs to man and not to some men. This same Shankaracharya asked a leading Western Theosophist why the Vedanta philosophy was not spreading more in the West, and what could be done to encourage it to spread. The Theosophist replied: "I will answer it by asking you a question: Why do you stand off from me twenty feet, and why do you refuse to eat with me? That is the reason why Vedanta does not spread. It has at the heart of its universality a snobbery." He was right, for nothing will spread that has at its heart a snobbery, however refined and subtle it may be. A thoughtful Black man said to me, "With very rare exceptions, the white man can no longer teach religion to the African-Americans. They will either get it from their own people, or straight from the New Testament, or they will reject it entirely, as many are doing, in favor of Communism. The white man by his attitudes has eliminated himself as a religious teacher of our race."

After a group of us had toured the United States we were asked to give a message to the American people. One of our suggestions was that a beginning of racial equality in religion should be made by each white church inviting at least one member of the black race to become a member of that white church, and that, vice versa, each black church should invite at least one member of the white race to become a

206

member of the black church, and that these representatives should be the center of good will and understanding. As far as I know, this suggestion was not mentioned in any religious periodical of America. That silence was terribly eloquent. These same papers printed many, many columns about our being missionaries to the black races across the seas, but were deathly silent when it came to printing anything about their own people being missionaries at home on this vital racial issue.

The following incident was related to me by an American pastor of a Japanese church in America: We invited the Japanese consular officials to the dedication of the new Japanese church in Los Angeles. As I showed the Japanese consul around the building he said, "I really do not care much for church architecture, nor for the sermons you ministers give. It is enough for me if someone would really show me Jesus Christ." He was in earnest and apparently heart-hungry, so I replied that I would like to undertake that mission. He asked me to come to his official residence, where we would not be disturbed. On the appointed evening I went as agreed, but found him quite changed. Something had happened. He quite impatiently broke out with a severe condemnation of the hypocrisy, the falseness, and the weakness of our so-called Christian civilization, and said that he would have nothing to do with such a powerless religion. I asked him what the trouble was, and he told me that he had gone that day to a barber shop and had politely asked the barber to trim his hair. The barber replied, "We don't serve Japanese persons here." The consul then said: "That is strange. Why not?" The barber answered, "It would ruin my business." The consul continued: "Why, that cannot be true, for usually I go to the Biltmore Hotel, where they serve me gladly. It does not seem to ruin their business. Come now and tell me the real reason." Just then a big policeman, called by one of the other barbers, came in with: "Shush now, boy; be on your way. We don't want no trouble here." The consul replied: "There will be no trouble. When he tells me I will go." The policeman urged him out. He went out. But as he went out of the door he was so angry and disgusted that he closed the door of his heart to Jesus Christ.

Within a few weeks the consul was transferred to a department in the Foreign Office, Tokyo, then to Manchuria. Today he is vice-minister for foreign affairs for Manchukuo and personal adviser to the new emperor, Henry Pu Yi. I wonder what he advises the ruler of that land about the Christian faith? In "God's country" we treat a guest that way!

It is of no use to say that we are clean and others are not, for every race thinks the same. Some European ladies were urged to allow some Indian Muslim ladies to sit down on their reserved berth in the train, but they objected, saying that they were not clean. But finally they consented, and when the Indian Christian lady who was the mediator, explained to these Muslim ladies that the European ladies were now willing to have them sit next to them, they replied that they were sorry but they could not sit down because the European ladies were not clean!

Each thought the other unclean! They were both right. All of us are unclean. All of us of every race are convicted before the judgment of the ideal of the Kingdom of God. We have failed to bring it in and to embody it. Arrogance is entirely out of place when we face the fact that we have failed to bring in a just and brotherly world. There is no messianic race and there is no messianic class.

When we hear that a Japanese professor has spent thirty years in experimentation to prove that the Japanese are physically and mentally and morally superior to all other races, we smile, for it sounds so familiar. We have heard it before—out of our own race. When a commission of Turkish doctors bring in a report that notes that after careful examination they find the Turk is in every way superior to all others, we again smile. For it sounds so like the statement of an Englishman to me, "You know we don't think of comparing ourselves with anybody else, for we don't think there is anyone else in the same class with which to compare." Or, again, a Frenchman: "Beyond that which is found in the modern Frenchman the human race will not progress." Fichte tells the Germans: "Among all modern peoples it is you in whom the germ of perfecting humanity most decidedly lies. ... If you perish as a nation, all the hopes of the entire human race will perish with you." Now the Bulgarian: "In the string of recorded events the biggest beads standing out most conspicuously are the literature and the culture created in Bulgaria." The American dares call his country "God's country." The New Zealander goes one better—he calls his country "God's own country." The Hottentots call themselves "the men of men;" the Eskimos call themselves "the complete people." The Dutch believe that "God talks Dutch," while the Armenians say that "you might as well learn Armenian; it will save you time, for the language of heaven is Armenian." A European lady said to me concerning a Hindu, "Doctor K— is a nice man; he has a European soul." Those two things, "European" and "nice," were synonymous! Any other soul would not have been nice. The Indian replies in the person of the Sikhs, who, when they went to America, took some of the holy soil of India with them, and wore it between their feet and the unholy soil of America, so that they were walking on the holy soil of India all the time as they were walking on the unholy soil of the West. An American was asked by a Scotchman in Scotland where he came from and replied proudly, "From God's country." The Scotchman looked at him in amazement and replied, "Then you must have lost your accent." The Santal tribe in India call the Santal people "men" and all others "enemies." This reminds us of the division made by the Communists of all men into "Proletariat" and "Enemies."

Let us grant that at the heart of that division into "Proletariat" and "Enemies" there is a sacred cause, and that through that cause they are trying to wipe out all exploitation and finally all classes. But we must remember that at the heart of every other division in the above statements was what, to the holders of those divisions, seemed to be a sacred cause. Let us grant that the Communist division into "Proletariat" and "Enemies" is as sacred as any, and perhaps more so, nevertheless that does not make it any the less dangerous. In the end the cause may be spoiled by the messianic class which attempts to bring it in. Therefore Jesus refused to identify his Kingdom with any special class or race. In doing so he set it into the very center of the world heart, for the Kingdom of God is the final standard and judges those who bring it in as well as those for whom it is brought in.

As Jesus said to the special messianic race which wanted to be the sole instruments of the coming of the Kingdom, that God was not confined to them and prophets were sent to those outside their race, so he would say to the proletariat today that God's prophets are going to those outside their class; that their class can be one of the instruments, but only one of the instruments, for the coming of the new day; and that the Kingdom judges the proletariat, their spirit and their methods, exactly as it would judge others. Man as man will bring in the new day, for it is going to be the new day of man and not the new day of a class. Since it belongs to man when it comes, it will have to belong to man in the coming. What he would say to the proletariat he would also say to the white races who are exclusive even in their charities—"You are willing to work for other races but not with them."

Turning from messianic races and classes to messianic denominations among Christians, the same thing may be said. The attitudes which the proletariat have taken in Russia can be paralleled in our religious denominations, both Protestant and Catholic. We are

210

willing for the new Kingdom to come, provided we can lead it in. Like the disciples of Jesus we forbid others from casting out devils from human society, "for they follow not us." The disciples of old were willing that the devils should stay in if the former were not to be the instruments of getting them out. In their minds the end was not the getting out of the devils, but their group staying on top through the getting out of those devils. They were afraid that the other group would get out more devils than they got out, and so receive a greater name and a greater place. Through the getting out of devils ran an ulterior purpose. There is scarcely anything holding back the new day so much as each denomination looking on itself as a messianic group through which the new day will especially, and perhaps exclusively, come. That is the core of the problem of divisiveness in religion. We all believe in Christ, we all believe in his Kingdom and its

> **If God should let us have our way, what we should have in the end would not be the Kingdom of man, but the kingdom of a denomination, which would not be the Kingdom of God.**

coming—so far we are one; but the divisiveness comes at the point of each denomination insisting, by its attitudes, that it be the special instrument of its coming. If God should let us have our way, what we should have in the end would not be the Kingdom of man, but the kingdom of a denomination, which would not be the Kingdom of God. The Kingdom would be reduced to something else by the very instrument of its coming. There is no messianic group—not even the Oxford Group! One of their members said that there was a race on throughout the world between Communism and the Oxford Group—

as if the Oxford Group were synonymous with the Kingdom of God! It is a very vital part of that Kingdom, and we are grateful beyond words for it, but it is not synonymous with the Kingdom.

I have come to the place where I do not want the Kingdom of God to come in as a Methodist Kingdom of God. Someone said over the radio that I had said that I did not want Mahatma Gandhi to become a Christian. What I had said was that I did not want him to become a Methodist. Unfortunately, or fortunately, those two terms are not synonymous! I am grateful beyond words for the contribution which the Methodists have made and are still making in their emphasis on warm, living, personal experience of God, but that is not the sum total of the Kingdom of God, and to make it a Methodist Kingdom would be to impoverish it. But just as strongly do I hope that the Kingdom of God will not be brought in exclusively, or even particularly, by any other denomination. That too would impoverish it. Each must give its contribution to that which is bigger than all, the Kingdom of God.

One hesitates to put his finger on a sore spot in such a sacred scene as this one. For participating in that scene were his honored friends and fellow Christians, the laces of whose shoes he is not worthy to unloose. But the hour to speak in behalf of real unity, and not a fictitious one, has come. This from the Church of England Newspaper of July 13, 1934:

> Last Sunday was an unforgettable day. It began with the Holy Communion for all the House Parties on one of the lawns of the beautiful Lady Margaret Hall. I wish I could describe this great service so that readers might get something like a correct picture and grasp its meaning and significance. More forcefully than ever it was borne in upon me that here was an illustration of the fulfillment of our Lord's Prayer— 'That they all may be one.' There must have been fifteen hundred people present. That in itself was an inspiring sight, but far more remarkable was the fact that not only many denominations, but many

nationalities were represented. Here was unity indeed—a marvelous, living picture of the great family of the one Father partaking of the one Bread and the one Cup—the perfectly cloudless sky symbolizing the joy of heaven at a sight so fair. I could not help exclaiming, 'Would to God that this were normal instead of being abnormal!' If it were, then the world would come to believe in the risen Christ as the world's Savior. What a tragedy that we persist in our devil-inspired divisions!

However, I noted that the *The Anglican Prayer Book of Service* was used almost in its entirety, the celebrant being the Metropolitan of India, assisted by eleven priests of the Anglican Communion.

Was no one else outside that Communion participating? Had anyone suggested that since we wanted unity, and that since there were members of many denominations present for the partaking of the communion, there should also be some of the clergymen of these denominations associated with the Anglican clergymen on the basis of equality—that simple and obvious suggestion would have derailed the whole affair. It would never have taken place. We want unity, provided we can be the messianic denomination to bring in that unity, for that would leave us at the top when the unity took place. The clergymen of the Anglican Church, and no others, leading in this unity, and leading themselves to the leadership of that Kingdom! That Kingdom would be something other than the Kingdom of God—it would be the Kingdom of Anglicanism. Our divisions may be "devil-inspired," but of this kind of unity the kindest thing one can say is that it is hardly more than denomination-inspired. As deeply appreciative of the Anglican Church as I am, it would stretch that appreciation too far to make that church synonymous with the Kingdom of God. No, this is not the unity offered by the Kingdom of God.

We shall have to wait till our eyes are open and we see the unity of that Kingdom.

I have seen some of that sort of unity in our Round Table Conferences, where Christians and non-Christians come together and tell what religion is meaning to them in experience. After listening in for fourteen years to what the Christians of the various denominations have said, I have noted that when we drop down beneath the level of organization and church polity and creed, down to the level of experience, there the Christians are the most united body on earth, if they only know it. They are united in the deepest thing in life, namely, in life itself. They share a common life, the closest bonds that ever bound men together. They do not have to seek for unity, they have it, not accidentally and marginally, but fundamentally and centrally. We have, then, the strange anomaly that the people who are most united at the center are most divided at the margin.

The fact is that in that scene at Oxford there was an amazing underlying unity in a common experience of the living Christ. It was a unity that underlay all their denominational differences. That unity was theirs, before that Communion service took place and after it was over. The medium of the expression of that unity—the Anglican Communion service and priesthood, and that alone—was too small to express that unity. As Leith says, "Under the sea the islands are one, under the surface humanity, under the creeds is the love of God."

In our Round Table Conferences we have discovered that the saints are about equally distributed among all the denominations. If you were to ask me where saints are most thickly congregated, for the life of me I couldn't tell you. No denomination has any corner on the saints. It seems as though God sometimes works through the denomination, sometimes in spite of it, but never exclusively or particularly in any one of them. If that statement hurts our denominational pride, it may help our Christian humility!

It seems certain that God is not going to use exclusively any

214

denomination—Protestant or Catholic—or any religious group, Oxford or otherwise— to bring in the Kingdom of God. If he did, it wouldn't be the Kingdom of God when it came. For the Kingdom is bigger than and deeper than any one of these denominations—or all of them put together. Each of them holds within itself a phase of the Kingdom, but must not be identified with the whole. The Kingdom of God stands above and judges every denomination or group.

In our Ashram we have discovered that there are two ways to find truth. One is to put forth your truth, press it to a decision, and the majority rules. But this always leaves a disgruntled minority with the feeling that their particular truth has been excluded or neglected. The other is to pool our truths and see if we cannot come to a common mind. In taking that attitude we usually find ourselves emerging with a larger truth than the one we brought to the group. But we have not only discovered a larger truth, we have also discovered a larger fellowship.

> **It seems certain that God is not going to use exclusively any denomination— Protestant or Catholic—or any religious group, Oxford or otherwise— to bring in the Kingdom of God. If he did, it wouldn't be the Kingdom of God when it came.**

The first attitude has been largely the attitude of the denominations. There is little hope in it, for there is little or no likelihood of the world deciding in favor of any one of them. The hope seems to lie in the second attitude. In that way the truth that each holds will be preserved and added to the common store. We should say to each denomination, "We do not want you to give up your special truth; we want you to give it to the rest of us." Out of these differing types of Christianity would grow a larger Christianity. It would be sufficient for its world task because it would have within it universal elements in a living blend.

I spoke in a Presbyterian College in North India and at the close the Presbyterian chairman said, "The speaker tonight has emphasized God's side in conversion, but I don't think he has sufficiently emphasized man's side." He proceeded to emphasize it. At the close I went to him and said: "My brother, the battle is all over. We have changed sides. You, a Calvinist, emphasize man's side in conversion, and I, an Arminian (whatever that is), emphasize God's side in conversion. The battle is all over." We had taken each other's truth and were the better for it. These battles must cease by our taking the other man's truth, and out of it all growing something that is more akin to the Kingdom of God.

As Jesus re-announces the Kingdom of God and sees that there are expectations among the denominational hearers that they will constitute the messianic group to bring in this new day, he says again that there have been many members of that denomination in the world and yet God has sent the prophets to those outside that denomination. As God is not going to bring in the new day by any messianic race or class, so he is not going to bring it in by any messianic denomination. For it will be a Kingdom of the Son of man, and it will take all the sons of men to interpret that Son of man.

But if there is to be no messianic class or race or denomination, neither is there going to be any messianic organized religion, even if that be the organized Christian religion which will bring in the new day.

In its ideal state the Christian religion and the Kingdom of God would be synonymous, a statement which I could not make of any other faith. But we are not now thinking of it in that ideal state, but in the real, the thing before us. We have built up around Christ what we now call Christianity. This system of creed and rite and culture which we have built up around Christ in the West only more or less reflects his spirit. Again and again it falls away from him and reflects anything but his spirit. In his name we have done some of the most wonderful things that adorn the pages of human history, also the most stupid and cruel. To the original Christian spirit we have mixed a good many other spirits—good, bad, and indifferent. It is this we call Christianity.

In its ideal state the Christian religion and the Kingdom of God would be synonymous, a statement which I could not make of any other faith.

Is this religion which we have built up around Christ to be the messianic religion through which the new day will come, and through it alone? I question it. For if that were true, then the organized Christian religion and the other religions would fight it out to a finish, with the organized Christian religion triumphant in the end. If what we have now as the organized Christian religion—if that were triumphant, would it be synonymous with the Kingdom of God? Surely not. The Kingdom of God judges the organized Christian religion just as it judges other systems, and again and again it stands condemned in the light of that judgment.

The fact is that Jesus never came to found a religion. He never uses the term "religion," either in its Aramaic form or in its Greek equivalent. He therefore did not come to set one religion over against

217

another religion. He came to set the Kingdom of God against all other ways of life, to judge them, to change them, and finally conform them to its reign. The Kingdom of God is larger than the organized Christian religion and breaks out beyond it.

Do not misunderstand me. I am persuaded that the Christian religion, even as it is now organized with all its faults, has more of the Kingdom of God within it than any other system. It has within it the noblest ideals, the finest character, and the most self-giving service to the human race of any religious system. Moreover, it holds within its very earthen vessel the greatest of all treasures, namely, the fact of the self-giving of God in redemptive act in the cross of Christ. Nevertheless, the Kingdom of God and the organized Christian religion are not synonymous, nor coterminous. I repeat that the Christian religion in its ideal state

> **The fact is that Jesus never came to found a religion. He never uses the term "religion," either in its Aramaic form or in its Greek equivalent. He therefore did not come to set one religion over against another religion. He came to set the Kingdom of God against all other ways of life...**

would be, but I am not dealing with that ideal system, but with the one built up around Jesus Christ which we have before us now. God was working through other systems of religion before the organized Christian religion came into being. Nor is he confined to it now. "God hath not left himself without witness among any nation." Nor is he leaving himself without witness in many an incomplete system of religion.

"Ah, then," you ask, "is Christianity only a way or is it the way?" My reply is that if we mean by Christianity that system which we have built up around Christ as his gospel has gone through the world, then I would say it is a way. But if you ask whether Christ and his Kingdom are a way or the Way, then I must reply that I am convinced that they are the Way. I put them together because Christ and the Kingdom are one. He embodied the Kingdom and interprets it in his own person and words. I believe him to be the final person and that Kingdom to be the final order. But the system which we have built up around him I do not conceive to be final. Christ's Kingdom breaks out beyond the borders of what we have built up as the Christian religion. Sometimes there is more of the Spirit of Christ in movements apart from the organized Christian religion than within it.

> Do not misunderstand me. I am persuaded that the Christian religion, even as it is now organized with all its faults, has more of the Kingdom of God within it than any other system.

God is not confined to this system in order to bring in his Kingdom. I am persuaded that it may be the chief instrument, but not the sole instrument of the coming of his Kingdom. When the Western world was sunk in armaments and the church seemed a part of that war spirit, God reached out and laid hold on Mahatma Gandhi and through him let us see some of the meanings underlying the Sermon on the Mount. A Hindu once said to me: "We should exchange sacred books—you of the West should take the Bhagavad-Gita, for it teaches war, and we of the East should take the New Testament, for it teaches men to love their enemies. It would suit us both better." India has learned to appreciate the ideas underlying the Sermon on the Mount through Mahatma Gandhi. Not entirely of course, but in very great measure. To the degree that the Mahatma has caught the meaning of the Kingdom, to that degree is he a part of that Kingdom. But the Kingdom of God judges Mahatma Gandhi just as it judges the rest of us.

When the Western world was floundering in an unjust and sub-Christian order, and the church was bound up with it and was a part of that order, God reached out and put his hand on the Russian Communists to awaken our minds and souls and to show a recumbent church what it has missed in its own Gospel. That does not mean that God, or we, can approve all they have in that order, nor all they have done to bring that order into being, but it does mean that God through the Communists is judging the injustices and wrongs inherent in our present system. To the degree that the Communists have caught the meanings of the Kingdom of God and have embodied them they are a part of that Kingdom, even if they repudiate that Kingdom in the very act of embodying some of its ideals. Borodin said to a Christian interviewer in China, "We Communists are trying to bring in the Kingdom of God by force, while you Christians are trying to bring it in by love." The Communists would in all probability repudiate that, but that does not mean that God may not use those who repudiate him when there are no other instruments at hand for him to utilize. Certainly the Russian Church could never have been the instrument of a new day. In Baku the Communists have closed the beautiful cathedral, but have left the picture of the Czar on the front of it, in order to let the people see how religion was bound up with the old discredited order. The Old Testament depicts God saying of Cyrus, the pagan

Persian King, "I have girded thee, though thou hast not known me." It may be that God is girding peoples today who do not know him, because those who do know him will not respond to him. But the Kingdom of God will judge the Communists and the Communistic order in Russia, just as it judges the rest of us, and while many a fundamental attitude will come under its approval, many an attitude and act will come under its condemnation and will have to be eliminated from the final order.

I believe that the Christian should work with anyone who is trying to bring in the new order, under whatever name he may work, believing that in the end the Kingdom of God will conquer us all. We believe the Kingdom of God is synonymous with the Kingdom of Christ. In that faith we work.

> **But the Kingdom of God will judge the Communists... just as it judges the rest of us, and while many a fundamental attitude will come under its approval, many an attitude and act will come under its condemnation...**

In thinking over the people who had influenced me particularly this last year three men arose above others: Kagawa, Gandhi, and Booker T. Washington. Not one of them was a member of my race, and one of them was not a member of my faith. But each of them introduced me to some phase of the Kingdom which I needed. How much poorer I would have been had these men never lived! And how much poorer a thing the Kingdom of God would be if only one class, or one race, or one denomination, or even one religious system, should bring it in. The adoption of that inclusive mentality will not be easy for some of us who have been brought up to believe in the finality of our religious system. But we can learn it if we feel that we are working for something beyond all of us. Someone asked an engineer in Russia how he could be content to work with men inferior to himself, and who though inferior were getting higher wages. He replied, "I can do it because we are making a new world." That is the spirit which should take hold of us as we make this new world-order.

That does not mean that we as Christians have a syncretism at the center of our faith. At that center we hold an undivided allegiance to Jesus Christ as sole Lord and Savior and as the Way. But that does not mean that, while holding that faith, we cannot work with those who do not hold it, but who are making some contribution toward bringing in the Kingdom of God in some of its phases. We must come together and welcome every man of every race, of every class, of every faith into the fellowship of those who work for the coming of the Kingdom of God. In our Ashram is this motto on the wall:

> Here we enter a fellowship,
> Sometimes we will agree to differ,
> Always we will resolve to love,
> And unite to serve.

A part of that motto came from China; we in India added the first line. Is this not what we are to do—take each partial conception of the Kingdom of God and add to it until it all grows to that which is beyond all, namely, the Kingdom itself?

Another motto on the Ashram walls is this:

> Leave behind all race and class distinctions,
> Ye that enter here.

That motto is at the threshold of this new Order we are about to enter. But it is not only written over the door of the Kingdom itself, it is also written over the door of the recruiting office where men are recruited as workers to bring in this Kingdom. Here too we must leave behind all race and class distinctions, for those distinctions will not be in the end if they are eliminated from the means.

"But," someone objects, "how can you get those classes to work together for the coming of a classless society without those very classes passing over into the end ?" But is there any way to get rid of those very classes except to get men of all classes to work together for something bigger than themselves? In discovering that Kingdom will they not discover themselves—and each other? Will not those who strive to bring in a classless society in all probability be converted away from classes as they strive to convert others? Will we not recognize that since we will have to live together when it comes we will have to live together in its coming? The only alternative is the supremacy of one class and the suppression of all others—a method which we reject. The Christian end is to produce a society where each is the servant of all. That end can be reached by inviting all to serve all.

Jesus was the great believer in man. He had an astonishing faith in people. He put together in his discipleship Simon the Zealot, the ardent revolutionary patriot, the communist of today; and Matthew, the tax-gatherer. And he expected something to happen to them—and it did! Each with his partial view finally emerged into something bigger than he brought to it: the Kingdom of God. In the end they belonged to that society which was of one heart and one soul, brethren who had all things in common and saw that no man had need. Working together they finally came together. They were far apart when they began, but were of one heart and one soul when they ended. The Kingdom had conquered them.

The method Jesus used was this: he let them see through himself into the heart of goodness, which was the Kingdom. And "when a man

223

has seen deeply into the soul of goodness, then the idea of distinctions becomes intolerable, and barriers of race, class, or government seem to him an affront to human dignity."

But the people in the synagogue had not yet seen into the heart of goodness—they saw only a good opportunity for racial self-assertion through the movement of this new prophet, Jesus, and were bitterly disappointed when he refused to identify his Kingdom with race or class. They listened to truth until it cut across their race and class distinctions, then they closed up.

We must now deal with situations and persons that close up when the Kingdom, in all its blinding glory, meets them.

CHAPTER 10

WILL CHRIST BEAR THE STRAIN?

Most of us are willing to listen to truth until it cuts across our race and class prejudices, and then we too close up. Thinking thus becomes for many of us just "a rearranging of our prejudices." But that morning in the synagogue these prejudices did not merely rearrange themselves; they flared into anger and into action. "To the brow of the hill with him!" They were blinded by the burning radiance of this new vision of new humanity, and being used to the dark they struck out blindly at the Light. If this were the meaning of religion, then away with it! To the brow of the hill with this Young Dreamer! So "they led him unto the brow of the hill whereon their city was built that they might cast him down headlong."

Stand with man as man, and man as class will stand against you. The Son of man would take all men to the heights of privileges and a full life, and therefore some men took him to the brow of the precipice. Strange world this! Religion in him would arouse impulses that would lead men to make a new world for all men; religion in them aroused impulses that led them to try to send out of the world the Man who would remake it. The light in them had turned to darkness, and how great was that darkness! On the sacred hill of Tirupati in South India the Brahmin will show you a black rock which was once a low-caste man who attempted to climb the sacred hill and was struck dead by the offended god whose sacredness was polluted by the aspiring outcaste. Thus has manmade religion into sacred privileges, and anyone who tries to share them is struck dead. Here in the synagogue that morning they tried to strike dead the Man who would open the sacred hills of life to all men as men.

But as they were about to cast Jesus down he turned and looked at them. He just looked at them. But that look was enough. It is said that Florence Nightingale, nursing the sick soldiers of the Crimea, broke the rules when the rules stood between her and the helping of sick and dying men. "What right have you to touch those stores?" thundered a mounted officer as he saw this slim young woman hurrying across a courtyard with a can of arrowroot in her arms. The young woman stopped and set her can down and looked at the impressive figure and continued to look out of her clear gray eyes, and said not a word. The officer silently turned his horse and drove off. Then Florence Nightingale picked up her can of arrowroot and went about her Father's business. Jesus did that. He looked at them. There was something so tender and yet so terrible in those quiet eyes. He had seen the sick and wounded world in those forty days of struggle, and he also saw what he could do for them, so there was a new world in those eyes. When the people saw it, they were afraid, so the crowd parted and fell back. "But he passing through the midst of them went his way." That blind, narrow, home prejudice closed in on him to block and to break him and his new Kingdom, but he passed through the midst of that gathered hate and blindness and went his way—went his way to the founding of his Kingdom. They could not stop Jesus then. Nor can we today. We can hinder him, but we cannot stop him. He passed through the midst of their littleness then, and he is passing through the midst of our littleness today. And as we see his eyes look into ours we see in them the new Humanity. And we are afraid—afraid of Sanity!

Note how again and again Jesus' disciples closed in on him and tried to block him and his Kingdom. The Samaritans refused to receive him into their village because his face was set toward Jerusalem. "Wilt thou that we call down fire from heaven and consume them?" angrily asked his disciples. They would meet race prejudice with hate and with fire. True, they put a religious aroma around their own race hate—it was "fire from heaven," and they quoted a religious precedent, "even as Elijah did." By their attitudes they closed in on him, and would block the broadness of his spirit, and would put "the day of vengeance" back into his program when he had deliberately left it out. "You know not what spirit you are of," Jesus quietly said, as he passed through the midst of them to go his way to the founding of a raceless and classless society, where Samaritans would be conquered not by hate and fire, but by love.

Again the disciples tried to block his plans and make them something other than he announced. They disputed which of them should be greatest in the new Kingdom, making the Kingdom into a Kingdom of the Privileged instead of a Kingdom of the Great-through-Service. He turned and rebuked them and told them that they could be great in the Kingdom only as they became the servants of all, and passing through the midst of their privilege-saturated thinking he went his way to the founding of the Kingdom of the Servers.

Then came the supreme attempt to block him and his Kingdom when the nation combined to stop him by a cross. Christ and Evil met face to face that day. There stood before him and his Kingdom incarnate Evil: the Pharisee—proud, hard outwardism; the Sadducee—shrewd materialism; the Chief Priests—vested interests; the

Herodians—political sycophancy; the scribes—letter-worship of the past; Pontius Pilate—imperialism demanding supreme allegiance; the People—apathy against change; the Soldiers—militarism, hard and unrelenting. They all combined to stop him and his subversive Kingdom. But even on a cross he was master of the situation: he opened the gates of paradise to a dying thief, dispensed forgiveness to his murderers, made provision for his mother's sustenance, and showed such regnancy that the officer in charge of the tragedy smote his breast and said that Jesus was the Son of God. God and the officer agreed, and the sign of that agreement is an Easter morning. Stop Jesus by a cross? He used that very cross to redeem a world. He passed through the midst of them to go his way to found his Kingdom and that in spite of!

For forty days after his resurrection he stayed with his disciples to implant within their minds the basic conceptions and the amazing sweep of his Kingdom—"He had . . . shown himself . . . and speaking of the Kingdom of God" (Acts 1: 3, Weymouth). At the end of these forty days of instruction the disciples showed that their hearts were too small for it: "Lord, will you at this time restore again the kingdom to Israel?" How his heart must have been stunned by the question! After all these years of patient instruction they still clung to the fundamental mistake the people had made in the synagogue in the beginning. His disciples did not reject the Kingdom, they simply sought to reduce it, to reduce it from a world Kingdom to a Kingdom of a race supremacy. He must have seen that his Calvaries were not over, that the deepest tragedies were yet to come, and that those tragedies would center in that very spirit, the spirit that would reduce this new Kingdom to the commonplace. They would not reject it; they would simply render it innocuous. They would inoculate men with a mild form of Christianity so that they would become immune against the real thing. I have used interpreters for languages which I understood sufficiently to know what the interpreters were saying. Some of them would heighten what I had to say and would make it more pointed and telling, and some would flatten it out into a dull commonplace set of platitudes. As I have heard my words thus flattened out I have looked at my interpreter and have inwardly said, "Is that all I said?" And in that hour I have almost always felt Christ looking at me and reminding me of the many, many times that I have flattened out his thrilling challenge into a dull commonplace, as he too has said, "Is that all?"

His disciples in that day and this try to reduce the Kingdom, but Jesus passed then and passes now through the midst of that smallness of soul to go his way to the establishment of his real Kingdom and not a reduced form.

In a new sense Jesus went his way when his disciples opened their spirits and consented to have them enlarged by the incoming of the Spirit at Pentecost. From that moment he did not need to go through the midst of them—he went

> **Stop Jesus by a cross? He used that very cross to redeem a world. He passed through the midst of them to go his way to found his Kingdom and that in spite of!**

with them, in the midst of them. They were going with him! A new society was emerging, the walls between Jew and Gentile were down, out of the two a new man was being formed, a new brotherhood; the barriers between economic classes were no more—they had all things common and to each was distributed as he had need; the inferiority and superiority based on gender was in the process of being dissolved, for in Jesus Christ "there is neither male nor female." At the basis of all this was love. A society had at last emerged out of which strife and jealousy and hate and classes and poverty and snobberies had been wholly eliminated: "They were of one heart and one soul."

Here was the Kingdom in miniature. It had within it the germs of a new world. Justin Martyr could say in 150 A. D., "We who formerly slew one another not only do not make war against our enemies, but, for the sake of not telling lies or deceiving those who examine us, gladly die confessing Christ." Christians even offered to serve the sentences of others. "Behold how these Christians love one another," cried the pagan in astonishment, and they might have added, "and others." It was a glorious day and the whole thing might have flowered into a new world. The germ was there. But, as Bernard Shaw once said, "The trouble with Jesus was that he had disciples," disciples who, instead of giving rein to the implications of the Kingdom, twisted it or reduced it.

A new cross awaited the Crucified. Jesus who founded the Kingdom on the basis of overcoming evil with good and hate by love and the world by a cross of suffering for the world had to see his Kingdom turned into something else. The attempt was made to militarize that very Kingdom. Cadoux says that "no Christian ever thought of enlisting in the army after conversion until the reign of Marcus Aurelius (161-180 A. D.), and with one or two possible exceptions no soldier joined the church and remained a soldier until that time." But by 416 A. D. no one but a Christian was allowed in the army of Rome! Christianity and the military spirit were fused until Christianity became the banner of aggressive chiefs. Lecky says that at the baptism of pagan tribes in Europe, "the arms of the males were carefully held above water that the more deadly blow might be struck." Those arms were not Christianized, for they were the fighting arms. Saint Bernard could say, "The Christian glories in the death of the infidel because Christ is thus glorified." And the matter of the sainthood of Bernard is not thereby called in question. Anselm could write of Ribermont in reference to the Crusades, "Our men returning in victory, and bearing many heads fixed upon spikes, furnished a joyful spectacle to the people of God." Statues of bishops, panoplied in armor, and sitting on their war horses with drawn swords, still adorn European cities. They still adorn these cities because that conception of Christianity has been in our hearts. It was there during the last war when we prayed to a tribal god instead of to the Father of our Lord Jesus Christ.

But something has got hold of us. It is the terrible fact of Christ. When the Peace Treaty was being signed at Versailles, I said in a church in Calcutta: "At the Peace Table stands Christ in the shadows— watching, noting. If they read his mind and spirit into that Peace Treaty, it will endure; but if they read hate and revenge into it, 'Time' will come along and tear it up as a scrap of paper." They did refuse to read his mind into it—did not Clemençeau sneer that "Wilson talked like Jesus Christ"? So they made the great refusal. Time has come along and has torn up that Treaty and today it is a scrap of paper. When Bernard Shaw was asked about Jesus Christ, he replied, "The recent revolt against Jesus Christ in the last war has turned out so badly that probably more people are thinking about Jesus than ever before." They are. The eyes of the world are being slowly but surely opened. The war lords may talk of war, but something has got hold of us. We see more clearly now. The Raja of ———, a tiny state in India, during a drunken feast ordered his men off to fight the British. The British got wind of it, marched out and sent the soldiers quietly back to their state. It seems ridiculous that a drunken Raja has the power to send off soldiers to fight against overwhelming odds, but it is no more ridiculous than what Lloyd George writes of General Neville commanding the Allied Armies: "General Neville in December was a cool and cautious planner.

231

By April he had become a crazy gambler. He was in a state of inebriated exaltation which destroyed his poise. . . . This state of mind accounts for the silly offensives of the war and for the reckless squandering of the youth of France." Between a drunken Raja and an inebriated general there is nothing to choose, and the mind of the world will one day eliminate both. Against that drunken insanity stands the awful sanity of Jesus, and one day men will turn to that sanity as the only way out.

The process of disentangling Jesus Christ from the war spirit is now taking place. The announcement of many of the churches of America that they withdraw from the whole war system, and will have nothing to do with it in the future, is a symptom of that disentangling. Jesus is passing through the midst of the war lords, and through his church which has betrayed him at that point, and is going his way to found a Kingdom in which war will have no place or part. We have hindered Jesus, we have crucified his spirit, we have shot his Kingdom to pieces on a thousand battlefields, but in the end we cannot stop Jesus. We may not be able to give up to him, but we certainly are not able to give him up. He has got hold of us, and we know that if we ever revolt against him again in another war, it will not be revolt—it will be ruin.

But it is not merely in the matter of the use of force that he is passing through the midst of us to go his way; it is also in the conception of authority. The question of what constitutes authority is basic in the new humanity. A wrong conception of authority may poison it. Jesus began his new society with the fundamental idea at the basis of it that only those shall have authority over the rest who win it by service to the rest. It was a society of the servers, and the greatest server would be inherently the greatest, and therefore would have the authority of that very greatness. Authority was not something given and invested from without, but something won from within. The spirit of subservience and slave-mentality would fade out, for all would be on an equal basis, since all could have this kind of authority if they earned it through self-giving. Alas, all this was changed and we have the spectacle of church dignitaries claiming supreme authority on various textual or tactual grounds, and lording it over others on that basis, and excommunicating where it was not implicitly obeyed. It is a sorry sight. Mahatma Gandhi coming back from Europe through Italy said, "And how I should have liked to have paid my respects to the representative of Christ, crucified at the Vatican."

The newspapers put in that fatal comma! And yet, and yet, there is truth in that comma, for Christ has been crucified at the Vatican, and all other Christian places, Protestant or otherwise, where a struggle for authority has gone on. It may be religious authority, but it is not Christian authority when we have to struggle for it. One does not struggle for it. One does not struggle for Christian authority; we serve it. There is a fundamental difference.

> **Jesus began his new society with the fundamental idea at the basis of it that only those shall have authority over the rest who win it by service to the rest.**

Two Indian Ranis (princesses) were anxious to succeed to the chairmanship of a Woman's Society, and they were both upon the platform. One moved her chair a little forward and the other, to be sure that the first one did not get ahead of her in any way, did the same. Again the first one moved her chair forward, and the second followed suit. This process went on till the audience, sensing the situation, was inwardly bursting with laughter. As church people have edged to the front with claims of validities and divine authorities the world has watched the spectacle with mingled amusement and contempt. They have seen themselves in all this, and what they wanted to see in Christians was something different.

All the time Jesus has had to go through the midst of a similar situation to go his way to found a Kingdom of the Servers. In spite of the crucifixion of his spirit by his followers he is winning. On a widespread scale men are sensing the inherent and final truth that no man should command who does not serve. The Rotarians see this, however dimly it may be, when they say that no one has a right to profits unless it is based on service. The British have decided that the Prime Minister shall have the greatest authority, because he is the Prime (First) Minister (Servant), the First Servant. The Communists have brought us a step nearer when they say that no one shall have the franchise unless he is a worker, a server. So in spite of the seizing of authority by dictators, and other manifestations of the same spirit, there is an undertone of world understanding that the future belongs to the contributors, that sooner or later all exploiters, all parasites, all who live on the toil and contributions of others must and will be eliminated, and those only can command who serve. When that spirit becomes universal, we shall all be at the feet of Jesus who came not to be ministered unto but to minister and to give his life a ransom for many. The facts in the end will drive us to Christ's feet. In a world where mutual service is the final law of survival the Son of Man will be king. If love is the end toward which all things must move, then in the end all things must lead us to Love.

There are other things on account of which he has had to pass through the midst of us. Jesus founded his Kingdom on open inquiry and moral and spiritual experimentation. He who was "willing to do the will" should "know of the teaching." He did not present a fixed creed which men had to believe or be damned. He presented himself and his new Kingdom, and as men trusted him and fellowshipped with him, and caught his way of living, they found upon their lips a new word— "Savior," for he was actually saving them here and now from gloom and despair and from themselves and from their sins. They found themselves there by actual experimentation. His words had come out of life and they spoke to life. Men believed him to be a revelation of God, because he actually revealed God. It was all so free and open and experimental and vital. Then came the period of hardening when orthodoxy became more important than orthopraxy. Most of the original moral and spiritual experimentalism gave way to tradition and to letter-conformity. Men's minds were not allowed to function in religion. Religion became in the minds of the more discerning the great docility, the great dimming, the great superstition. Galileo had to repent on bended knees of his scientific discoveries.

> **Jesus founded his Kingdom on open inquiry and moral and spiritual experimentation.... He did not present a fixed creed which men had to believe or be damned.**

Then came the great awakening— the Renaissance. The mind of man was loosed from its fetters and told to inquire. It did. And religion seemed doomed. The goddess of Reason was set up by the French Revolutionists as the new deity of the new day. But a strange thing happened. Instead of this blinding light of reason dimming Christ, he stood out as never before. He had been dimmed in the atmosphere of tradition and closed-mindedness. His gospel was gasping for breath in this stuffy atmosphere. It was not its native air. It longed for the open air, for the hillsides where men could look around at God's world and could think his thoughts and inquire with open mind after Christ's purposes. When the bands were removed from the minds of men, they found their thoughts turning to him as the needle turns to the pole. More men accepted him in the last century as their guide in life than they had in the previous nine centuries. On the very day that the French Revolutionists were tearing down the image of the Virgin from the Cathedral in Paris, William Carey was sailing up the Hooghly River to found this new Kingdom in India; and that Kingdom was founded on enlightenment. Carey published, published, and published again. He laid the foundation of this Kingdom which I see growing up before my very eyes in India. It was no chance that the foundations of modern education in India were laid by Christian missionaries. Nor was it a chance that ninety per cent of the colleges of America were founded by religious denominations. Christ instead of being overthrown by the broader knowledge was coming back through that very knowledge.

A child of this Renaissance was the movement of Biblical Criticism. This new movement seemed to destroy the very foundations upon which the gospel rested. The battle has been fierce and bitter. In the midst of it one critic in dying said, "I am glad to die, for there won't be a rag of faith left by the next generation." At this period Carlyle stopped by a wayside shrine in Italy and gazed at an image of Christ hanging on his cross and then thoughtfully said: "Poor Fellow! You have had your day." It seemed that Jesus had had his day. But Carlyle lived to see that he had made a mistake, that Christ's day was just beginning. This critical movement, instead of preparing Christ for burial, as many thought, was in many ways loosing the grave clothes to let him go. We saw that it left "free from mists the permanent stars behind." Voltaire said that within a hundred years there would not be a Bible in existence. On the very spot where he said this there is a Bible House selling what today is "the best seller" of the world. The house

236

where Ingersoll wrote his *Mistakes of Moses* has been torn down and a Y.M.C.A. is in its place. Why? Well, men saw that this critical movement, instead of overthrowing Christ was really uncovering him. The wounds of knowledge were being healed in the only way they can be healed, namely, by a deeper knowledge. As men found verbal inspiration slipping away, they found vital inspiration taking its place. They began to believe the Bible to be inspired, for they found it to be inspiring. God must have gone into the account, because they found him coming out of it. When men exposed themselves to the mind of Christ, something happened to their minds: they were cleansed, enlightened, converted. The possibility and the fact of this infallibility arose: if a man would take the way that Christ would ask him to take, he would infallibly find God.

Jesus is passing through the midst of this critical movement to go his way to found a Kingdom based upon open frankness, and upon knowing the truth, which alone can make man free.

> **When men exposed themselves to the mind of Christ, something happened to their minds: they were cleansed, enlightened, converted.**

But another child of this Enlightenment seemed to close in on Jesus to stop him and to throw him down from the brow of the hill— Science. The conflict between science and religion has been fierce, but the smoke of the battle is now clearing and some things stand out. Between some science and some religion there is a real conflict. But between real science and real religion there is no real conflict. We now see that science has its province and religion has its province. Science has reference to that which can be weighed and measured, religion to that which can be evaluated. Science has reference to facts, religion to values. Science has reference to the quantitative aspects of life and religion to the qualitative. But religion does not merely evaluate; it changes values and the persons holding them, and uses both the persons and the values for its ends. Science comes to the poetry of Wordsworth and explains it in terms of the physical structure of the sentences, the number of feet in the meter, the components of the ink and paper upon which it is printed. Having done so, has it given an adequate answer to the meaning of the poetry of Wordsworth? "No," says Religion, "there are ideas, emotions, aspirations, and urges using the physical structure of the poetry. I interpret and evaluate them." Obviously, each answer is necessary, but incomplete without the other. It will take the answer both of science and of religion to give an adequate answer to the meaning of the poetry of Wordsworth. Someone has defined a violin solo in not very elegant language, but true as far as it goes: "A violin solo is the scraping of a horse's tail across the guts of a dead cat." The violin soloist will probably object! There are urges, emotions, and aspirations beating through the physical structure of the violin. Religion would interpret and evaluate them. It would thus take the definition both of science and of religion to give an adequate answer to the meaning of a violin solo.

> **Science has reference to that which can be weighed and measured, religion to that which can be evaluated. Science has reference to facts, religion to values. Science has reference to the quantitative aspects of life and religion to the qualitative.**

The situation between science and religion is clearer now. Each has its province. But while we are grateful for that clarification we are not satisfied, for we do not want a compartmentalized world. We want a universe instead of a multiverse. Can these two come together into closer relationships? They can. Religion can give to science a new spirit, a new altruism so that the powers of science may be used for the purposes of the collective good. On the other hand, science can give to religion the method of experimentation. I accept that method whole-heartedly. I believe that we should apply the method of experimentation to the realm of value just as we apply it to the realm of quantity. We can test Jesus Christ and his way exactly as we test any other hypothesis, namely, by trying to see whether it will work. I am persuaded that it does work, to the degree that it is worked and on as widespread a scale as it is tried. It works! I find by actual experience that when I obey Christ without reserve, then life catches its rhythm, its harmony, its peace, its song. But when I do not obey him, or obey him only partially, then something snaps within; life sags and loses its music. A very modern young woman of the West said to me: "I don't believe in a single thing—I don't believe in God, in myself, in life, or in other people. There is no purpose to life, or meaning." "Well," I replied, "it doesn't seem to have done you much good, does it? At twenty-five you are bored, cynical, critical, and out of joint with yourself and with life in general. At twenty-five you should just be beginning to live gloriously, but now you have run through your resources and don't know what to do next. At fifty life for me is getting better and better, every year is finer than the last and the adventure of living is glorious. I don't know what it is to have a bored or cynical hour. My way seems to be working, and yours doesn't—isn't that true?" She admitted that it was. "Then try Christ, and I give you my word of honor that it will work to the degree that you work it." She said she would and went away. A few hours later the telephone rang and someone came from the

239

telephone saying that there was a lady at the other end of the telephone and that she says to tell you just two words and you would understand: "It works!" A year later she wrote me that "it still works." It does, with everybody who really tries it.

As I have sat in our Round Table Conferences and have listened to what men have said about the way their ways of life have worked I have watched Jesus Christ rise to moral and spiritual supremacy. Men in fellowship with him had hold of resources by which to live that other men did not have. If I did not know the New Testament says that Jesus is the Way, I should know it from my Round Table Conferences. Whenever men sincerely and simply make Jesus Christ the Lord of their lives, then something happens to light up life, to coordinate it, to cleanse it from evil and strengthen it at the center, and to make it want to be of service. That is not argument—it is fact, and that fact is attested on as wide a scale as it is tried. Depths of life are reached and satisfied that a person does not even know are there. Henceforth the individual lives, lives in every fiber of his being. It works! We are therefore persuaded that the more men become scientific the more they will become Christian. We are not afraid that they will become too scientific; we are afraid they won't be scientific enough. We are persuaded that in the end the facts of the moral and spiritual universe will lead us to the fact of Christ. A great scientist said to us: "We scientists can make a hen's egg with exactly the constituent elements of the ordinary egg, and to all intents and purposes it is the ordinary egg, but the difficulty is that it won't hatch. It lacks life." Science cannot give life either at the lowest place or at the highest. In the end men want life in its highest qualitative form. Christ gives life at that highest place, therefore men cannot do without him—and live.

But, says Professor J. B. S. Haldane, "Science is the free activity of man's faculties of reason and imagination. It is just because even the least dogmatic of religions tend to associate themselves with some kind of unalterable moral tradition that there can be no truce between science and religion." Here he set up a straw man—and a very old one at that —and then knocks it down. It is true that the church again and again has hardened in authoritarianism. But the Christ who is at the center of it did not. Jesus offered himself as the Way of life, and as men walked out on it they found him actually saving them, saving them from themselves and from their sins, so they called him a Savior. We do that today and find the same result. It is the authority of a constantly verified fact. But the whole thing is open: it is a Way. It is an opening way. He provided that it should be: "Howbeit, when he, the Spirit of truth, is come, he shall guide you into all the truth." The Spirit of truth! Not fixed, unalterable, bound-up truth, but the Spirit of truth! This goes beyond science, for science seeks for truths, but this is the very Spirit of truth.

No, Christ is at home in the atmosphere of science, even if scientists are not yet at home with Christ. One day they will be.

No, Christ is at home in the atmosphere of science, even if scientists are not yet at home with Christ. One day they will be. But in the meantime Jesus is passing through the midst of them to go his way to the founding of the Kingdom of Facts—the Highest Facts.

But as Jesus is challenged by science in the West as being bound up with unalterable authoritarianism, so he is being challenged in the East with being bound up with imperialism. He came to the East at the time of the imperialistic expansion of the West. He seemed to be the religious side of that expansion, hence hated. In South America the missionaries had to change their names when they went among the Indians who had been exploited and betrayed by the white men. The Indians would kill any "Christian" at sight, but they distinguished the missionaries as "Jesus men." These persons were different. The name of Christian stank in their nostrils. For many years it did in the nostrils of the East. They were ready to cast Christ down from the brow of the hill on which their civilization was built.

But things are changing. The Hindu principal of a Hindu college tells of the change in these graphic words: "There was a time when the name of Christ was poison to us. But we have been going through certain stages in our attitude toward him. First, he stood at our doors in company with a trader and knocked. We looked out and said to ourselves: 'We like you, but we don't like your company.' So we shut the door. Again he presented himself, this time with a diplomat on one side and a soldier on the other. Again we said to ourselves, 'We like you, but we don't like your company.' And again we shut the door. Then he came and stood at our doors in a different role—this time as the dispenser of bounties to the outcaste. We liked him better in this role, but we were not sure what was behind the whole thing, so again we shut the door. But now he comes again, this time disentangled, standing in his own right, speaking directly to our hearts in his own person. To this Christ we say, 'Come in, our hearts are open to you.'"

It is true that many still see him with the old entanglements in mind and cry out against him, but an increasing number are welcoming this disentangled Christ. One Hindu put it this way to me: "Krishna is upon our walls, but Christ is in our hearts." India is beginning to see in Christ the fulfillment of the past and the hope of the future. "When we hear him present Christ," said a Hindu chairman, "we feel we hear the notes of Buddha, the ancient sages, the notes of Positivism, of Humanism—all seem to sound and to blend in his message." And yet I had mentioned none of these, I had only presented Christ. But this Hindu saw that in Christ all the good of all the ages came into concrete reality and was fulfilled.

Christ is passing through the midst of the searching, palpitating East and is going his way to found his world Kingdom, for the East not only sees that he meets her present needs, but also gathers up all that was noble and great in the past.

Just a few years ago China, feeling that Christianity was bound up with the imperialisms of the West, lashed out and nearly every missionary was forced out of China by the Anti-Christian Movement. They led Christ to the brow of the hill on which their civilization was built to cast him down headlong. But a strange thing has happened. The Anti-Christian Movement has spent its force, the missionaries are back again, and China is face to face with the question of whether she will build the future on Christianity or Communism. There is a race on in China between Christianity and Communism and the prize is one quarter of humanity. China is in the moment of the Great Hesitation. She has decided not to be anti-Christian, but she has not yet decided to be Christian. At least this much is sure: Christ has passed through the midst of the Anti-Christian Movement of China and is going his way.

In the West, Christ is facing another group who would take him to the brow of the hill—the nationalists. The totalitarian state which claims supreme authority over conscience is a direct and positive challenge to Christ and his Kingdom, for that Kingdom by its very nature is totalitarian and final. Hence arises one of the living issues of the world today—two totalitarian claims meeting. "Is the modern state God, or is the Lord God?" As I went into the Exposition celebrating the tenth anniversary of the founding of the Fascist state in Italy in the very front of the Exposition entry, was a figure of a peasant as he was before the Revolution, bowed down by the weight of heavy volumes on his shoulders. One of these volumes was "Internationalism." Thought for other nations was looked on as a danger to the peasant and to all others in the state. Christ opposes this. He was put to death by nationalism: "Your own nation and the chief priests delivered you unto me," said Pilate. "Your own nation"—nationalism was behind his death. The Jews wanted the Romans to put Jesus to death for telling the Jews to love their enemies, the Romans. As Jesus stood before Pilate he revealed another kind of Kingdom based on new principles: First, his Kingdom is nonviolent. "My kingdom is not of this world: if my kingdom were of this world, then would my servants fight: . . . but now my kingdom is not from hence." Its genesis is not in this world-order. Those kingdoms, which have their roots in this world-order, fight. It is their distinguishing characteristic. Second, his Kingdom is truth: "You say that I am a king. To this end have I been born, and to this end have I come into the world, to bear witness to the truth." "Yes," Jesus says, "I am a King, for this cause I came to bear witness to the Truth." A King in the realm of truth! This is in direct line with the modern tendency that fact and truth are king. "Everyone that is of the truth hears my voice"— "I shall be king over the heart of every lover of truth." Christ will draw every lover of truth to himself. Now note that Mahatma Gandhi says that his movement is "truth" and "non-violence"— startlingly near to the Kingdom of Christ at these two points. But this conception of Christ's Kingdom is just as startlingly opposed to the rampant nationalisms of today. They are not "truth"—their loyalties are based on suppressions of good about other people and the magnifying of the good about themselves. They are not "nonviolent"— they are founded on the sword, and to the extent they are they perish with it. There can be no truce between Christ and this kind of a state. Christ will be crucified by it, but in the end he will break it as he did the Roman Empire.

244

On the Chalice of Antioch, which some have supposed to be the original cup of the Last Supper, the carving represents Christ seated above the Roman eagle. Early Christianity put Christ above the state. Where there was a clash between the two the Kingdom claim was supreme. It must be so today. Modern nationalisms would put the state above Christ. They will try to make him fit into the state—a Nordic Christ in a Nordic state, for instance—or they will cast him down from the brow of the hill on which their state is built.

In the end Jesus will pass through the midst of them to go his way to found his Kingdom based on brotherhood and the equal worth of human personality. The modern state may hinder him, but it will not stop him, for this Man met Rome in the very first skirmish—and conquered! He will conquer again, for in the long run truth and nonviolence are stronger than untruth and violence.

I do not think that the rampant nationalism, even in its Hitler and Mussolini forms, presents such an issue, a lasting issue, as Communism. There we are face to face with the supreme question of the future. Christ has passed through the midst of everything so far in the founding of his Kingdom, but will he pass through this new, and it seems to me, supreme test? For this goes deeper. Communism does not merely criticize the Christian movement, as many in the past have done, but it offers an alternative program to it, detailed, decisive, and anti-Christian.

It is plain that the structure of the Russian Church had to come down, for it was obstructing the vision of Christ and his Kingdom. That structure was something other than his Kingdom, though here and there it contained elements of that Kingdom. But I feel that the Communists have really not yet come to grips with Christ. When I finished going through the Anti-Religious Museum in Leningrad I turned to my intelligent and poised guide and said to her: "To your mind is this an adequate answer to religion? I can quite see that it is a very telling blow to the church, the structure that has been built up around Christ in Russia, but you have really not touched the issue as yet. You have not come to grips with Christ and his ideas and his Kingdom. This museum is no answer to that."

"I agree," said my guide, "that this is not an adequate answer to religion, but our scientists are putting up another Anti-Religious Museum, and that will be an adequate answer, for they will trace the genesis of religion and show how it comes from magic and superstition and fear."

No, neither will that be an adequate answer, for by that method you could dismiss the modern scientific surgeon or physician, for his antecedents were the medicine man dancing around the fire and muttering incantations to get rid of disease. Can you explain the water lily by the slime from which it came? No, Christ must be explained in terms of the fact that there is in everything—from the lowest cell to the highest man, an urge for life, for completion, for perfection: everything is lifting up strong hands after a fuller life. Christ stands at the center of that urge and says, "I am come that they might have life, and that they might have it more abundantly." His Kingdom is that urge expressed in its highest qualitative form and turned toward the highest goal. Bergson says that the élan vital which is through the universe came into its highest expression in Jesus and the prophets. The fact is that when this urge for completeness is given full rein, then Christ becomes inescapable, because he stands for the highest life manifested on this planet. The Communists have not yet faced him and his Kingdom, for he was covered up with the awesome glory of the Russian Orthodox Church.

But when the issues have been cleared, they will have to face him, for he is passing through the midst of them as well to go his way. But as he goes he pauses to approve much that is in their system. I think he would approve the Prophilactoria, the houses where prostitutes are treated with respect and trained for some job, then given one and sent out into the world again. This is nearer to the mind of Him who treated the woman caught in adultery with infinite respect and said, "Neither do I condemn thee; go . . . and sin no more," nearer than our Pharisaical attitudes of segregation and legality. I think that Jesus would add, offer the changed woman conversion which would give a new center for her life.

Again, I think Jesus would approve the prison system of the Soviets—prisons without walls, without revenge, without stigma, where the inmates are free to run away, but do not; where they are taught to work and to become useful members of society, and do so; where they can marry and raise families and are in every way treated as persons with future possibilities. That system seems to me to be nearer the mind of Christ than our system based on

> **The fact is that when this urge for completeness is given full rein, then Christ becomes inescapable, because he stands for the highest life manifested on this planet.**

hardness and revenge and "an eye for an eye." True, this type of prison is only for those who commit crimes within the system; those who commit crimes against the system are treated as harshly as political prisoners of bourgeois countries, and perhaps more so. Even to the model prison system mentioned I believe that Jesus would add that the prisoner can and should become a child of God, and hence capable of an inner self-respect.

I think that Jesus would also approve of the school system, where the children are taken over and looked after during the day, while the parents are at work, only allowing them to go home when the parents are there ready to take care of them; schools where the children are fed during the day with a free meal, put to bed in clean dormitories attached to the school after the noon meal for a rest, and treated in every way with intelligence and care.

I am persuaded that Jesus would also approve of the hospital system where the mother is given prenatal care, and then the child cared for by specialists for that particular age, through the different stages of its life, all of this done free and seemingly with enthusiasm. This is done for the child, but each person is attached to a hospital where he can be looked after when ill.

I think that Jesus would approve the holiday homes by the seaside and in the mountains where workers can go and recuperate, privileges which were once only accorded to the rich.

I think that Jesus would approve of the attitudes they are taking toward different races, giving each race the chance of its own cultural development and yet a part of a great fraternity, where to speak disrespectfully of a Jew, for instance, is a criminal offense.

I am sure that Jesus would be more at home in this atmosphere than he would have been in the old Christianity of pogroms and cathedrals and where the people of his race were kept within the Pale, or in the atmosphere where they are being hounded out of Germany on the basis of a Nordic superiority.

I think that Jesus would approve of a society where there is an attempt to produce an order where there are no parasites living on others, without toil or contribution. He who said, "My Father works and I work," would say to all men and women who are able, "You also must work."

I think that Jesus would approve of "The People's Court," in which a professional judge sits with two associates, elected by the Trade Unions, one a man and one a woman, where in an atmosphere free from legal quibbling questions, are faced on their equities and decided at once, and almost without expense. I think that he would approve of the attempt to produce a society which is co-operative instead of competitive, one in which the success of the one would not mean the failure of another.

It is possible that Jesus would approve many more things that you and I, in his Name, are not prepared to approve. But as he goes on his way to found his Kingdom I am sure that Jesus would pause to lay his finger on the dangerous sore spots in that society. Some little children stand looking wistfully through the cracks of the fence at the other children at supervised play, but they cannot get in, for they are the children of the former bourgeoisie and must therefore pay the penalty. That is revenge. Jesus looks at that and in his eyes we can read his burning condemnation.

Sherwood Eddy tells of a young man who was imprisoned for his refusal to join an anti-religious collective. He wanted liberty of conscience, and so when freed from prison he and his friends, one hundred and forty-nine persons in all, tried to cross the ice on the river Amur at night to escape from Russia. Only nineteen of them escaped, four of them being wounded. The rest were shot or captured and taken back to be shot. A land from which you cannot get away if you do not like it is a prison house, no matter by what name you call it. A professor taught that "the natural sciences cannot explain the mystery of life," and that "naturalism is not a complete philosophy of life." He was ordered to be watched and disciplined. This is tyranny. Jesus would look at that tyranny and say, "Ye shall know the truth, and the truth shall make you free."

The Communists say that any means can be used to further their ends. So "hatred, lying, falsehood, misrepresentation, and violence are and must be freely used." But this dishonesty in the means passes over into the situation after the achievement of the end. I asked a headwaiter in a large hotel in Russia where the guests were, as the dining room seemed to be empty. He replied, "The hotel is full, mostly by Soviet officials; but they do not eat in the dining room, for they want to drink and have girls with them, so they eat in their rooms, lest they set a bad example by doing it in public." I think Jesus would look through all this untruth and dishonesty and would condemn it as unscathingly as he condemned it in the religious system of his day.

I think Jesus would watch in Russia the growing corruption that comes through absolute power. This absolute power instead of loosening its hold, as they say it should, is becoming more and more tyrannical and all-pervading. Einstein says: "I am convinced that degeneracy follows every autocratic system of violence, for violence inevitably attracts moral inferiors. Time has proved that illustrious tyrants are succeeded by scoundrels. For this reason I am passionately opposed to such regimes as exist in Russia and in Italy today." And now Einstein must add his own Germany. Jesus stands today as he stood before Pilate and is being condemned to crucifixion again by this tyrannical power. He stands silent now as he stood silent then. But that silence is more terrible than insolent tyranny.

Jesus would note that "every prophetic voice in religion is silenced in Russia, and that every effective preacher or dynamic religious worker is either exiled, or banished, or placed under a ban of strict silence." He would note that while once the constitution guaranteed "freedom for religious and anti-religious propaganda," it now only says, "freedom for religious confession and antireligious propaganda is recognized for all citizens." Tyrannical unfairness.

No, if the regime of Capitalism is not the Kingdom of God, neither is the Union of the Soviet Socialist Republics the Kingdom of God. That Kingdom judges both of them. Jesus must pass through the midst of them to go his way to something better. We have delayed him terribly. He would have built this new Kingdom into human society in those early Christian centuries had we not twisted it into something else. That "something else" is being shaken to its depths. In Russia it has almost collapsed. It is well that it has. It dealt in tinseled splendor and left little but awe in the souls of the people. When the magic of that splendor was broken, the inner life could not sustain it, for that inner life had not been ministered to. Protestantism in Russia has held up better under the impact of the atheistic propaganda because it had more teaching, more inner building up. It is apparently holding its own. Three thousand congregations are registered with the government. But neither the Orthodox Church nor Protestantism was big enough for its task. Then is everything gone ? No. I said that when I emerged from Russia there were two passages upon my lips and in my heart, "For we have a Kingdom which cannot be shaken," and, "Jesus Christ, the same yesterday, today, and forever"— an unshakable Kingdom and an unaltering Person; a Program and a Person.

I am persuaded that amid the wreck of things of the old order these two things will survive. But many things in our churches and in our "Christian" civilization are being shaken to their depths. They will collapse, many of them because they are unchristian, and many because they are merely irrelevant. They should collapse, for they obstruct the view and encumber the ground. This is God's purging hour. He is sifting the heart of our civilization and the soul of the church. God's besom (broom) of destruction is upon us. Out of the crash of things two things are emerging intact and resplendent—the Kingdom and the Person. This Kingdom has been "built from the foundation of the world;" it has been laid within the very nature of things. The deeper we go into the very nature of things, the more we shall discover its foundations; the more we want to live, the more we shall have to live by the Life. Jesus made "life" and "the Kingdom" synonymous. "It is better to enter into life maimed." . . . "It is good for you to enter into the kingdom of God with one eye" (Mark 9: 47). We are more and more discovering that they are synonymous. If, as Marx says, "The only goal worthy of humanity is the greatest possible enlargement of all human capacities," then the Kingdom of God stands for the highest enlargement of all human capacities. But it stands not only for the enlargement of all human capacities; it stands for their having a certain quality as well, and that quality is Christlikeness. Without that inner qualitative basis of Christlikeness, "Communism must inevitably collapse, for at bottom it is then only a confraternity of collective selfishness." The Kingdom of God is Life, life in its highest quantitative and qualitative form.

The Kingdom of God will survive all others because it completes all the good in others. Jesus said, "I will not eat this Passover with you until its full meaning is brought out in the Kingdom of God" (Luke 22:16, Weymouth trans.). But not only the Passover, but the full meaning of Community will be brought out in the Kingdom of God, because it will not then be a Community shot through and through with force and compulsion and hate and intolerance, as Marxist Communism is and must undoubtedly be from its premises, but a Community based on love, good will, sharing, and a Common Life.

To see how the Kingdom fulfills and completes in itself many tendencies at work in the world let us look at the fact that there are three great emphases in the Synoptic Gospels. Matthew's emphasis was upon the Kingdom of Heaven (Matthew 3: 2); Mark's emphasis was on the Person, Christ (Mark 1: l); Luke's emphasis was on the human changes which Christ's coming would mean (Luke 3: 4-6). The first has its emphasis on the organization, the second on the Person, the third on the persons. The New Order, or the Organization, was inaugurated by the Person in behalf of the persons. In the Kingdom these three are held in a living blend, no one snuffing out the rest. At the end we see the Person, the persons, and the new Order. In these three emphases we have three great types of government according as one element of the three is emphasized: when the emphasis is upon the Person, there is Autocracy; when upon the persons, there is Democracy or Communism; when upon the Organization, there is Constitutionalism. In every age men arise and say that salvation lies in one of these three. When the emphasis is upon one single element, the rest are subordinated and often lost sight of. In history men have fought for one single type, excluding the other two. So governments swing from one to

> **Without that inner qualitative basis of Christlikeness, "Communism must inevitably collapse, for at bottom it is then only a confraternity of collective selfishness."**

the other, and each fails because it has only one element in it to the exclusion of the others. Autocracies fail because they do not have in them the willing consent of the people. Democracies fail because they do not have enough centralized power. Constitutionalisms fail because they cannot command loyalties which we give to persons and cannot give to mere organizations.

253

In religion we find these exclusive emphases on one or the other. The High Churchman emphasizes the Organization, the Evangelical the Person of Christ, and the Liberal the persons, the human side. Each has persisted because each has contained a truth, but each has failed to satisfy because it did not contain the whole truth.

The Kingdom of God gathers up all these within itself and holds them in a living blend. God is the Sole Ruler in this new Kingdom, but he develops initiative and freedom in the subjects of that Kingdom, for the rulership really issues from within— "the kingdom of heaven is within you"; and he preserves amid this freedom the Organization, the New Order. The Kingdom of God is an Organization which does not swamp people with its over organization. It uses organizations, but it goes beyond them. It uses the Quaker in his revolt from ritualism and organization, and the High Churchman in his love of the continuous order in ritual and organization, but it is not confined to either. It uses both and breaks out beyond! The Person of Jesus is the corrective to over organization, for he brings everything to the bar of the judgment of his own Person, thereby keeping everything fluid. Besides, the Ruler is the Son of man—one who rules because he identifies himself with every man; hence man, at the very moment of being ruled, is the ruler. In the Kingdom man is a member of an Organization, but he finds himself an organism, developing through life from within. The Kingdom of God becomes the Kingdom of Man. In being a subject he finds his freedom. The Kingdom thus fulfills all lesser ways and completes them.

"But," says the critic, "the Kingdom of God is too vague—too large and too vague to gain the allegiance of man." Mussolini, in criticizing internationalism, says, "Your unit of allegiance is too large." This would be true of the Kingdom of God were it not personalized in Jesus Christ. There the unit of allegiance is not too large. It is made definite and personal, but set in a framework of universality—the Kingdom of God. So we have the combination of something that is warm and personal and definite with something that has the sweep of time and eternity in it. The unit of allegiance is so definite that we no longer grope, and yet sufficiently indefinite to encourage our growth.

Jesus stands amid the crash of things unmodified, the same yesterday, today, and forever. He stands unmodified, but forcing modification on everything. He is vital and vibrant and in the end will be victorious. Jesus says, according to the Aramaic translation, "The Son of Man is going through" (Matthew 26: 24). He is. But many things built around him are not going through. They cannot go through; they are temporary and have no survival value. But the Son of Man—note the phrase—not the Son of the East, nor the Son of the West, nor the Son of the Nordic, nor the Son of the Jew, nor the Son of the Bourgeoisie, nor the Son of the Proletariat, but the Son of Man, the Man who embodies in himself all that men have yearned for, and who presents his Kingdom as the way those yearnings will be realized—he is going *through*. Jesus is going through just because he is the Son of Man—nothing temporary, nothing national, nothing racial, nothing local, but identified with the needs of man as man and able to meet those needs.

A man arose in one of my meetings in India and said, "I am opposed to all religion, not merely Christianity, all religions; but it is men like you who are our difficulty."

"I am not your difficulty, my brother," I replied, "but the thing I am standing for is your difficulty. For you class religion as superstition, and this is the highest kind of experimentalism; you class religion as an opiate, and this stabs one broad awake; you class religion as escape-mentality, and this new Kingdom makes one corporately responsible for the last and the least; you say religion makes you long for heaven, and this Kingdom makes us long to make the earth a heaven of good will and brotherhood. No, it is Jesus and his Kingdom which embarrasses your propaganda."

In India the gods lose their vitality and vigor every fifty or sixty years and have to be revived by certain reviving ceremonies and rites. "Ishwar [God] is growing old and decrepit and is not of much use to us now," said a Hindu to me. But while systems grow old and have to be renewed, there stands One among those systems who is eternally young. I saw some Hindu girls stand before an audience and entertain them by singing songs about the gods, but above these girls was a picture of the Christ with one of his hands on the shoulder of a youth, and with the other pointing to the future. We may praise whatever gods we like— Success, Mammon, Acquisitiveness, Race, and War—but in the end his hand is on the shoulder of youth and he is pointing to the future. That future belongs to him, for he has something to give to man, and especially to youth, that no one else can impart.

In the city of Baku in Russia, in a public park, I looked at a statue of Youth, standing on a globe, with an iron bar in his hand, breaking the chains which were binding the world. It was a noble statue, nobly conceived. Upon a bench nearby sat a youth looking straight at this statue of youth breaking the chains of the world, but seemed unmoved. Unresponsive while looking at liberty? Statues, however noble, cannot redeem. Only a Person, living and present, can do that. Statutes, however true and nobly conceived, cannot redeem; at best they can only point the way; they cannot give strength to walk in the way. "Why don't you preach to us the principles and leave out the Person, Christ?" inquired a Hindu of me one day. My reply: Shall we take the stream and leave out the fountain? Shall we take the rays of the sun and leave out the sun? If so, we shall soon have no fountain and no sun. No, we shall take Jesus and his principles, Jesus and his Kingdom. Both of them areas necessary for the survival of the race as the light is necessary for the survival of the eye.

H. G. Wells, in his *Outline of History*, in surveying human history as a whole ends up his statement about Christ in these words, "The Galilean has been too great for our small hearts." He has been. Jesus gave us a Kingdom which was the new and final order breaking into and changing this whole present world order, and we have made it into a fold into which we run and are safe until Jesus takes us home to heaven. Jesus gave us a Brotherhood which would bring all races and classes together in a great Fraternity, and we have damned it into the religion of being white. Jesus gave us the Spirit of Sharing, which would have made a just and happy and well-ordered world, and we have made it into a scramble for wealth at the expense of others. These continuous scrambles have turned the world into shambles. We have reduced the Kingdom so that a millionaire in dying could say that, although he had been hard and driving and a shrewd business man, he had never drunk and had never kept a mistress, and probably felt that by being able to say this that he was a good and model Christian. The Kingdom into that! Jesus gave us a Kingdom which is entered by the narrow gate of self-losing for the sake of him and his brothers, and we have made that narrow gate into a narrow message, a narrow outlook, a narrow program and narrow-souledness.

> **Unless we enlarge our hearts to this Galilean and his program, he will have to pass through the midst of us who are called by his name to go his way to found his Kingdom.**

Unless we enlarge our hearts to this Galilean and his program he will have to pass through the midst of us who are called by his name to go his way to found his Kingdom. This is our chance to rethink our whole position, to right our attitudes, to turn with dedicated wills to him and to his Kingdom, and to start afresh. What a world renewal would happen if we did! In the words of a very able man, himself not a Christian, a chairman of one of our meetings in India: "As the speaker has gone on, two thoughts have been going through my mind. One was, 'What a tragedy it was when Christianity broke with Christ!' and the other was, 'What a world-awakening would come if Christianity and Christ should come together again!'" It would.

CHAPTER 11

THE NEXT STEPS

There are many who may be prepared to accept the Christian way as the only finally workable program but who feel rather puzzled and hesitant as to how to begin. How shall we dig into the situation and make a beginning? "It is a law of the mind that that which is not expressed dies," so it will all die unless we express it. But in this case it cannot be a mere oral expression—it must be a vital expression, or it will die, and we with it.

I think that we can do exactly what Jesus did when he announced his program. He closed the book, gave it back to the attendant and said, "Today this scripture has been fulfilled in your ears." In other words, "Today, so far as I am concerned, this program begins." And it did.

Jesus embodied that program. He was the Kingdom of God in operation. If you want to see what the Kingdom is like, look at Jesus. In his attitudes to God and man, in his relationships to people of all classes and races, in his spirit toward the weak and the fallen and the dispossessed, in his uncompromising hostility to all exploitation of man by man, in his belief in man and in his capabilities to rise, in his way of sharing life daily in a brotherhood with his companions—in the whole outlook and temper of his life we see the Kingdom in operation. In his cross we see the method by which he resists evil. It is not a passive acquiescence, it is a positive resistance, but a resistance on a higher level —he overcomes hate by love, he attacks ill-will by the weapons of inexhaustible good will, he takes it all into his heart and turns it back as redemptive love, he conquers the world by a cross.

> **We have the immense advantage over every other way of life in that we know beforehand just exactly the kind of life we want to live. We have seen it in operation in Jesus.**

His contacts with men were vicarious. His love insinuated itself into the lives of those about him so that everything that affected them affected him. He was guilty in their guilt and degraded in their degradation. When the apostle said that he "bore our sins in his own body on the tree," he was simply expressing as a final crisis fact what was a continuous everyday fact. Jesus thus showed us that the very nature of the Kingdom is vicarious. He showed us that society also must take the attitude of the vicarious in relationship to its members—the sin of any is the sin of all, the hunger of the one bites into the heart of the rest, the chains of the least bind the whole.

We have the immense advantage over every other way of life in that we know beforehand just exactly the kind of life we want to live. We have seen it in operation in Jesus. We are not following a Utopian dream, we are endeavoring to universalize an accomplished fact. So when we are told that the Christian plan for the remaking of the world is Utopian and not scientific, we reply, the Christian's plan is probably

more scientific than Marxist Communism, for Marx evolved
Communism out of his own brain, and it has yet to prove that it will
work in the long run, while the Kingdom of God has been
accomplished in a life and in an emerging society in the early days, and
needs only to be rediscovered and applied on a universal scale. We
know what we want—a Christ-like society. We know nothing higher, we
can be content with nothing less. "Who is the greatest man in the
world?" I asked an audience of Hindu students, and received the reply,
"A Christ-like man." Those non-Christian students knew nothing that
was higher. In the end we shall all know nothing higher than a Christ-
like society, and in the end we shall be content with nothing less.

Professor Macmurray says that "the central thing in Marxism is its
principle of the unity of theory and practice. It is this principle which
makes Communistic philosophy not so much a particular philosophical
system among others as a new type of philosophy altogether." Marxism
says that there is no theory apart from practice—your practice is your
theory, your only theory. This, of course, is very searching. You cannot
hold one set of views and practice another. If you practice them, you
hold them and nothing else. Hence the constant purging within the
Communist party, not on the basis of beliefs, but on the basis of
practice. Their members are tested publicly and periodically on the
question of their practice during the year. This is all very searching to
the hypocrisies of society where many hold high beliefs in mental
compensation for low practices.

Professor Macmurray says that this union of theory and practice is
new among philosophies. It is—among philosophies. But I wonder if it
is new when we think of Jesus and his conception of the Kingdom of
God. This is all very near to Christ— not I grant you to organized
Christianity, for in it we have built up vast theories apart from practice.
But Jesus gave no set creed. He called men to follow him, to follow

261

him, note—not merely to accept his ideas, but to follow him as he went forth to put into operation the Kingdom of God. His theory and his practice were one. You could not tell where his words ended and his deeds began, nor where his deeds ended and his words began, for his deeds were words and his words were deeds, and they both came together with what he was and became the Word, not a spoken Word, but a Lived Word. Jesus laid down no philosophy (the Hindu senses at once that there is no philosophy in the Christianity of Christ and objects to it on that ground), but he met life day by day, and as he met life he interpreted his own life. But it is the interpretation of a practice and not of a theory. It was a lived-out Word and not a spelled-out Word. When he said that the Kingdom of Heaven is at hand, it was at hand, in the very person of the Speaker and in the emerging society growing up around him. He did not speak of a co-operative society, but he produced one. Jesus and his disciples practiced one long before it emerged into the co-operative society in the Acts of the Apostles. That was just an enlarging to include other people about what Jesus began with himself and his disciples. When he sent out his disciples he said, "As you go, preach, saying the kingdom of heaven is at hand. Heal the sick, raise the dead, cleanse the lepers, cast out devils: freely ye have received, freely give. Get you no gold, nor silver, nor brass in your purses, . . . the laborer is worthy of his food." Note that he says that your contribution to society is your claim, your only claim for sustenance from that society. To each according to his need—"the laborer is worthy of his food." From each according to his ability— "heal the sick." He forbade acquisitiveness—"get ye no gold"—and practiced it. He said that society should support you according to the degree of your needs, since you are contributing to society. Here, then, are the three things which economists are increasingly saying are necessary for the foundations of a just society: (1) The elimination of acquisitiveness; (2) the provision for support according to need; (3) the contribution to that society according to the ability given—as freely as ye have received, freely give. In the kind of society in which we have been living these statements of Jesus seem quixotic and impossible and only intended as an interim ethic. So we have rejected them, or damned them with faint praise. But lo, the stones which the builders of civilization have rejected are now becoming the head of the corners. These three principle-practices of Jesus will become the stones upon which we shall build in the future, or the rocks upon which we shall stumble to our doom.

Jesus embodied this theory-practice in everything. He did not say to his disciples, "Love one another"—that would be theoretical and abstract, but, "Love one another even as I have loved you"—that is concrete and worked out. So the Kingdom of God is an intense realism. It is as far away from philosophers spinning theories about life as can be. It is

> **Jesus gave no set creed. He called men to follow him, to follow him, note—not merely to accept his ideas, but to follow him as he went forth to put into operation the Kingdom of God. His theory and his practice were one.**

life, a new kind of life emerging from the decaying shell of life around it. This is why Luke says Jesus came "preaching and bringing" the Kingdom of God. Jesus brought it in his own Person and in the society which was being formed. The people heard it and saw it in actual operation. They saw it in the joy, in the fellowship, in the creative, healing love and in the new freedom from acquisitiveness in Jesus and in the new society. They saw the difference between this new Jesus-society and the religious society they knew—at the doors of the temples they were used to treasury boxes, money-changers and temple tax-gatherers—that that religious society was acquisitive; it had its hands stretched out to receive. This new society had no hands stretched out to receive, but hands stretched out to give and to heal and to lift. We have preached the Kingdom of God, we must now bring it. We must match against the realism of Marxist Communism a deeper and more comprehensive realism. "I suppose you are an idealist? If you are, then *au revoir*, for I am a realist," said a Communist actress to me in Russia as she dismissed me with a wave of her hand. Thus will the world dismiss us in very fact with a wave of the hand if we are not realistic bringers of the Kingdom of God.

If we restored this theory-practice to our modern world, and counted only those as Christians who were actually bringing the Kingdom of God, then we should cut through the vast hypocrisies which have been built up around this new Kingdom, and an air of reality would come upon the whole movement. We should have less numbers, but more driving force in our Christian movement which would send us further into the soul of the world than we can now go, shackled as we now are with the dead weight of unchristian Christianity. But in so doing we would convert many of the theory holders of Christianity to the practice of the Kingdom of God, for then they would see something to which to be converted. Now they see little or nothing because they are respectable members of a theoretically Christian, but practically unchristian society.

"But," someone objects, "these practices of Jesus were on a small scale and in a comparatively primitive society, and can thus hardly be applicable to the complexities of modern life." Our answer is that in the nature of the case they had to be small. Jesus was not giving us a completed society, but a revelation of the nature of the new Kingdom.

"The burden of the Gospels is not how we ought to behave, but to portray for us his disclosures of the meaning of goodness itself, the inmost quality of life." "Many assume that a perfect disclosure of goodness would embrace all forms and species of what is good. That would mean in the end that the best man is the man who has done the greatest number of good things; that is to say, has responded to life on the widest conceivable front. That assumption is radically false. What gives a man his place in history is not the number of things which he has done, but the quality of his response to life. It is not those who have done something of everything who have most set men's hearts afire, but those who have done something supremely well. Jesus did not do everything good that can be done. He revealed the meaning of goodness itself."[1]

> **What gives a man his place in history is not the number of things which he has done, but the quality of his response to life.**

In these simple day-by-day happenings Jesus was disclosing as in a flash the meaning of life itself, and incidentally the meaning of the way to live. The happening was small, but it had on it the feel of the eternal and the universal. He was fulfilling what Kant suggested: "So live that your actions may be a universal rule of life." His deeds had the setting of Palestine, but the quality of a world movement in them.

Since Jesus made theory and practice one, we must do the same. He announced his program and then said, "Today it begins." That is the first thing we can do.

---

1 Canon Barry.

265

1. We can say, "As far as I am concerned it begins right now."

We cannot wait until everybody is ready for it before we begin to practice it. We can anticipate the completed Kingdom by acting in our own persons, and as far as possible in our relationships with others, as though it were already here. We can begin to live now as we expect to live when the Kingdom is fully operative. Of course that practice of the Kingdom will be limited and partial, for it cannot be fully practiced until it is embodied in society. It is a good thing that we cannot fully practice it until basic wrongs are righted. If we could practice the Kingdom without those wrongs being righted, then we should probably leave the wrongs untouched. God holds us up and makes its full practice impossible until we face the whole basic injustice underlying life. Nevertheless, in spite of this limitation, in spite of the fact that we shall be thwarted at every turn, we can begin the practice of the Kingdom. Though the practice is limited we are letting men see what the nature of the Kingdom is, so that while furthering that Kingdom we are also revealing its nature.

Just what would it mean to say that it begins in us right now? The first item in the program was good news to the poor. Applied to our lives it would mean that we should live economically as though the Kingdom were already here in full operation. The basis of that new order is that property is for use and not for acquisitiveness. We should therefore renounce acquisitiveness and take as much, and only as much, of material things as will make us mentally and morally and spiritually and physically fit for the purposes of the Kingdom of God. We will draw a line in our lives and say, "Up to that line is use, and therefore legitimate and right, but beyond that line is luxury, and therefore un-Christian territory for me." Just where that line shall be drawn every man must decide in quietness of his own heart before God. It will not be the same for all people. For all men's needs are not the same. To discover that line is not an easy thing, and a good deal of "rationalization" is liable to creep in at this point. This line must be decided upon in full view of and in relationship to the under-privileged.

No man can decide that absolutely alone, even though it be alone with God. We carry too many prejudices in our own favor, even into our holiest of moments. Each one needs the counsel and judgment of a group who are also striving to find that line for their own lives. The judgment of the group would correct some of the prejudices of the individual in favor of himself. The Christian life is a co-operative endeavor and cannot be worked out individually.

"Fit for the purposes of the Kingdom of God"— that is a qualifying phrase which should help in making that decision. The Kingdom of God is the final order and therefore the final authority. Whenever the personal, family, or state claims conflict with the Kingdom claim, then they must give way before it. "Seek ye first the Kingdom of God." Whatever will make me and my brothers more fit for the purposes of that new society is allowable, even, obligatory; whatever I want for a purpose which will not fit into and not further the purposes of that new society must be rigidly excluded. That would mean that we must give to society everything beyond what is required for our Kingdom fitness. That giving of the surplus beyond our needs would help to bring about the fitness of others.

In regard to the second item of the program— release to the captives—it would mean that if we are to anticipate the full coming of the Kingdom, we must release every captive as far as we are concerned. If we are a member of the white race, we will treat every man as though he were of our race. It is easy to feel class pain and race pain, but not so easy to feel human pain. A member of the white race, cultured and recently "changed," said of the people of a non-white race: "They cannot be so badly off, because their numbers are increasing. When the numbers of any people are increasing, you know that they are above the subsistence level." Would he have propounded that theory had he been dealing with the white race in general, and his own nation in particular, and his own class specifically? Would he have felt that he and his family were "not badly off" if they were on the living side of the "subsistence level"? This man, obviously sincere and really in the Kingdom, had brought over the mentality of the old into the new way of Kingdom living. We as sons and daughters of the Kingdom must dismiss from our minds all excuses and apologies for exploiting and treating people differently by saying that they are members of another race or class. To us there can be no more race or class. The Kingdom is classless. It is also color-blind.

Some white children on the west coast of America were debating the question of whether they would rather be born blind or born non-white. They decided that they would rather be born blind. But the fact is that any society in which children have to come to that conclusion is blind. It is blind to the fact that they themselves were once despised as impossible barbarians by the cultured Romans. It is also blind to the fact that unless you give to others the liberties which you have received from others you yourselves cannot retain them. The moment you deny liberty to any man that moment you put yourself into bondage. We must regain the attitudes of the early church at this point. The early church knew no lines of race or color. Paul was ordained by a black man. In the church at Antioch were prophets and teachers, among whom was Symeon, who was called "Niger"— "the dark," or "the black." This man among the rest laid his hands on Paul and sent him forth. Paul did not merely give to the persons of other races, he received from them. We must all become recipients of the good that comes through every race. We must be willing to receive from every race as well as give to them. As long as we give only we are "a brother bountiful," but when we receive as well we are a brother.

If we cannot give full effect to this freeing of the captive, since society as now organized will not allow us, nevertheless we can give full freedom mentally as far as we are concerned. In our minds we can look on them as free, and treat them as free in our relationships as far as it depends on us. We shall mentally disarm in regard to all classes, all races, all colors. We can say, "As far as I am concerned all captives are free right now."

2. We can form groups for the practice and study of the new Kingdom life.— These groups will be the Kingdom in miniature, Kingdom "cells." These cameos of the new day will help us and others to see something of the nature and meaning of the new Society when it does come. These groups should not be exclusive in their mentality and spirit, but should recognize themselves as explorative portions of the Kingdom, which includes them and others. They should welcome every differing attempt to bring up phases of the Kingdom not emphasized by them. Whole churches might decide to become such groups.

3. While we shall look on the church as the probable center of the Kingdom, we shall not confine the Kingdom to the church, even if we could. We shall welcome those outside organized Christianity, who, however limited they may seem to us to be, nevertheless are striving for the New Day, at least in some of its phases. This "informal Christianity" may be able in this crisis to see more clearly and act more decisively than organized Christianity. We shall look on these brothers and sisters of the margin as just as truly brothers and sisters as those whom we think of as brothers and sisters of the center. It may turn out that they are nearer the center than we.

4. We can help develop the co-operative spirit instead of the competitive by organizing co-operatives of various types and kinds. Denmark has led the way at this point, for she has widely distributed the wealth of her people by means of cooperatives. There are scarcely any rich and scarcely any poor in Denmark. Within the framework of the present order they have done much to change conditions and to prepare for the new order. In the midst of an armed world they have voted to disarm, they who were once one of the greatest free-booting (piracy) nations of Europe. They are moving toward a cooperative society and are doing it without recourse to the brutalities of the class war.

The fact of the matter is that we are now facing an entirely new situation. Stuart Chase calls attention to the fact that technological inventions and the use of electric power have created a new situation in today's economy which must revolutionize the action patterns and social theories that were appropriate to the economy of scarcity that existed all over the world until now. Mr. Chase says that the production of physical energy in the United States is today forty times as much per inhabitant as it was one hundred years ago. With such energy applied to the natural resources there is no need that any human being should suffer from lack of material things, or that he should be exploited by long hours of labor. Sayre, commenting on this, says: "The fruits of security can be had by all. They need not be restricted to a small possessing class, riding, as Tolstoy said, like the Old Man of the Sea upon the backs of the poor. All can ride on the back of electric energy." Mr. Chase continues: "Suppose that two men are traveling across a desert and that one has a full water bottle while the flask of the other is empty. If the first refuses to share with the second, a fight is likely to ensue. Suppose the two men are in a boat on a great fresh-water lake, which they believe is salt sea. If they discover that the abundance of water within easy reach is fresh, they need not fight for the little in the flask. The desert is the economy of scarcity in which our forefathers lived; the lake is the economy of abundance on which the craft of civilization now floats."

Sayre comments, "If this is anything like a true description of the facts, it should alter radically the Marxist picture of the inevitable class war." Class war under those circumstances becomes absurd. We must learn to co-operate in producing and distributing that abundance and renounce the notion that we should fight over the little bit we now have. Christ's method of co-operation becomes the only realism under these changed circumstances.

> The desert is the economy of scarcity in which our forefathers lived; the lake is the economy of abundance on which the craft of civilization now floats.

We can prepare for the public ownership of public resources and utilities, to which society must come if we are to stop selfish exploitation, by training the group mind in the handling of collective projects through cooperatives.

Kagawa of Japan, in forming cooperatives among various types of people in various occupations, is improving the economic and moral condition of vast numbers and training them for the new Cooperative Society—the Kingdom of God on earth.

5. Christian business men can change the basis of their business from competition to cooperation. A profit-sharing basis with employees would still leave them in competition with the outside world, but within the business itself the change would be in the direction of co-operation, and therefore nearer to being Christian.

6. We can teach this New Order, frankly, persistently and with a burning passion. We need not apologize for something so big, so compelling, so utterly necessary as the New Crusade, for this time "God wills it!" As we proclaimed the message of individuals being saved only to desert the wreck of things, our tongues stammered. As we called men to a church program that ended in itself, we felt the sense of futility. In Travancore, India, I saw alongside of the road an old motor bus as broken-down as Oliver Wendell Holmes's one-horse carriage. But the sign on it was still intact: "Please Step In." I inwardly said, "No, thank you." We have asked men to step into programs that were broken-down and played out, and have wondered at their refusal. But as we rediscover the meaning of the Kingdom of God on earth, with the uttermost conviction we can invite a confused world to consider this way as the only workable way.

I cannot be grateful enough that Jesus gave us the conception of the Kingdom of God on earth as the central item in his teaching, for if it were not there, and Jesus had only taught a way of individual release, it would now prove itself too small and too inadequate for its world-task. Mahatma Gandhi has seen the necessity of some such idea for his movement to reconstruct India, so he calls men to "Ramarajya"—the Kingdom of Rama. But the Kingdom of Rama has embarrassments attached to it, it lacks content and illustration and has no depth or meaning such as Jesus put into the Kingdom of God. Men are everywhere feeling after just such a conception, and lo, Jesus has given it to us! Upon its rediscovery world rehabilitation awaits. We must all become centers of the New Order— "cells" of the Kingdom of God, multiplying like a living cell. We must teach it until every man, woman, and child shall become aflame with it.

7. We must teach it as though we believed in the inevitability of the Kingdom of God. I know that we can preach the certainty of a coming event in such a way that it will take away all sense of responsibility for its coming. We have often done this with the Kingdom of God, so that it has left us with a sense of paralysis instead of initiative. But the very nature of the undertaking, an undertaking to renew the world within and without, is liable to leave us paralyzed by its vastness. We must be inwardly motivated to meet that tendency. We must get hold of the belief in the inevitability of the Kingdom of God.

One of the things that gives driving force to Communism is the belief that Communism is the inevitable outcome of economic forces. In the doctrine of the dialectic, in which they apply Hegel's thesis, antithesis, and synthesis to the economic order, they believe that Capitalism is the thesis, of which the inevitable deterioration of the working classes under Capitalism is the antithesis. This deterioration gets so bad that there is revolution and society comes to the synthesis— Communism. They feel that they can stand off and watch the situation move to its destined end by the very economic forces of the universe. These forces back the Communistic goal.

Of course that belief in economic forces moving on to an end that is moral makes it akin to a belief in

> ... a divinity that shapes our ends,
> Rough-hew them how we will.[2]

To them God is out of it, but economic forces themselves lead inevitably to Communism. That gives the Communists the sense of being the agents of the universe. It gives driving force.

---

2 *Hamlet: Act V, Scene II.*

We must match that Communist assumption, and go beyond it, by the feeling that we are the agents of a universe that is wider and deeper than an economic universe. We believe that the sum total of everything good and true is behind the Kingdom movement, that the very stars in their courses fight in behalf of it. If the Marxist believes that the working of the dialectic is toward Communism as a goal, we think we see the dialectic working toward a greater goal. We think we see Communism as the thesis creating Fascism as the antithesis, and that these two, becoming unworkable and breaking down through inherent weakness, will lead in the end to the synthesis—the Kingdom of God on earth. We think we see the pageant of human history moving, with many a setback and many a disastrous turning into roads with dead ends, which have to be laboriously retraced, but on the whole and in the main, toward a higher order of human living, and that higher order is the Kingdom of God. Of course it may be that the Kingdom within us reads the Kingdom outside of us, and in the reading heightens it, but nevertheless this does seem to have the feel of the real upon it. A young Communist professor who had insisted that the New Order could come only by force, held to this until he found a new inner spiritual conversion while at the Ashram, and then he said: "Now I see what you are talking about. I believe it can be done by the method of Christ." And he arose with joy to try it. He felt such a New Order was inevitable!

We believe in the inevitability of the Kingdom because, as one sociologist put it in one of our Round Tables, "I find in my study of sociology that the fundamental tendencies of the universe are in Jesus Christ." They are. And we may add: His Kingdom is the embodiment of and the inevitable meeting place of all the tendencies that make for human betterment.

We could not believe in the inevitability of the Kingdom if we saw the Christian Church as the sole medium of its coming. It is perhaps the chief, but certainly not the sole medium. Said a leading Hindu of an Indian state: "You Christians think that Christianity can only be lived inside your Mission Compound walls. I assure you that there is more Christianity outside your walls than inside them." That may be an overstatement, but it calls our attention to the fact that the Kingdom is both within and without the Christian Church. "Other sheep I have, which are not of this fold," said Jesus. Everything that tends toward the good is to that extent a part of the Kingdom. We must include within it whatever are the fine and noble things in Communism. And they are not a few. There is a growing number of persons who are willing to swallow the hate, the compulsions, the ruthlessness, and the materialistic atheism of Communism to get to that good. We cannot and must not swallow those evils, for they would poison the body of society, and may lead to its death, but we must not refuse to take the good that is present in the current model of Communism, for that good will one day lead to the Good. A Hindu, returned from Russia, while discussing Communism, said: "The Communists act as though their idea is new. It is not. It arose with Christianity. The Communists would take the Communism from Christianity and throw out Christ. One day they will have to bring back Christ to make the system work." The fact is that we are all having to bring back Christ to make our individual and collective lives work. The Kingdom of God is inevitable—if men would live. "If this is Christianity," said a Hindu chairman, the head of a large college in the central city of Hinduism, "then I don't mind if all India becomes Christian, in fact, all the world." This is a conclusion to which we are all going to be driven sooner or later.

We must lay aside a defeatist mentality, for the stars in their courses, the fundamental tendencies of the universe, the results of trial and error in human living, the very pressures of the human spirit after a workable way to live—all these, and more, work in behalf of the new Kingdom. "Fear not, little flock; for it is your Father's good pleasure to give you the kingdom." We must catch the stride of victory. We must preach the inevitability of the Kingdom not as a paralyzing inevitability, but as one that constitutes a call, for the Kingdom is ours only if we individually and collectively will it. We must will it! A great statesman once said, "If I believed that Jesus Christ died for me, I should be able to think of nothing else and speak of nothing else." Some of us profoundly believe just that, and we must therefore let it possess us completely until it shall become a contagious fire. A Hindu chairman said this, "If what the speaker has said tonight isn't true, it doesn't matter; but I tell you if it is true, then nothing else matters." If the Kingdom isn't true, let us forget it and dismiss it—it doesn't matter; but if it is true, then nothing else really matters. It is the one compelling idea which should possess us and the one compelling motive which should gather up all lesser motives within our lives and point them toward the one business of making the Kingdom a realized fact.

> **This higher Kingdom presses upon us, awakens us to aspiration, to prayer, to yearning after social and individual completeness.**

Against the economic interpretation of history we match the Kingdom interpretation. Man is not merely conditioned from below, he is called to from above. This higher Kingdom presses upon us, awakens us to aspiration, to prayer, to yearning after social and individual completeness. It is Life pressing upon life. We interpret man in terms

276

of this higher life and not in terms of his economic roots. If man is only an economic animal, then "service to each other is only the scratching of the back of one hog by another hog," and nothing more. But we are something more. I stepped up to a youth on the streets of a Russian city and asked if he were a student. "I am an aspirant," he replied. "I am an aspirant"—in these words is the interpretation of history, for we aspire because of the pressure of the higher Kingdom upon us. Our aspiration is an answer to God's inspiration. The aspirations can only be fulfilled in the Kingdom of God. The Kingdom is inevitable. God wills it. And in the end man must will it—or perish.

8. One of the next steps is the uniting of the Christian forces of the world into a Christian Internationale. I have said that, with all its faults, the Christian Church is the best serving institution on earth, and that while it has many critics, it has no rivals in the work of human redemption. While this is true, it is not now a fit instrument for the coming of that Kingdom. It is too divided. A divided church has little moral authority in a world seeking unity and unable to attain to it. The next great step in putting into operation the Kingdom of God is for each Christian church to conceive of itself as a part of that Kingdom, without exclusive rights and standing, and to recognize all other Christian bodies also as integral parts of that Kingdom. We must recognize as a fellow Christian every man, whatever his name or sign, who recognizes Christ as his Lord and works for the coming of the Kingdom. I am persuaded that we will get together only on a common task—any other attempt is hopeless. The tragedy of Lausanne showed us that. To try to fit in ministerial validity with ministerial validity ends in the invalidity of the whole thing. A common task awaits us! Let that suffice us to begin with. A Roman Catholic priest, after some correspondence with me on the matter of church union, said, "I suppose the first step which we as Roman Catholics could take would be to recognize you Protestants as Christians." "Good," I replied, "and we will reciprocate and recognize you as Christians!" Does any man give his loyalty to Christ and does he work for the Kingdom? If he does, he is my blood-brother and I give him my hand. We can and must have a Christian Internationale. The Communists' Third Internationale would seem small and unimportant before this Christian Internationale. Six hundred million Christians could do anything they decided to do!

Fireflies are interesting to watch as they flick on their individual lights in the darkness, but one night in India I was thrilled as I saw a whole tree filled with fireflies, and all of them lighting up their lights in unison like a pulse beat. It lighted up the surrounding region. Individual Christians have been interesting points of light in the darkness, but they would become more than interesting if they should pool their lights and let them shine as one —they would then lighten the world.

Our divisions have largely lost their meaning. We must transcend them in a common loyalty to a common task. In our Ashram estate stone walls still run through it, but they have lost their meaning, for they are relics of the days when the estate belonged to different owners. We are now taking them down and using the materials to build bigger and better buildings. Christ, as the one Lord of us all, renders these stone walls of division still standing between us an absurdity. The Kingdom is one! If we do not tear down these walls and build a new temple of unity, then a world catastrophe will shake them down.

The task of providing a new world program awaits us. Let us be done with the trifling and the unimportant! A British airman, in charge of keeping the peace in the Persian Gulf, told me how they kept the Arabian Sheiks quiet. When they become restless, and want to fight the rest of the world, they take them up in an airplane and let them see the extent of their dominions which take days and days to traverse on a camel, but can be flown over in an hour. The Sheik comes down chastened and sobered—his dominions are small and unimportant when viewed from above. When we look at the world task awaiting us, when we look at the whole thing from above, then we see the comparative insignificance of our tiny denominational patches, and the futility of acting as though we were the whole.

Christians of the world, unite! We have nothing to lose except our dividing walls. The truth of each will then belong to the whole. A Christian Internationale is one of the most important next steps toward a Christian alternative.

9. When we have a sufficient majority to make this Christian program effective, we should not hesitate to put it through the political order. Obviously, we cannot make a Christian world if the state remains pagan. If we put the Kingdom into operation in the economic and the social, it is obvious that we must put it into the political as well. If we repudiate as unchristian the slogan, "Business is business," we must also repudiate the slogan, "Politics is politics." They must both be made Christian. We would not capture the machinery of the state by a *coup-d'état*, and set up a dictatorship by a minority; but where there is a majority who stand for the Christian program we should not hesitate to put it into operation through the state. A non-Christian officer in Feng's army, when that army was probably the most Christian army the world has ever seen, said, "You might as well be a Christian in Feng's army, for you have to act like one anyhow." We want the state to be so Christian in its outlook and spirit and program that the citizens of that state will feel that it is the normal and natural thing to be Christian.

Now we have to be Christian in spite of the social, economic, and political order, then we may be Christian on account of. Whether we shall be able to use any of the existing political parties or create a new one must be decided by the enlightened judgment of the united Christian forces. If it now seems impossible to get those forces together for such a decision, let us be reminded that the pressure of the future is going to be so great, the crisis will be so acute, the alternatives will be so sharp, that we shall be driven together where now we hesitate. When the world choice shall have to be made between the Kingdom of God and Marxist Communism, then the Christian Communions will vividly realize what they do not now, namely, that they will have to present a united front or abdicate. We "will have to hang together or hang separately." The fact is that we have now the largest body in the world centered around one Idea and one Person. Can we not get together? We are together—if we only knew it!

Our individualism in religion may revolt at first at the idea of Christianity functioning through the state, but the conscience of Christendom is more and more deeply revolting at the unchristian mess into which pagan economics and pagan politics have landed us.

I was refused a place in a car by a French consul on my journey through Persia, though we were traveling through the same agency. He said in haughty grandeur, "I am a diplomat." I inwardly replied, "I am an ambassador." But some of the haughtiness of the diplomat wilted when on board steamer a distressed wave of the hand and more distressed French pleaded that I rescue him from the bathroom, the lock on the door of which had treacherously locked him in. I released him. The diplomats of the world may still talk haughtily and act loftily, but they know in their heart of hearts that they have locked themselves into a world impasse by their competitive selfishness. They know no way out. One day they will have to call to the ambassadors of the Kingdom of God to open the door and let them out. For the Kingdom of God is the only final way out.

10. The next step that each of us can take is to lay hold of the resources of the Spirit of the Lord— the dynamic behind the whole program. Each of us must take these resources for several reasons.

(1) *We must be made new by the impact of the Spirit of God upon our inner lives.* After all, we must have new men for the new day. We "cannot make the golden age out of leaden instincts," for "men made Babylon out of their own Babylonian hearts." When "he that sits on the throne" said, "Behold, I make all things new," he laid his hand upon the human heart. He was right. A professor friend reports that Professor Giddings, eminent sociologist, once said to him that although he was not a Christian he blamed the Christian Church for its abandonment of its chief asset, radical conversion. The growth and appeal of the Oxford Group Movement witnesses to the fact that men everywhere are feeling the deep necessity of "changed lives." That "change" is in the process of being enlarged from an intensely individual thing to include the social order. That enlargement is accompanying our enlargement of our views of Christ and his Kingdom. At our Ashram we volunteer to take the place of the outcaste sweeper one day a week in order to give him a holiday. It is not an easy thing for either the white "Brahmins" or the brown "Brahmins" to do this scavenging work, the cleaning of the latrines. I found one Brahmin convert hesitating and when I asked him when he was going to volunteer, he drew a long breath and slowly replied, "Well, I'm converted, but I am not converted that far." Many of our conversions have been real, but limited. We must now be converted as far as our relationships extend. But changed we must be! This is the rock upon which any movement will be built or broken—its capacity to produce changed characters who can sustain the movement during periods of backwash and discouragement and moral sag. Wherever men expose themselves to Christ something happens to renew their inner

natures, and to toughen the fiber of their characters. When the Christian Church can no longer produce the miracle of the changed life, it has lost its right to be called Christian.

While we believe in changed lives, we must not overlook the fact that the very channels for a cooperative society are laid within our very natures. We are sometimes told that as long as human nature is what it is we will never get a cooperative order, for the essential nature of man is selfish. But we forget that while the egoistic impulses are there, the altruistic are also there. The herd instinct is deeply implanted within us. That is the natural channel along which the Kingdom of God, which is a cooperative commonwealth, will come. The fact is that Kropotkin has shown us that the law of survival is not in selfish, isolated competition, but in mutual aid, that this is the law by which all higher life survives. If what Drummond calls "the struggle for the life of others" is the final method of survival, then the Kingdom of God is the inevitable end of human living, if we are to survive at all.

Therefore the Spirit of the Lord upon us means not only the changing of our natures into new channels, but also the taking of the very channels which are there, now clogged by selfishness, and making them to be the very means along which this new day shall come. We said that this Kingdom is built within the foundation of the universe— it is also built within the very foundation of our own being. When the Kingdom comes we shall be truly natural; now we are trying to live unnaturally and are breaking ourselves in the process.

Many bring the objection against the possibility of the New Order by asserting that it is against human nature and human nature never changes. But Professor Hocking rightly says: "That is a hazardous refutation of socialism, or of any other proposed revolution, which consists in pointing out that its success would require a change in human nature. Under the spell of particular ideas monastic communities have flourished, in comparison with whose demands upon human nature the change required by socialism, so far as it calls for pure altruism ... is trivial. To anyone who asserts as a dogma that human nature never changes it is fair to reply, 'It is human nature to change itself.'" And we would add what Professor Hocking would himself add, that it is divine nature to change human nature. Put together the fact that it is human nature to change, and that it is divine nature to change human nature, and you have the stage set for vast changes.

(2) *We must have the Spirit of the Lord upon us not merely to change our lives, but also to realize them.* One of the great fears about a collective society is the loss of individual freedom. It is a real fear with a real basis for that fear. For while Communism in Russia gives a sense of freedom to the man who fits into the system, nevertheless, when all is said and done, it is a Kingdom of the Mass Man. The individual is molded every moment of his life by mass

> **When the Christian Church can no longer produce the miracle of the changed life, it has lost its right to be called Christian.**

suggestion, mass propaganda, and mass action. Individual freedom is reduced to the vanishing point. Professor Macmurray, who has a deep sympathy for the basic principles of Marxism, says: "There is only one way to escape from some form of State Communism, maintained by a dictatorship of force which would destroy freedom and with it individuality, and that is by creating a form of community life which is compatible with the individuality of its members."[3] The Communists of Russia see this necessity, and they say that after social attitudes are

---

3 *Communism*, p. 96

established in the Russian people, if necessary by force, then they intend to emphasize the development of the individual. But how can you, when the whole thing is maintained, and has the prospects of being maintained, by a dictatorship based on force? Individual freedom seems a remote possibility in those conditions.

It is at this point that the Kingdom of God scores, and scores heavily. It is a Cooperative Society, but it has individual freedom at its heart. "The Spirit of the Lord is upon me"—when a man can say that, then he is no longer in bondage to any man, to any society, to any circumstance. He has direct and individual relations with the Spirit of God. No man can ever again bring him into bondage—he is free at the center. He is bound up with every man by the closest of ties, and yet he is inwardly free from every man. He belongs to all and yet to none. At the center of his being he is conscious of a relationship that makes him alone in any crowd, individual in any group.

To see this blending of belonging to every man and belonging to no man, look at Jesus. How brotherly he was! The crowds "throng" him, the lepers push past laws to get to his feet, the children climb into his lap. He is so brotherly that he winces at every pain that darts through the being of any man. And yet, and yet, how aloof he was! He is so close to me that I feel that I can put my hand on his shoulder and say, "Brother Man," and yet when I am about to do it, I cannot. He is the Alone. In a lesser degree we partake of this sense of identification and isolation—we are alone with the Alone. There is a sense of fellowship with the Highest that puts meaning, dignity, and worth into human living. Intimate communion with the Spirit of God saves our personal liberty, and thus saves us from being merged into the mass man. It is no chance that those who have held to an evangelical Christian faith have had the strongest sense of personal liberty. Their direct communion with God has done it. It will do it again in a collective society, and thus save both our liberties and our unity. Without this sense of the Highest in the depths of our being collectivized life would mean not much more than a glorified anthill. With it collectivized life would mean the Kingdom of God on earth, the perfected man in a perfected society. The Kingdom of God would mean individual liberty amid collective living. The meaning of individualism and the meaning of collectivism are both "fulfilled in the Kingdom of God."

(3) *We can depend on the Spirit of God to back this movement to the utmost if we set it in the direction of world redemption.* One missionary said, "Everything depends on whether the Holy Ghost will come up to the mark." Everything does. But we can depend on the backing of the Spirit of God only when our directions are clear. For centuries God has not been able to back religion, except on a personal and limited scale. The

> **It is no chance that those who have held to an evangelical Christian faith have had the strongest sense of personal liberty. Their direct communion with God has done it.**

organized church has been set in the direction of autocratic power, as in Roman Catholicism, or in the direction of divisive denominationalism, as in the case of Protestantism—suppose in either case God should have backed them with his power? The result would have been disaster. Moreover, where the church has not been set in the direction of autocracy or divisiveness it has been very personal in its attitudes and lacking in social vision. God could not back these attitudes with power on a vast scale, for it would have driven his Kingdom inward, and would have made it specialize in inward states.

285

But now the issues are becoming clearer. The Christian movement sees more clearly than before that we must have both individual and collective salvation. We are being headed in the directions which God can back to the utmost. You do not apply power in your car when the car is headed toward the ditch —you wait till you have the open road. The vistas of the Kingdom of God are now opening before us. God's power can now be given to us. If the Christian world will take God's program, it can depend on God's power. If we catch the spirit of the Kingdom, we can depend on the Spirit of the Lord of that Kingdom. The line between the lower Kingdom and the upper Kingdom may become so thin that the upper Kingdom may break upon us with power and collective redemption.

(4) *But this expectation must not make us glance off from the fact that we need the Spirit of the Lord upon us to energize us to change entrenched and ancient wrongs.* We may expect a collective Easter morning to dawn upon us, but in the meantime we must face the cross that lies before us. The founding of the Kingdom cost Jesus a cross; the fulfillment of it will cost us the same.

We are in the birth-pangs of a new order. We must welcome those pangs and guide them. They may lead to senseless, useless, and unfruitful disorder and chaos, or they may lead to the birth of a new day. We must combine Christian daring with Christian sanity. Many a hesitating Peter will be afraid as we announce our decision to go to the cross to get a new day and will say, "Be it far from you, Lord: this shall never happen to you," but we must say with, the Master, "Get behind me, Satan: you are a hindrance to me; for you are not on the side of God, but of men." (Matthew 16:23). For God thinks and is arousing men to think in terms of this new Kingdom, while men have been thinking in terms of the old order based on exploitation, hence Satanic. Anything now that is static is Satanic, for it stands for the old, and the old has an injustice at its heart, however softened that injustice may be.

We must relearn hardness. We have become too soft. "The soft ["effeminate," A. V.] shall not inherit the Kingdom of God," nor shall they bring it in. A Chinese student was sentenced before a Chinese court to die for his Communistic convictions. As he was about to be led away he said to the court: "I am dying for a cause. What are you living for?" We must answer the challenge of that youth and say, "We will live for this Kingdom-Cause, and if necessary die for it." We must say that, and say it on a large scale, or be prepared to abdicate in favor of the cause which that youth represents. The Christian must relearn that spirit — and more.

> **This cross that faces us is not merely an abstract cross; it is an actual one. The theory of the cross and the practice of the cross must coincide.**

This cross that faces us is not merely an abstract cross; it is an actual one. The theory of the cross and the practice of the cross must coincide. Only those who believe in it are prepared to act on it. The hour for testing how Christian we are has now come. The cross again divides. If that division leaves us with only a minority, still we must not be disconcerted. It was a sure and determined minority that swung the whole of Russia to its views and program. A Christian minority, sure, determined, and united, might turn a confused and hesitant world situation to the Christian program. The foundations of the Christian way have been laid in the world mind—it is latent, awaiting the touch of Christian daring.

The matter of tempo in acting collectively upon the Christian program is of vital importance. The world decision between atheistic Communism and the Kingdom of God will probably be made in the next twenty-five years. The struggle may linger on at the edges for many years to come, but the strategic places in the world mind, and in the world situation, will probably be held by one or the other by that time. The time may be much shorter. We are now in the moment of the Great Hesitation. The situation is fluid. In the next few years it will probably turn in one direction or the other. The tempo of this whole matter is therefore important. The Communists realize this. The keynote of the Cleveland Convention, which looked toward the Sovietization of the United States of America, was struck by Secretary Browder in these words: "Our task is to win the majority of the working men to our program. We do not have unlimited time to accomplish this. Tempo, speed of plan, becomes the decisive factor in determining victory or defeat." It does, for either program.

The hour for piously passing resolutions has gone by. A Christian convention was reported as "resolutionary" when "revolutionary" was meant. The mistake was probably nearer the facts. We must get beyond the resolutionary temper of mind to the revolutionary. We must act. A little girl went up to a famous film actress in a hotel and said, "You're an actress, aren't you?" When told that she was, the little girl replied, "Then why don't you act?" We must say that to every Christian, including ourselves, "You're a Christian, aren't you? Then why don't you act?" The world situation awaits a collective Christian act. It is the one thing that can save us. "If you Christians should really be Christian, and should take your program seriously, the Communists wouldn't have a chance," said a thoughtful Hindu to me. Another Hindu, at the close of one of our Round Table Conferences, said, "Well, if you Christians are finding what you seem to have found, then I don't see why you haven't Christianized the world long ago." It is astounding that we haven't done it long before this—with such a program and such a dynamic. The time has come for us to do it. H. G. Wells says, "A resolute push now for quite a short period might reconstruct the entire basis of our collective life." That resolute push may be either a bloody revolutionary push by force, or it may be an intelligent, concerted Christian push of collective justice and brotherhood.

Macaulay used words of his day which we can use with more point of this day: "You may make the change tedious, you may make it violent; you may, God forbid, make it bloody, but avert it, you cannot. Agitations of the public mind, so deep and long continued, as those we have witnessed do not end in nothing. In peace or in convulsion, by the law or in spite of the law, through Parliament, or over Parliament, reform must be carried." Blood and confusion and chaos can be averted. The Christian way is the way out. Halevy's *England in 1815* shows that here was a society moving toward class war, and asks how it can be averted, as averted it was. He answers, "Through the Wesleyan Revival and its far-reaching effects on religious and social life in England." If that spiritual awakening averted that bloody revolution coming out of the class war in that limited sphere and to that limited extent, we can avert world chaos by a Christian push which will not merely avert class war, but obviate the necessity of it, for we can accomplish by Christian means everything good the class war seeks to accomplish—and more!

Before the world decision is made we have this breathing space to set our house in order, to unite our forces and to launch our program. The whole thing may be upon us sooner than we dream. The fact is that it is at our very doors now. I put it at twenty-five years. It may be longer than that, but it may be very much shorter. In 1917 Lenin, addressing a group of students in Switzerland, said, "This revolution may not come in my lifetime." A few months later he was leading the revolution that has shaken the world.

We Christians may be standing nearer the world decision than we know. The means of communication are now so rapid, the world mind is now so quickly and easily influenced by world movements, the scattered, isolated thoughts of the world are being replaced so fast by world thought, that we must forget the tempo of past world decisions. Things are now different. The world stage is more and more being set for a world decision.

The Kingdom of the Atheistic Mass Man and the Kingdom of God are at the door of the world. This generation may have to decide which one it will take.

AFTERWORD

BY DR. JOSEPH B. KENNEDY, SR.

Retired Missionary Evangelist to China

To the reader who has completed what I consider the most enlightening Christian book on Communism, I want to ask a question. It is based on one of Stanley's wisdom teachings condensed into a few words…a gift above most others: "Impression minus expression equals depression." My urgent and prayerful question is: "What do you plan to do with this knowledge?"

The reason I ask is that today, perhaps as never before in human history, the wisdom in this book is needed. I have toured Russia with Sherwood Eddy in early 1956 and spent years in China. Unredeemed mankind has, by its very nature, the possibility of destroying itself. The next war will likely not only be the last war, it may be the end of civilization. Little has been taught in Christian churches, seminaries and fellowships world wide on the example Jesus gave us when tempted by Satan, as he was during his fast in the desert. (Matthew Chapter 4) The fact of temptation is very clear. How to deal with that experience is one of the central needs of mankind. "Know your enemy," a phrase in *The Art of War,* is good advice. Jesus taught us in Matthew 6:13 to pray, "Lead us not into temptation." He met evil with scripture. Few today have studied the Bible enough to be able to do that. One can Google and find much help in this, and for sources to gain insight to almost any aspect of life. I mention this here to give aid in the answering of the question on **what you plan to do with the knowledge you have just received.** I will not seek to determine the *best order* of importance in the following suggestions, as yours may be in a different order than mine are here, as well as many more.

First, for me, I have set aside a part of my tithe to give as many copies of this book as possible to friends, family, my pastor, seminaries, colleges, as well as government leaders.

Second, I suggest that each of us visit www.christianashram.org and attend an E. Stanley Jones Ashram, with as many of your family and friends as possible. My first Ashram, meeting Dr. E. Stanley Jones, was a dynamic life-changing experience for me. It will provide spiritual growth as well as help you answer the question I have presented above.

Third, I will think of all that happened to me, after reading *Christ's Alternative to Communism* many years ago. What I did then was take the second reading, marked copy and now re-read it again the third time. This time, I will make notes on what I can use for further growth in my own spiritual journey, as well as what I can share with others in the time I have left here on this planet. I am ninety-one years old in 2019. I had recently found my first copy of this book, and was led to call Dr. Anne Mathews-Younes, Stanley's granddaughter. She is President of the E. Stanley Jones Foundation and also has served for a time as the Vice President of the United Christian Ashram Board. As she discovered the story of my long relationship with her grandfather, she asked me to write an Afterword for the new publication of this book. I am humbled by such a request, and smile as I know Stanley would approve. Dr. Mathews-Younes has done a remarkable job going forward from that moment when the world lost one of the most gifted, dedicated disciples of our Lord. The vitality of the Christ-centered content and awesome challenge to dedicate one's life to our Lord in each Ashram still lives! Don't miss this experience!

Fourth, please gather a few members of your church, or those in your community not attending any church, or even those who are atheists and unbelievers to study this book over several months. Such a study fellowship is one of my plans, at least to start and help those interested find the wisdom in this book, as well as the truth about Communism. Few know that the first people to hold all things in common were some of the early followers of Jesus. (Acts 2:44 – 4:32) And from your reading, you will discover the secret to this possibility. It is possible only with the born-again, conversion experience found in Christianity. When you re-read and study this book, you will discover the truth, the understanding, and the logic of that statement. May I add something I wrote in a class assignment while a student at Emory University. "In Communism, the ends justify the means. In Christianity the means determine the ends."

Fifth, I believe that each Christian reading this book prayerfully and carefully will want to re-dedicate his or her life to Christ. Regardless of how far you have come in your journey with our Lord, there is yet another level waiting. John Wesley, founder of the Methodist Church in England, called it, "Moving on to perfection." Sanctifying grace may not be something you are familiar with but Google that phrase and do some reading. It is the concept of continuing growth in Christian living as we seek to follow the only perfect person ever. I might mention here if you take this seriously, Stanley's book, *The Way* will take you forward day by day from where most of us are in our present moment, nearer to where our Lord would have us live and witness to his Presence and Love.

I wish I could share in great detail several other experiences of my friendship with Dr. E. Stanley Jones. He was my friend and my mentor. He once asked me to go with him to India to study to take his place

293

when he had to pass that leadership on. I sat for a period with him, not knowing how long it was, for I was overwhelmed with the love, the honor of his offer, and the understanding that no person could take his place. I then shared with him the following: "Dr. Jones, the night I was converted, I was a gang leader in Birmingham, lost, and an atheist." Coming from a Christian home the story of how I arrived is not for now. I continued "May 6, 1947, I attended a meeting at the North Highlands Methodist Church in Birmingham. Dr. Harry Denman, a friend of yours, was preaching. After his sermon, on the third verse of the invitational hymn, 'Just As I Am,' I found myself moving with several others toward the altar. The Pastor, Rev. L. E. Price and Dr. Denman prayed for me with the laying on of hands. When I had accepted Christ and my prayer of confession was completed, I stood and Rev. Price said, "Lucky, (my nickname) how do you feel?" I tried to describe that which was beyond words. "I feel as a great weight, a burden, was lifted from my shoulders, and I am so light I think I could fly." After a moment of silence, I heard myself say: "Tonight I give my life to serve the Chinese people." Dr. Denman stepped back, putting his hand on me, and prayed I would serve as a missionary to China. I felt strange for I did not know one Chinese person. Stanley smiled, leaned forward, putting his hand on my shoulder, as I wiped tears away, saying, "I understand Joseph," and then he prayed a blessing on my life and the fact that I had been faithful to that calling to serve China.

I share that story, for Stanley later helped me on my first trip to Singapore and Malaysia, where I had been invited as the National Chairman of Methodist Youth to speak at the All Malaysian Youth Conference on April 7, 1952.

Kagawa, the great Japanese saint and another friend of Dr. Jones, that I had the joy and privilege of knowing, has these words written by his biographer, William Axling: "Kagawa is a social engineer, absorbed in actual programs rather than academic speculations. His programs however, are built on deep-going, strongly buttressed principles. He believes in communism, but it is the communism of the early Christian church and of Tolstoy rather than of Karl Marx, as against the class hatred of Russian communism. He pleads for and passionately practices brotherly love. As against Marx class conflict, he advocates Tolstoy's non-resistance. And the building of a finer and fairer social order. He believes in evolutionary rather than revolutionary processes."

Let me close with something that has never been published. I was in Los Angeles, in a hotel, on my way back to Singapore after the afore-mentioned trip in 1952. I was sitting in my hotel room praying, for I did not have the funds for the ticket back to Singapore. A breeze blew the *LA Times* newspaper off the table spreading pages across the floor. I got up and noticed no window was open. Amazed I stooped to pick up the pages scattered a good three feet across the floor. There in the middle on one page was a picture of Dr. E. Stanley Jones, who was to speak that evening at the Methodist Church. I took that page, put it on the desk and began to dress. I was sitting on the front pew at 6:00 when the program was to start at 7:00 pm. When the time came all the pews were full and the pastor with Stanley behind him came to the stage. As he sat down our eyes met, he smiled, and the evening proceeded. His message, as always, was beyond measure. I waited for almost another hour after the service as people came forward to meet and greet Dr. Jones. When all were gone, he came and sat with me. We found we were staying at the same hotel. We went back in a cab and up to his room. Asking what I was doing there, I told him the story. He had heard of the success of the first trip when a Wednesday night prayer meeting in the Paya Lebar Chinese Methodist Church with 12 people, growing week after week to a meeting in the Happy World Stadium with five thousand nightly for four nights. I shared with him the Straits Times News with one showing four hundred accepted Christ the first night, and another clipping showing five hundred the next. Stanley said "Last I heard you were in Singapore. I had received your request for prayer and from what I heard much indeed was accomplished." Smiling he said, "Why are you here now?" I explained and he asked when I would be leaving. I replied, "Well, I am not sure. I do not have the funds necessary for my plane ticket. I cashed in the remainder of my Comer Scholarship at Emory for the first trip. Now a local church could be a source, but I have to meet with the pastor, they are also hoping to get some funds for my car. I am going back on a mission for the Methodist Church to preach in every city in Malaysia where we have a church." He looked at me, then closed his eyes. In a moment, he said, as he got up and went to his briefcase and returned with a checkbook. "Joseph, you must give me your word this will never be mentioned until I am with the Lord. I am on the Mission Board and you are not going under the Foreign Mission Board of the Methodist Church. I would be in much trouble were they to know I was supporting a Methodist Evangelist to Malaysia." I assured him I would keep the secret as he handed me a check for three thousand dollars. I sat, in tears unable to speak. I might add, we had eight hundred men, women and youth join the Methodist church in that preaching tour. Only in heaven will we know the full extent of the souls brought to Christ through his gift to me, and the untold stories of his support for others like me. This is the Dr. E. Stanley Jones I knew, loved, and who blessed my life in so many ways. God bless you as you go forth from the time you have spent with him in this great book. I now sit praying you will not only give a positive answer to my question, but go beyond with the help of many of the great books by Dr. E. Stanley Jones.

DR. JOSEPH B. KENNEDY, SR.
Chairman and CEO
Society for Advancement of Global Education, Inc.
US-China Education Foundation

ABOUT THE AUTHOR

A Portrait of E. Stanley Jones
by Shivraj Mahendra

(Acrylic on canvas [16"x20"]. This portrait was presented
by the artist to The E. Stanley Jones School of World Mission
and Evangelism at Asbury Theological Seminary,
Wilmore, Kentucky on May 17, 2017)

297

E. STANLEY JONES (1884-1973)

E. STANLEY JONES was described by a distinguished Bishop as the "greatest missionary since Saint Paul." This missionary/evangelist spent seventy years traveling throughout the world in the ministry of Jesus Christ. Jones wrote and spoke for the general public and there is little doubt that his words brought hope and refreshment to multitudes all over the world. As a well-known, engaging, and powerful evangelist, Jones delivered tens of thousands of sermons and lectures. He typically traveled fifty weeks a year, often speaking two to six times a day.

Jones worked to revolutionize the whole theory and practice of missions to third world nations by disentangling Christianity from Western political and cultural imperialism. He established hundreds of Christian Ashrams throughout the world, many of which still meet today. E. Stanley Jones was a crusader for Christian unity, a nonstop witness for Christ, and a spokesman for peace, racial brotherhood, and social justice. He foresaw where the great issues would be and spoke to them long before they were recognized... often at great unpopularity and even antagonism and derision to himself. Many consider Jones a prophet and his honors – and he did receive them — were all laid at the feet of Jesus Christ. Jones would readily admit that his quite ordinary life became extraordinary only because he fully surrendered his life to Jesus Christ!

Jones' writing and preaching did not require people to leave their intellect at the door; his presentation of Jesus engaged both the intellect and touched humanity's desire to experience the living Christ in their lives. When Jones wrote or talked about Jesus, it was as if he knew Jesus personally and could reach out and touch him. Jones described himself as an evangelist... the bearer of the Good News of Jesus Christ. The countless illustrations found in his books and sermons speak to a cross section of humanity and demonstrate, in a multitude of ways, the transformative impact of Jesus Christ on human existence. Few readers or listeners could miss identifying with one story or another — virtually all would find stories that touched their lives. All were offered hope that they, too, could experience the transformation available through self-surrender and conversion.

In presenting Jesus as the redeemer of all of life Jones used his wide ranging study of the non-Christian religions, medicine, psychology, philosophy, science, history, and literature to make the case that the touch of Christ is upon all creation — that the totality of life was created by Christ and for Christ. We were all created to live upon Christ's Way. Jesus' Sermon on the Mount lays out both the principles and the Way.

Jones wrote twenty-seven books. More than 3.5 million copies of his books have been sold and they have been translated into 30 languages. All proceeds from his books have gone into Christian projects. He gave all of his money away! Now more than 45 years after his death – his books and sermons (many written in the 1930s and 40s) are not out of date and with few exceptions are entirely relevant to today's world.

According to his son-in-law, United Methodist Bishop James K. Mathews (1913-2010), "the most salient and spiritually significant characteristics of Stanley Jones were the spiritually transparency, clarity and persuasiveness of his personal witness for Christ. For thirty five years I knew him intimately and had occasion to observe him closely for prolonged periods. He rang true! Once when I asked a Hindu how he was, he replied, 'As you see me.' So it was with Brother Stanley, as he was called. He was as you saw him."

Even after a severe stroke at the age of 88 robbed him of his speech, Jones managed to dictate his last book, *The Divine Yes*. He died in India on January 25, 1973.

Jones' monumental accomplishments in life emerged from the quality of his character cultivated through his intimacy with Jesus Christ. As he lived in Christ, he reflected Christ. That experience is available to us when we invite Christ to live in us!

Follow E. Stanley Jones

on social media

OTHER BOOKS
By E. Stanley Jones

The Christ of the Indian Road
1st edition: Grosset & Dunlap/Abingdon Press, 1925.
New edition: Abingdon Press, 2010.

Christ at the Round Table
1st edition: Abingdon Press, 1928.
New edition: The E. Stanley Jones Foundation, 2019

The Christ of Every Road: A Study in Pentecost
Abingdon Press, 1930.
New edition: Coming soon.

The Christ of the Mount: A Working Philosophy of Life
1st edition: Abingdon-Cokesbury, 1931.
New edition: The E. Stanley Jones Foundation, 2017

Christ and Human Suffering
Abingdon Press, 1933.
New edition: Coming soon.

Christ's Alternative to Communism
Abingdon Press, 1935.
New edition: The E. Stanley Jones Foundation, 2019

Victorious Living
1st edition: Abingdon-Cokesbury, 1936.
New edition: Abingdon Press, 2014.

The Choice Before Us
Abingdon Press, 1937.
New edition: Coming soon.

Along the Indian Road
1ˢᵗ edition: Abingdon Press, 1939.
New edition: Coming soon.

Is the Kingdom of God Realism?
1ˢᵗ edition: Abingdon-Cokesbury, 1940.
New edition: The E. Stanley Jones Foundation, 2018

Abundant Living
1ˢᵗ edition: Abingdon-Cokesbury, 1942.
New edition: Abingdon Press, 2014

The Christ of the American Road
1ˢᵗ edition: Abingdon-Cokesbury, 1944.
New edition: Coming soon.

The Way
1ˢᵗ edition: Abingdon-Cokesbury, 1946.
New edition: Abingdon Press, 2015.

Mahatma Gandhi: An Interpretation
1ˢᵗ edition: Abingdon-Cokesbury, 1948.
New edition: Abingdon Press, 2019.

The Way to Power and Poise
1ˢᵗ edition: Abingdon-Cokesbury, 1949.
New edition: Coming soon.

How To Be A Transformed Person
1ˢᵗ edition: Abingdon-Cokesbury, 1951.
New edition: Coming soon.

Growing Spiritually
1ˢᵗ edition: Abingdon Press, 1953
New edition: The E. Stanley Jones Foundation, 2019

Mastery: The Art of Mastering Life
1ˢᵗ edition: Abingdon Press, 1955
New edition: Abingdon Press, 2018

Christian Maturity
1st edition: Abingdon Press, 1957.
2nd edition: Abingdon Press, 1980.
New edition: Coming soon.

Conversion
1st edition: New York & Nashville, Abingdon, 1959.
New edition: The E. Stanley Jones Foundation, 2019

In Christ
1st edition: New York & Nashville, Abingdon, 1961.
New edition: Seedbed Press, 2017.

The Word Become Flesh
1st edition: Abingdon Press, 1963.
New edition: Abingdon Press, 2006.

Victory Through Surrender
1st edition: Abingdon Press, 1966.
New edition: The E. Stanley Jones Foundation, 2018

A Song of Ascents: A Spiritual Autobiography
1st edition: Abingdon Press, 1968.
New edition: Coming soon.

The Reconstruction of the Christian Church
1st edition: Abingdon Press, 1970.
New edition: Coming soon.

The Unshakable Kingdom and the Unchanging Person
1st edition: Abingdon Press, 1972.
New edition: The E. Stanley Jones Foundation, 2017

The Divine Yes
1st edition: Abingdon Press, 1975.
New edition: Coming soon.

ABOUT

The E. Stanley Jones Foundation

Our Mission

The E. Stanley Jones Foundation (ESJF) exists to reach today's generations with the life-transforming message of Jesus Christ, and to equip effective Christian evangelism by making available to all, the relevant and rich works of Dr. E. Stanley Jones, whose Christ-centered preaching, teaching, and prolific writings continue to enlighten and bless millions of people worldwide.

Our Vision

- To ensure that E. Stanley Jones resources are available to the public from trusted retailers and online providers, as well as directly from the E. Stanley Jones Foundation.
- Fully equip disciples of Jesus Christ for effective evangelism.
- Use all available technological and media platforms to update, create, and distribute worldwide, the full array of Dr. Jones' books, sermons, and teaching tools to entities, including but not limited to universities, seminaries, churches, groups, and individuals.
- Create new opportunities for teaching and equipping leaders, using our timely, effective teaching tools, curricula, and training resources.
- Develop partnerships and nurture relationships with others of like mind to help ensure resources are available to implement and perpetuate our mission.

The E. Stanley Jones Foundation is a nonprofit 501(c)(3) organization. The US Internal Revenue Service Code permits the amount that US residents donate which exceeds the fair market value of the material(s) a donor receives from the Foundation to be tax-deductible. Proceeds from the sale of books and materials remain in the Foundation to continue the work of the Foundation. For more information please visit our website:

www.estanleyjonesfoundation.com

Follow us on social media

The E. Stanley Jones Foundation
10804 Fox Hunt Lane
Potomac, Maryland 20854
Phone: 240.328.5115

OTHER PUBLICATIONS
From the E. Stanley Jones Foundation

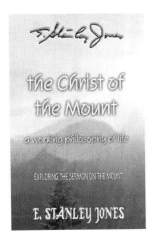

The Christ of the Mount:
A Working Philosophy of Life
Authored by E. Stanley Jones
List Price: $15.99
6" x 9" (15.24 x 22.86 cm)
312 pages
ISBN-13: 978-1542896030
(CreateSpace-Assigned)
ISBN-10: 1542896037
BISAC: Religion / Biblical Meditations /
New Testament

The Life and Ministry of Mary
Webster: A Witness in the Evangelistic
Ministry of E. Stanley Jones *Authored by*
Anne Mathews-Younes
List Price: $14.99
6" x 9" (15.24 x 22.86 cm)
286 pages
ISBN-13: 978-1544191799 (CreateSpace-
Assigned)
ISBN-10: 1544191790
BISAC: Religion / Christian Life / Spiritual
Growth

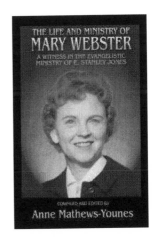

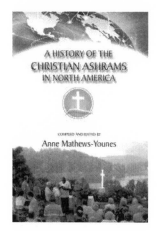

A History of the Christian Ashrams in North America
Compiled and Edited by Anne Mathews-Younes
List Price: $34.99
6" x 9" (15.24 x 22.86 cm)
528 pages
ISBN-13: 978-547229017
(CreateSpace-Assigned)
ISBN-10: 1547229012
BISAC: Religion / Christianity / History / General

Is The Kingdom of God Realism?
Authored by E. Stanley Jones, Foreword by Leonard Sweet, Afterword by Howard Snyder
List Price: $19.99
6" x 9" (15.24 x 22.86 cm)
428 pages
ISBN-13: 978-1976151514 (CreateSpace-Assigned)
ISBN-10: 1976151511
BISAC: Religion / Christianity / General

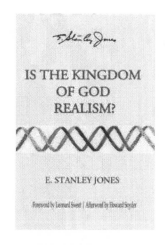

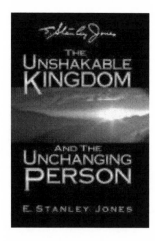

The Unshakable Kingdom and the Unchanging Person
Authored by E. Stanley Jones
List Price: $18.99
6" x 9" (15.24 x 22.86 cm)
408 pages
ISBN-13: 978-1974132935
(CreateSpace-Assigned)
ISBN-10: 1974132935
BISAC: Religion / Spirituality / General

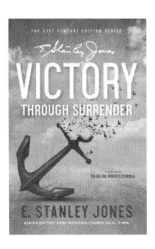

Victory Through Surrender
Authored by E. Stanley Jones, Preface by
Anne Mathews-Younes
List Price: $12.99
6" x 9" (15.24 x 22.86 cm)
166 pages
ISBN-13: 978-1717548474
(CreateSpace-Assigned)
ISBN-10: 1717548474
BISAC: Religion / Christian Life /
Professional Growth

A Love Affair With India: The Story
of the Wife and Daughter of E.
Stanley Jones
Authored by Martha Gunsalus Chamberlain,
Preface by Anne Mathews-Younes
List Price: $14.99
6" x 9" (15.24 x 22.86 cm)
250 pages
ISBN-13: 978-1984960276
(CreateSpace-Assigned)
ISBN-10: 198496027X
BISAC: Biography & Autobiography

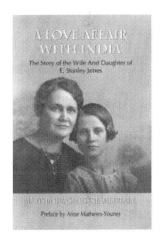

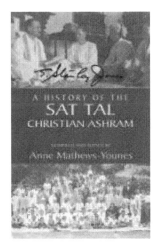

A History of the Sat Tal Christian
Ashram (USA Edition)
Authored by Anne Mathews-Younes
List Price: $15.99
6" x 9" (15.24 x 22.86 cm)
238 pages
ISBN-13: 978-1722847524
(CreateSpace-Assigned)
ISBN-10: 1722847522
BISAC: Religion / Christianity /
History /General

Living Upon the Way: Selected Sermons of E. Stanley Jones
Authored by Anne Mathews-Younes
List Price: $24.99
6" x 9" (15.24 x 22.86 cm)
454 pages
ISBN-13: 978-1724745736
(CreateSpace-Assigned)
ISBN-10: 1724745735
BISAC: Religion / Christianity / Sermons

Conversion
Authored by E. Stanley Jones
List Price: $15.99
6" x 9" (15.24 x 22.86 cm)
284 pages
ISBN-13: 978-1726458702
(CreateSpace-Assigned)
ISBN-10: 1726458709
BISAC: Religion / Christian living / Personal growth

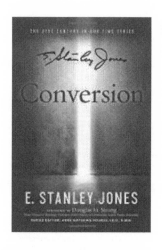

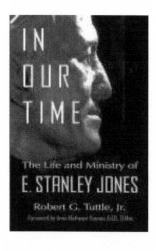

In Our Time: The Life and Ministry of E. Stanley Jones
Authored by Robert G. Tuttle, Jr
List Price: $22.99
6" x 1" x 9" (15.24 x 22.86 cm)
440 pages
ISBN-13: 978-1793813237
(KDP-Assigned)
ISBN-10: 179381323X
BISAC: Nonfiction / Biography and Autobiography / Religious

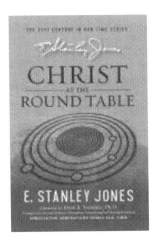

Christ at the Round Table
Authored by E. Stanley Jones
List Price: $15.99
Dimensions: 6 x 0.8 x 9 inches
Paperback: 320 pages
ISBN-13: 978-1791766481
(KDP-Assigned)
BISAC: Religion / Christianity /
Christian Ecumenism

Tailwind: The Robert E. Miller Story
Authored by Jennifer Tyler and Nicholas
Younes
List Price: $15.00
6" x 0.8" x 9" (15.24 x 22.86 cm)
173 pages
ISBN-13: 978-1092213172
(KDP-Assigned)
BISAC: Nonfiction / Biography and
Autobiography / Religious

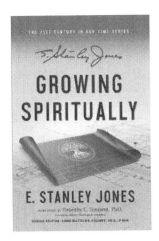

Growing Spiritually
Authored by E. Stanley Jones
List Price: $16.99
6" x 1" x 9" (15.24 x 22.86 cm)
400 pages
ISBN-13: 978-1090885302
(KDP-Assigned)
BISAC: Nonfiction / Self-help/ Christian /
Personal Transformation / Devotional

ALL PUBLICATIONS OF

The E. Stanley Jones Foundation

are available for purchase from
estanleyjonesfoundation.com, amazon.com

and other sellers worldwide

Order your copies today!

Made in the USA
Coppell, TX
04 December 2019